INVESTMENT-CENTRIC INNOVATION PROJECT MANAGEMENT

Winning the New Product Development Game

STEVEN JAMES KEAYS

M.A.Sc., P.Eng.

J.ROSS
PUBLISHING

ISBN-13: 978-1-60427-151-5

Printed and bound in the U.S.A. Printed on acid-free paper.

10 9 8 7 6 5 4 3 2 1

Library of Congress Cataloging-in-Publication Data
Names: Keays, Steven, 1963– author,
Title: Investment-centric innovation project management : winning the new
  product development game / by Steven Keays.
Description: Plantation, FL : J. Ross Publishing, [2018] | Includes
  bibliographical references and index.
Identifiers: LCCN 2018011371 (print) | LCCN 2018013385 (ebook) | ISBN
  9781604277982 (e-book) | ISBN 9781604271515 (hardcover : alk. paper)
Subjects: LCSH: Project management. | Creative ability in business. | New
  products.
Classification: LCC HD69.P75 (ebook) | LCC HD69.P75 K426 2018 (print) | DDC
  658.4/04—dc23
LC record available at https://lccn.loc.gov/2018011371

Phone: (954) 727-9333
Fax: (561) 892-0700
Web: www.jrosspub.com

CONTENTS

FOREWORD

We are entering an era of technological transformation. There is a global call to action for innovators. This book, entitled *Investment-Centric Innovation Project Management: Winning the New Product Development Game* by Steven Keays, provides us with the knowledge and grit needed for us to overcome the numerous obstacles that innovators will face in what many are calling the golden age of automation and artificial intelligence.

I met Mr. Keays over a year ago when he joined the National Research Council of Canada as an Industrial Technology Advisor. I invited him to a technology session to discuss innovations in gas power systems. I was impressed. There was a broad range of technologies represented and Mr. Keays was able to quickly identify sticking points in the innovators' presentations. It was clear to me that he had a rare and unique perspective on innovation and that he brought a diverse range of valuable insights to the discussion. I would later learn of his formative past in aircraft engineering, systems engineering, and pipeline capital projects.

Steven has an engaging writing style that will resonate with many innovators as he artfully lays out the ground rules for innovation and product development. Drawing in part from his own innovation experiences, Keays gives readers the tools needed to navigate their way to faster success and sometimes, yes, early failure.

This valuable handbook for innovators is a survival pack to be used on your journey through the innovation landscape. Mr. Keays has pared down his vast knowledge from years of experience in the innovation game to ensure that you get the most valuable advice and guidance to prepare you for what lies ahead.

Take the helm and enjoy the ride.

Anouk Kendall
President, Decentralised Energy Canada
Calgary, Alberta

PREFACE

"You have all the reason in the world to achieve your grandest dreams. Imagination plus innovation equals realization."
—Denis Waitley

"An important scientific innovation rarely makes its way by gradually winning over and converting its opponents: What does happen is that the opponents gradually die out."
—Max Planck

The inspiration for this book came about in the early days of the summer of 2016 when I was hard at work on the completion of *Investment-Centric Project Management*. The other hours of my day were filled with the business affairs of NAIAD Company Ltd., an engineering and management consultancy that I founded in 2000. The business of innovation management, product development, and technology R&D had been at the core of NAIAD since its inception. Almost from the outset, it was clear to me that the innovation journey had to go beyond engineering or manufacturing, albeit to an extent that eluded me in those early days. Even when the viewpoint was pulled back into the mechanics of design, of engineering, of material selection, and of manufacturing methods, I could not escape the realization that NAIAD and I were not all that enlightened on the artful execution of a technology development program. Despite the patents that came to life for our clients and for ourselves over the years, there lingered a feeling that we could have gotten there faster, at less cost, and with more elegant outcomes. In essence, we had fumbled our way to success by trial and error, in fits of creativity, and bouts of stagnation. We earned our innovation chops, in other words, in the school of hard knocks. I was an avid consumer of books on the topic, ranging as far as management science and the art of artistic creativity. Yet, I was left none the more enlightened for it. The innovation journey seemed to be imbued with a persistent dose of wishful thinking tied to the exhortation to maintain one's faith in the idea through thick and thin. The recurring emphasis on creativity seemed to make sense, but too often came at the expense of any formalism in the *process* of developing an idea into a commercially successful offering.

This is where the summer of 2016 ties into the storyline of this book when I began to write it in parallel with *Investment-Centric Project Management*. The insights from that book turned into a realization that should have been obvious all along: *innovation projects are capital projects*. They are not, as the literature would have it, the point of some lyrical mission to change the world or invent a better mouse trap. While innovation projects can, of course, change the world and alter our own, they do not succeed primarily on the merits of some new-fangled, whizbang technology. Indeed, the history of failed innovations by giant corporations throughout the decades dwarfs, in size, the failure statistics of failed capital projects discussed in *Investment-Centric Project Management*. However, the goal of innovation projects is the same as capital projects: to realize a profitably performing asset that will generate sustained investment returns to its shareholders throughout the economic life of that asset. In the case of a capital project, the asset is an operational plant. In the innovation case, it is the business selling the product resulting from the innovation journey. The uniqueness and physiognomy of the plant or product matter *only to the extent that they propitiate the profitability objective*. The corollary to this insight was equally telling: it makes absolutely no difference that an innovative solution displays the greatest technological wizardry since the invention of digital sliced bread: if nobody buys it, it will amount to a complete waste of time, money, and patience by those who bankrolled its development. If the thing doesn't make money, it makes no investment sense.

The decade between 2001 and 2011 saw a multitude of technology projects come to NAIAD. These projects afforded me the unique opportunity to investigate, on my own, the mechanics and mechanisms of technology development. What was once a very limiting viewpoint dominated by engineering had expanded into the realms of market research, buyer psychology, finance, supply chains, business start-ups, and management theory. The glaring zones of ignorance that had plagued me in the early days of NAIAD have, by now, amply shrunk to manageable levels. By November 2016, I had joined the Industrial Research Assistance Program organization, administered by Canada's National Research Council, where this vastly expanded mind space would be put to the test. My new role as industrial technology advisor effectively put me on the other side of the innovation game; rather than develop an idea, my job was to assess the technical and commercial merits of ideas by would-be innovators.

The premise of this book posits that the successful development of an idea into a commercial business must be corralled by a formal execution framework. This framework allows creativity to roam freely in the early stages of the innovation journey. As the work progresses, the execution effort must switch focus from *ideation* to *development*, which is where formalism necessarily comes in. The name of the game is not to obsess about technological novelty but *sellable* technology. The ultimate objective is always just below the surface: to get to a profitable commercial operation. The need for structured creativity and development formalism calls forth a repeatable, controllable methodology that can be managed effectively and *valunomically* (a concept introduced in *Investment-Centric Project Management*). This book means to introduce such a methodology. The result is a single, unifying management framework for transforming an innovative idea into a commercially viable product or service, and to morph the latter into a successful business. The contents of the book are divided into two parts. Part 1 caters to the innovation process proper, starting with the idea and ending with the commercially ready product. Part 2 switches focus and is intended for readers who want to understand what is involved in getting a business up and running in order to sell the product. Together, the two parts form a coherent innovation project delivery system. The system is inherently flexible so that one can tailor its prescriptions to the scale of the effort anticipated, from the simplest of widgets to the most complex enterprise-wide solution.

A comprehensive implementation of the elements found in Part 1 will apply to innovation projects that target complex applications found in large commercial and/or industrial applications. Such an implementation will entail a heavier management hand print than more limited projects that are intended for retail markets. It establishes a definite level of formalism over the execution strategy, the technology development plan, and the administration of the financing requirements. Such formalism cannot be avoided if one wishes to pursue innovation projects in a repeatable, predictable, and controllable fashion. Winging it, as some suggest, in the name of unshackled creativity isn't a recipe that leads to commercial success. When other people's money is involved, the innovator does not have the freedom to follow his whims. Nevertheless, the methodology proposed herein is not so rigid as to prohibit any relaxation of that formalism. Indeed, the innovator can be served equally well by picking and choosing the elements of Part 1 that fit his circumstances, especially in the detailed execution of the technology development program (explored in Chapter 4). As a matter of fact, the methodology will be most effective when it is tailored to the particular environment of the innovator. For example, the innovator who is an employee of an established firm will have different needs than the one who is starting up from scratch, as will be the case for business start-ups. The savvy innovator will therefore maximize his benefits from this book by extracting from it the prescriptions that best serve his purpose and set aside the others.

Part 2 is equally malleable in terms of implementation. Its target audience is comprised of the people within an organization who are invested with management and leadership mandates tied to money and budgets. Part 2 will be useful to all readers of Part 1, but will prove especially useful to those who are newcomers to the management game. Part 2 highlights the importance of financial literacy to the effectiveness of daily management. It is an unfortunate fact that most employees pay little heed to their employers' financial state. Budgets, accounting numbers, and financial management are viewed with skepticism by many, even loathing by some! The business of business numbers is not glamorous or inspiring to most people, it is true. However, a lack of glitz does not imply an absence of merit. As the reader will discover, Part 2 makes the case for educating one's entire workforce on the basics of financial accounting. Other topics of paramount importance will benefit managers and subordinates alike, such as management mindsets, corporate culture, product rollout, and commercialization planning. Part 2 ends on a positive note through a discussion about what the immediate future holds in store for us all. The reader is invited to read between the lines: he will surely find there a fertile ground for a myriad of innovation seeds.

The innovation journey is exactly that, a journey. It is neither for the diffident or the fearful; the game is played on a battlefield dominated by belligerent competitors who will defend their turfs at whatever costs. Think of it as a pirate ship with you, the reader, as captain. The treasure that awaits you glitters in the sunlight, but only if you are prepared for the fight. It is also a glorious adventure that will inspire you and your crew. The world in which we live exists because someone, somewhere, at some point in the past imagined what it could be. The marvelous thing about the world of innovations is the fact that everyone is invited. It is the great opportunity equalizer—unfazed by entrenched interests, economic superpowers, mercantile giants, or global corporate cyclops. It is not, however, a field where one strolls leisurely toward easy riches. While its doors are open to all, its rules are enforced in the throes of competition. Opportunities are offered but never given. Success will be earned from within, never bestowed from without. In the immortal words of Eleanor Roosevelt:

"The future belongs to those who believe in the beauty of their dreams."

Steven Keays
Calgary, Alberta, Canada

ABOUT THE AUTHOR

Steven Keays, M.A.Sc., P.Eng., is a 30-year veteran of the aerospace, defense, manufacturing, and energy sectors. He is the author of the acclaimed book *Investment-Centric Project Management* and is the founder of NAIAD Company, a consultancy that specializes in capital and innovation project delivery. He is also an industrial technology advisor for the National Research Council of Canada and an engineering graduate of the Royal Military College of Canada and the University of Ottawa (M.A.Sc., turbulent fluid mechanics). He is a specialist in large-scale project planning and delivery, global execution strategies, innovation programs, and machine sciences. He is a registered professional engineer and a member of the Project Management Institute. Mr. Keays resides in Calgary, Canada with his wife, Margaret, and their younger children Gabrielle and James.

This book is dedicated to my son, Michael Pankowski,
who is a wonderful young man, human being, and wise old soul.

ACKNOWLEDGMENTS

It takes a village . . .

The writing process is tedious, lonely, and absorbing. It takes a very special type of person to put up with the constant isolation of the author from his own world. One singular such person is my wife, Margaret—and doubly so since she has had to put up with my writing two books back to back. Through it all, her patience, support, and integrity never wavered. What I wrote in the first book, I write again unequivocally: *I would not be me, without you with me.* This second time around, I had the pleasure of calling upon the help of our daughter, Gabrielle, and our son, James, to make real contributions to the book: she, with the structure and he, with the illustrations. This goes to show that being 15 and 13 is never too young to be entrusted with grown-up expectations! Our oldest son, Michael, contributed in thoughts and insights amid a hectic university schedule punctuated with summer work.

Writing, however, does not amount to a hill of beans without the means to put it in the hands of a reading audience. It is very much akin to the innovation game itself: nothing has happened until the first sale is made. And like any innovation, it takes a special individual to be the first to willfully take a chance on it. This book, as with its predecessor, *Investment-Centric Project Management*, came to commercial life through the priceless ministrations of two key people at J. Ross Publishing: Drew Gierman and Stephen Buda. Drew was the motivating force behind the first book and its first enthusiastic champion. Without his faith in the two projects, neither would have come to light. He was gracious with his time, patience, and wisdom of the literary trade, in spite of my condition of budding amateur author. The structure and semantics of the two books emerged from his generous guidance. Translating the idiosyncrasies of my writing style into proper English fell upon Steve's production team, whose task it was to figure out how to correlate my French thinking (French being my first language) into English—no enviable task in the best of circumstances. They did not shy away nor give up on this arduous task; their handiwork permeates the end result that is in the reader's hand. Steve's team was also instrumental in morphing my hand-drawn figures and sketches into the efficient clarity of the images comprised in both books. Their guidance and feedback were also imbued with the kind of diligent patience and professionalism that made the necessary back-and-forth exchanges a rewarding experience (speaking strictly for myself, of course, as the net beneficiary of their ample experience).

A great many insights found in the book came about from the generous relationships of colleagues and professional acquaintances. First among them is Robert Faulder (Director of the Industrial Research Assistance Program (IRAP), National Research Council of Canada), who was instrumental in bringing me on board the IRAP train. My thanks go to my IRAP colleagues Ron Quick, Dr. Arvinder Kainth, Bob Golding, Gordon Jolly, Peter Basnak, Calvin Koskowich, and Nikki Butcher, who shared with abandon their own experiences with the innovation process and its many pitfalls. Poonam Tauh, Ph.D., a patent agent at MBM Intellectual Property Law, outlined the lay of the land for the patent discussion in Chapter 3, while Shawn Abbott, a partner at iNovia Capital (and co-inventor of the ubiquitous USB computer connector) supplied precious guidance on dealing with IP infringement cases. Richard May, venture capitalist, shined a light on the mysterious workings of angle investors and venture capitalist organizations. Bruce MacArthur (founder and CEO of Tesera Systems) generously shared his business philosophy on culture, employee strategies, and officeless operations. Alan Swanson (past executive at Newalta Corporation, now General Manager at Klimer Platforms) bluntly made the case for paying attention to the financials and choosing cash flow over vision integrity in Chapters 10 and 11. John MacDonald (founder and director of The Sulphuric Group and also a past client of NAIAD Company Ltd.) painted—in exacting yet painful detail—what the actual reality of the battlefield looks like in a highly competitive and unleveled marketplace, which is discussed in the first three chapters.

Additional thanks go to Michael Kerr (technical development advisor with Alberta Innovates), Joe Lukacs (CEO of CETAC-West), and Jeremiah Lindstrom (then VP of Business Services with CETAC-West and now Industrial Technology Advisor at IRAP) for their respective views on technology maturity levels and commercialization challenges. Last, but not least, I thank Darren Massey (program leader of GE's Global Growth Organization) for his help in uncovering the lay of the digital land that is explored in later chapters.

Last, in the tradition started by *Investment-Centric Project Management*, I tip my hat to Fraser Brooks and his crew at Starbucks in Britannia Plaza (Calgary, Alberta) who kept the brain lubricants flowing by the corner near the bay window. I raise my coffee cup (my very own, really, kept on the shelf above the coffee machine) to Alphonso Camaya, Cheyenne Ockey, Jerica Rollinmud, Gemma Maglaque, Jeremy Masson, Ainna Javier, Greg Vanderbeek, Yasmin Abdulkadir, Christophe Landry, and Yenimar Badell.

CHAPTER SUMMARIES

PART 1—THE INNOVATION JOURNEY

Part 1 is comprised of six chapters. The first two chapters lay out the global perspective of the innovation process: from this the reader will garner a thematic understanding of the forces with which an innovator must contend. The next pair of chapters introduces the concepts that underlie the work of planning and scoping the development process. Together, Chapters 5 and 6 deal with the transition from technology development to asset creation.

Chapter 1 introduces the reader to the unsuspecting complexity of the innovation process.

Chapter 2 strives to paint the true reality confronting the innovator. The object is to open the reader's eyes to the real nature of the opposition that will stand in the innovator's way, which is essential to formulate a suitable innovation development strategy.

Chapter 3 discusses the key factors that propitiate the probability of success of the project. It also introduces the reader to the *technology readiness level* methodology, which breaks down the sequence of activities to transform the idea into the product.

Chapter 4 presents a detailed road map to determine what work needs to be done when, in what order, and for what purpose. The reader will find the techniques for quantifying the scope of work, the time and cost estimates of each task, the timelines, the budget, the resources, and the go/no-go decision schemes to progress the development work.

Chapter 5 brings the reader to the critical stage of the prototype's pilot test to secure the very important first customer sale.

Chapter 6 discusses the innovation journey from the perspective of the outside champion—our would-be buyer of the innovative product.

PART 2—THE BUSINESS JOURNEY

Part 2 switches the orientation of the text from innovation to business. It assumes that product development has succeeded and that the product is ready to start making money.

Chapter 7 starts things off with the issue of management. The text addresses the general features and dangers of managing the project as seen by the project or business manager's point of view. The reader will discover the concept of the project management framework and understand how that framework can be used to corral risks, mitigate off-the-rail situations, and show the value of investment capital over time.

Chapter 8 is concerned with the issue of culture and its relationship with the concepts of vision, mission, strategy, and value proposition.

Chapter 9 segues from this theme to explore what is involved in getting the business ready to sell the product, a stage that is called *pre-commercialization*.

Chapter 10 walks the reader through a selection of marketing topics that are imperative to the external communication of the firm.

Chapter 11 contrasts the aspirational character of Chapter 9 with the bareknuckle inflexibility of cash flow demands. The arrant importance of paying diligent, constant attention to the flow of money in and out of the firm will be unequivocally stated. *The vision thing is subservient to the cash king as long as it cannot be inverted.*

Chapter 12 switches the focus to business survival in the face of adversity and an unpredictable future. It introduces the idea of the *antifragile organization*, an organic construct meant to enable an organization to not only survive a threatening event, but grow in strength from it.

Chapter 13 concludes the text through a parallel between the innovation process and the mechanics of natural selection and evolution.

Web
Added
Value™

This book has free material available for download from the
Web Added Value™ resource center at *www.jrosspub.com*

At J. Ross Publishing we are committed to providing today's professional with practical, hands-on tools that enhance the learning experience and give readers an opportunity to apply what they have learned. That is why we offer free ancillary materials available for download on this book and all participating Web Added Value™ publications. These online resources may include interactive versions of material that appears in the book or supplemental templates, worksheets, models, plans, case studies, proposals, spreadsheets and assessment tools, among other things. Whenever you see the WAV™ symbol in any of our publications, it means bonus materials accompany the book and are available from the Web Added Value Download Resource Center at www.jrosspub.com.

Downloads for *Investment-Centric Innovation Project Management: Winning the New Product Development Game* include a Unit Transformation Worksheet, a Direct Accountability PowerPoint, a Technology Development Plan, and a set of slides presenting 40 TRIZ Design Principles.

Part I

The Innovation Journey

From the idea to the first sale: in this first part of the book, the reader will be taken along the innovation journey—exploring the pitfalls, land mines, waterfalls, and windfalls of the development process—all the way up to making that all-important first sale of the commercially ready innovation.

1

THE BIRTH OF A NOTION

"Adversity reveals genius; prosperity conceals it."
—Horace

THE BETTER MOUSETRAP

A Star Is Born

Ours is a world filled with ideas that came to be. Take a look around you right now. It doesn't matter whether you are lying in bed, traveling on a plane, driving, or sitting on a park bench reading this book; you will see just how much your existence is affected by the things in and around it. This very book is the sum total of wondrous technologies that conspired to put it in your hands. This book, seemingly so innocuous, embodies the very essence of the innovation process which, in this case, was so momentous that in the hands of Guttenberg it once changed the world. This book may look like an unlikely standard-bearer of innovation; but, when you pause to think about its coming to life, it conceals all the marvels of modern life. This book simply would not exist without the awe-inspiring power of innovation.

We go about our daily routine without ever giving a second thought to the seminal influence of innovations on the world. We see things as they are and take them for granted. Sometimes, we ask why they should be so. Sometimes, we ponder why indeed, and imagine how else they could be. Everyone has lived a moment when the invention of a new device seemed so evident that it made you wish that you had thought of it first. Humans seem to be genetically predisposed to detect flaws in their environment as a survival reflex. To the brain, flaws are a threat—be it a risk of pain, a danger, a denial of access, an absence of safety, or simply an annoyance. Whatever the case, it is the flaw that spurs people to let their minds wander and stumble upon a way to fix it. A thought leads to an idea, which becomes a concept, from which is molded a reality in many iterations, until a final design is at hand. This is the quintessence of the life of an innovation. Everyone (well, most of us) is born with this innate gift of observation and deduction to spawn new visions of how things can be. We need not ask where ideas come from; instead, we wish to know how to make them real and get rich in the process. What this process is and how to carry it out successfully is the central thesis of this book.

The innovation process is multifaceted, tedious, long-winded, and fraught with frustrations. The idea is just the starting point. To get from the starting point to riches demands time, patience, money, persistence, and luck. Sweat and steadfastness will make the idea into a reality. But transforming that reality into a profitable business calls for something more. It needs a formal framework to execute all that must be done, in the right sequence, to reach the end in a minimum of time and budget. Large companies have two competitive advantages over everyone else in this realm: money and access. *Money* empowers them to marshal whatever resources they already have unto their own innovation pursuits. *Access* enables them to hire whatever expertise or company necessary to do the work on their behalf. IDEO, the product design company that is the standard-bearer of Planet Innovation, is the top of this particular consulting business. As for the rest of us, i.e., the overwhelming majority of the players in the innovation game, we must make do with what we can get. Dwarfed by resources and strained by cash flow, the silent majority is left to its own device to figure out the mechanics of transforming an idea into a commercially successful product.

This book intends to swing the lopsided competitive advantage of big business back toward the little guy. So what is the *good* news? It is possible to overcome the hegemony of money through the agency of a formal development process that is both potent and economical. There are myriad ways by which an idea can be transformed into a product, a service, a process, or a procedure. Most ways will take too long, run out of money, or fail to gain traction with buyers. This book presents one empirical way that avoids these pitfalls and leads to commercial success *without breaking the bank*. Note where the emphasis lies: on the commercial success rather than the wizardry of the innovation. The idea behind the innovation is but a seed that must be nurtured to blossom into the commercially successful product. The product is the cornerstone of the business that we intend to create. The business is the ultimate aim of the innovation journey, one that will become profitable. This way of moving from idea to profits has a name: *investment-centric innovation project management* (ICIPM).

An Ancient Game

The preponderance of the word *innovation* in the geopolitical discourse speaks to its importance to the broader discussion on free trade deals, economic hegemony, and income equality. There is no denying the role of innovations to the wealth of nations. As Thomas Piketty remarked in his seminal book, *Capital in the Twenty-First Century*, the widespread impact of innovations has always led to dramatic changes in their times. Back in 1980, there was no *modern* internet, nor were there smartphones, CAT scan machines, or nine-speed automatic transmissions. Flying was still reserved for a minority of well-to-do travelers. Attending a university was reserved for a minority of high school graduates. Piketty remarked that up to a third of the jobs in today's economy did not exist thirty years ago. That's what we call impact.

The subject has taken on the mantle of economic orthodoxy on par with those of Marx, Keynes, Schumpeter, and Deng Xiaoping. It peppers the political discourse to such an extent that national governments everywhere latched onto its economic promises as a vehicle of GDP growth, wealth creation, and tax revenue inflation. To gauge from the media coverage, one could think that the mechanics of innovation was itself a recent innovation of the post-industrial revolution. And one would be forgiven for this impression—for innovations are as old as humanity. Call them ideas, call them concepts, or call them flashes of genius; in the end, they are all incarnations of the instance of a point in time when what came after was different than what came before. Fire, the wheel, counting, writing, agriculture, clothing, bricks, metal smelting, threads and needles, knives, cups, plates, pipes, oil, music, paint, the Sistine Chapel—all of these are examples of an innovation that was imagined or discovered by someone, and then manifested into being. Every single artifact that you can touch, smell, hear, or taste began at inception as a thought which became an idea that eventually became reality. Some changed the world (think fire, wheels, languages), while others made it just a tiny bit better (the fork, toilet paper, shoes); some came out of someone's mental triumph (geometry, buoyancy, croissants); and others developed as improvements upon the extant (corsets, ballpoint pen, money). The word *innovation* conjures up visions of something totally new and novel. The bulk of them do not represent the majority. In the majority of cases, the innovation arose incrementally by integrating existing bits and bytes.[1]

Ironically, despite years of first-hand exposure to the phenomenon of innovation, most of us would be hard-pressed to explain the *mechanics* of innovation. This lack of understanding perhaps explains why so many innovative adventures end in failure. The evidence indicates that close to 90% of novel products and services will fail in the marketplace. Mark Payne, President and Founder of Fahrenheit 212, points out that most companies begin to fail when they neglect to deal with the toughest challenges first.[2] Failure or success will often be dictated by the choice between focusing on the widget's features (failure) rather than on the needs of the eventual buyer (success). The former emphasizes the better mousetrap as a means of attracting buyers; the latter builds a mousetrap that will solve their problems.

The Burden of Proof

The better mousetrap almost never works out as a business motive. For sure, the merit of an idea is what gives the ensuing development the impetus to proceed, but that's about it. The history of commerce is littered with examples of great products that went bankrupt. Think of Newton (Apple), New Coke, Google Glass, Bikes (by Smith and Wesson, the gun manufacturer), DMC-12 DeLorean (of *Back to the Future* fame), Zune (Microsoft), Betamax (Sony), LaserDisc (Phillips), Zima (Coors Brewing Company), Lisa (Apple), Pinto (Ford Motor Company), and Wave (Google). There is even a museum in Sweden dedicated to the glory of past failures that were so bad, they are good (see http://museumoffailure.se). The reader is invited to check it out at this time and then again at the end of Chapter 3 to get a stronger appreciation of the importance of being attuned to the market before launching into the development of a supposed better mousetrap.

Conceptually, all innovations labor under a burden of proof that must be proven beyond any reasonable doubt in order to reach the land of plenty. This burden of proof goes something like this:

Proof of need > proof of physics > proof of system > proof of installation > proof of economics >>> make money.

Before any labor and treasure is spent on developing the purported innovation, the proponent must demonstrate the terms under which the marketplace will embrace it. That's the *proof of need*. Next, it is necessary to demonstrate that the product is feasible *practically* in terms of the physics (which implies chemistry, mathematics, and any other pertinent scientific basis) involved. The key word is *practically*. For example, if the operating principle requires rare and esoteric materials, its commercial viability may be mortally wounded from the get-go. It is not enough to show that the science permits the principle; the economics must also permit the science at production scales. This is the *proof of physics*. It is followed by the *proof of system*, whereby the working principle is integrated into a working model of the device and tested in the laboratory. At this stage, the aim is to uncover the side effects stemming from the interplay of the integrated components. Once proven, the system is scaled up to the actual size intended for sale, then tested once again for interactions and emergent complexities within a controlled environment (the lab, a field test, or a pilot plant). This is the *proof of installation*. The final stage, *proof of economics*, must prove out the business case for the product. In other words, are the economics of the business required to sell the innovation worth the investment?

The secret of innovation success lies within the burden of proof. The innovation process begins with the correct assessment of what the market needs and the conditions under which the market will buy the product. This is what Mark Payne[3] means by choosing to do the toughest challenges first. Make no mistake about this: the commercialization of a product is order of magnitudes more difficult than coming up with a good product design. Take the Segway mobility device, a two-wheeled scooter that remains to this day a marvel of engineering and simplicity. Unleashed initially with great fanfare, it failed to gain wide traction in the marketplace. Why? Because its proponents never took the time to assess the regulatory environment surrounding its use. You see, most city by-laws would not allow its use on sidewalks because it was motorized, nor allow it on city roads because of safety. With no obvious field of joy upon which buyers could gambol away with glee, the Segway failed utterly in its initial vision of a world-changing urban transportation solution.

A FEW DEFINITIONS

The Product

In this book, the term *product* will encompass both product and service innovations. In either case, the definition will imply that a user spends money to acquire or use it. The product, as an entity, is either physical or algorithmic. For instance, this book was written on a laptop—a physical product—through the agency of a word processing application—an algorithmic product. A service, on the other hand, has no weight. It is essentially an activity that produces an output bought by the user. From the user's perspective, a product answers the question, what can I buy from you?—whereas a service answers the question, what can you do for me? Clearly, the inner workings of a service may involve physical and algorithmic products. Buying an airplane ticket online and getting it printed through a kiosk at the airport involves both; however, their respective inner workings are invisible to the buyer who does not care about the software or the machine that prints it. The user in this case is purchasing a service, namely transportation.

The *Integrated* Product

The *product* comes in three flavors: *integrated, ready,* and *schema.* The *integrated product* must be incorporated into an existing infrastructure before it can be used. The integration implies that the product is controlled through signals and commands that are transacted within the infrastructure. It also implies that the inputs and outputs of the product are dependent on the inputs and outputs of other existing products. A solar power system, complete with battery storage connected to the main distribution grid is a good example. Another example is the game app on a smartphone—the underlying code must be compatible with the phone's operating system, work with the physical user interfaces, and not place excessive demands on the battery.

The *Ready* Product

On the other hand, things like a screw, a sensor, a control panel, a clothespin, a button, a smartphone, a car, a light bulb, and a laptop are not integrated in the sense that was previously laid out. These product instances can be used at once and perform their function independently of their environment. They are called *ready products.* Whereas an *integrated product* gives priority to function over form, the *ready product* will tend to flip the priority in favor of form over function. Retail products are of the *ready* type, for which color, feel, and finishes matter to the user. Industrial products are usually of the *integrated type* and are less prone to whims and fancy in matters of buying decisions. What matters is that they work as advertised. This distinction will become critical to the discussion of pilot demonstration in Chapter 5.

The *Schema* Product

The third product type is the *schema.* The *schema* product has no immediate tangible form. It is first and foremost a process through which information and interactions flow. The *schema* product is akin to the mechanics of a transaction. What must be done to approve a request? Whose signatures are required to release a payment for an expense report? How to file an income tax return online, without paper? How to best handle long lines at an amusement park? These are examples of *schema* products. The April 2017 edition of the magazine *Wired* includes an intriguing example in the form of a high-efficiency office floor layout.[4] In all of these instances, the *schema* product differs from the integrated and the ready products in one key aspect: it generates no sales revenues from users—it exists as a cog in the wheel that makes an organization's world turn. Yet, while it generates no direct sales revenues, the *schema* is fundamental to the profitability of the business, through process and transaction efficiencies (more on this in Chapter 5). Within the realm of a business' operations, the *schema* product constitutes the broadest source of internal innovations from which higher profits can be wrung out.

The Players

The term *innovator* will designate the individual leading the innovation journey. That person may also be the idea's originator in most cases. The innovator is the driving force behind the vision and is the overall leader of the activities throughout the development's phases. The innovator may be the inventor, the development manager, the eventual business manager, or even the company underwriting the project. Over time, the innovator will be forced to make a choice between managing the development process and managing the business underlying the development. In all instances, the innovator will be understood to carry the ultimate decision-making power over the innovation journey.

The term *buyer* will refer to any party who is independent of the innovator and is willing to buy the innovator's product offering. The buyer can be a person or a company, but *not* related to the innovator through family or friendly ties. The buyer will represent a commercial entity distinct from the innovator's firm for *integrated* and *ready products*. For *schema* products, the buyer will in most instances belong to the organization intent on implementing them.

The term *owner* will designate the organization employing the buyer. Finally, *investors* and *shareholders* will be used interchangeably to designate the providers of funds to the innovator, including government funding programs.

THE POINT

The Aim of the Game

The book will not dwell into the mechanics of idea generation, which is already amply served by a surplus of excellent books.[5] The text assumes that the reader's idea has merit from the get-go. From there, it proceeds to guide the reader on a journey toward the objective of a profitable business. The text follows the chronology of the development process. It will introduce the reader to the variegated techniques for assessing the merits of the idea and its commercial potential; for turning the idea into the set of functions necessary to achieve commercial success; for avoiding dead ends, pitfalls, and wasteful chases; for constructing a development plan that is controllable, predictable, and without risk; for executing the work at the least cost and time; and for managing effectively the randomness that is inherent to the process while staying steadfastly on course. The reader will discover a comprehensive methodology for conducting research and development and for executing an innovation strategy that yields the greatest probability of success in the least amount of time. Incidentally, notice the emphasis on the business outcome rather than the wizardry of the gadget. This is on purpose and will be a recurring theme throughout the book. The end game is making money, not making flashy gadgets.

The book explains to the reader the mechanics of transforming an idea into a business. The transformation mechanics go by the name *development process*. The set of activities required by this process will comprise the *project*. This particular perspective allows us to characterize the evolution of the innovation process in terms of project management, from which we can extract the necessary tools and techniques to manage the scope, the timelines, the budgets, the risks, and the outcomes. The management approach will borrow heavily from the *investment-centric project management* (ICPM) philosophy expounded on by Keays.[6] ICPM states that the point of a project is to develop a profitably performing asset (that which generates revenues for its shareholders over the asset's economic life). Analogously, we posit that the point of the innovation process is the *realization of the commercially successful business* based on the sale of the product. The product becomes the asset when it begins to generate revenues. The asset is driven by the prime objective of delivering a return on investment (ROI) to its shareholders throughout the economic life of the product. This perspective sets the tone for the book and frames the end game of the innovation process as *making money from the asset*. The development process is thus seen to be the *investment vehicle* to realize the *asset*.

Two Solitudes

As we will see in Chapter 2, an innovator is quite distinct from an inventor. Suffice it to say that the inventor exists in juxtaposition to his idea, while the innovator exists as a counterpart to his buyer. Without a buyer, the innovation journey is futile. The people who have the innovator's well-being at heart cannot be counted as arbiters of an idea's merit. The sole measure of that merit stems from the commerce that it engenders (or not). For that reason, the buyer is the logical arbiter. The buyer performs two vital functions: (1) define the purchase criteria (why a buyer would purchase the innovation); and (2) buy the innovation once it is offered.

> *The innovator-buyer relationship is the driving—external—force underlying the innovation journey. Commercial success is possible only through the willing agency of the buyer, whose needs must be satisfied by the innovation. No buyer, no business.*

What about the investors? It is a self-evident truth that the innovation journey requires money. As air is to a scuba diver, so is money to an innovator. The investor fulfills two vital functions during the innovation journey: (1) supply the money; and (2) enforce the focus on the end game: the commercially successful business. The investor will most often be a collection of sources such as wealthy individuals, venture capital firms, government programs, and would-be buyers. Observe, once again, the absence of family members and friends. Although these people can contribute money to the cause, these ties will often taint the cold, rational calculations that are required to make tough but necessary decisions (like firing the innovator, for example!). The innovator is best served by the discipline imposed by independent minds marching in unison to reach the summit together.

> *The innovator-investor relationship is the driving—internal—force behind the innovation journey. It is the source of energy required to power the development works.*

THE AUDIENCE

From Innovation to Corporation

This book is divided in two parts: Innovation and Business. Part 1, The Innovation Journey, discusses the innovation process, its techniques, and its developmental sequence. Part 1 will therefore appeal to the reader who is interested in the transformation of an idea into a commercial product, but may lack the experience to see it through. The reader may already be employed in an established firm, or be the founder of a one-man start-up company. Part 1 is not—*and this is important*—about techniques for coming up with the idea in the first place or for looking around for opportunities to innovate. Part 1 is about equipping the reader with a detailed road map for transforming an idea into a commercially successful business. The road map creates a formal product development framework to carry out the innovation process in accordance with professional project management principles. These principles are necessary to maintain investment discipline—without which the project will devolve into a morass of tinkering and improvisation.

The emphasis is on the process of evolving the idea over time, expounded in a prescriptive style, to enable the reader to apply the methodology immediately to his own circumstances. The prescriptions will thus empower the reader to:

- Engineer a product development strategy that will minimize investor risks (costs, time, performance);

- Put together a project execution plan that will maximize the probability of product success *in the shortest time* possible; and
- Devise a commercialization strategy that is aimed at accelerating the attainment of profitability for the business thus created.

Part 2, The Business Journey, will switch the focus from innovation to business. The appeal of Part 2 will resonate with readers who are in the early stages of their own business, perhaps as start-ups or as recent buyers of a small business, and who are relatively new to the intricacies of everyday mechanics. The text will point the reader in several directions and bring to light the hidden traps and dangers of ramping up a business. Topics will span a broad range of business functions from manufacturing, warehousing, and logistics, to supply chain management and marketing; from corporate strategy to execution tactics; and conclude with important pointers for the often-dreaded realm of finance and money matters.

Multiple Personalities

The reader will note a constant evolution in the innovator's immediate focus as the text progresses through Parts 1 and 2. From the outset, that focus will be placed on figuring out the viability of the idea, then switch to a market perspective that is driven by external imperatives. The focus will once again be transformed into management discipline while the innovation development takes places. Over time, the development will near completion and require yet another focus adjustment to embrace the all-important monetization planning before product launch. The discussion at this point will adopt a more descriptive style, and paint in broad strokes a high-level visualization of such big picture items as production setup, marketing development, sales strategy, after-sale support, and business operations. Each one of these subjects is a topic of study unto themselves and is beyond the scope of this book. The text is meant to alert the reader to the importance of these enterprise functions for the success of the business.

Taxonomy

The text will rely on a number of common terms that are familiar to most readers. Nevertheless, within the ICIPM context, several of these terms will take on specific meanings defined in Tables 1.1, 1.2, and 1.3.[7]

A consequence of these definitions will be that some of the material may not apply to all readers, depending on the scope of an envisioned product. When the latter is a component or an assembly, pursuant to Table 1.1, the development

Table 1.1   Physical taxonomy

Product	The generic term referring to a product, service, process, procedure, or other objective of the innovation process.
Asset	The sum of the final, ready-for-sale product and the business functions enabling its selling and servicing.
Innovation process	The activities carried out during the development of a product, comprising the TRL spectrum.
Project	The shorthand name for *innovation process.*
TRL	Technology readiness level. Method of estimating the technology maturity of a product during development.
Design	Set of related deliverables representing the theoretical features of the asset.
Product	The product is the version of a sales-ready design.
Unit transformation	A process that converts one or more input variables into one or more output variables. The process can be physical, procedural, or algorithmic. Together, the inputs, transformation process, and outputs constitute a product function.
Element	Generic term representing the constitutive part of a set of connected parts. For example, components are the elements of an assembly. Both are the elements of a system. And all three are elements of an installation.
Primary	An element is said to be primary when its unit transformation directly contributes to the revenue stream. For example, a gas compressor moving natural gas down a pipeline is a primary system.
Secondary	An element is said to be secondary when it acts as an enabler of a primary element. The fuel gas supply to the engine driving the gas compressor is a secondary system.
Tertiary	An element is said to be tertiary when it belongs to the operation of a system, an installation, or a plant. The access road to the compression station and the ground rainwater drainage network are tertiary installations.
Component	The smallest, indivisible physical element of a design; a component performs a single transformation. For example, the components of a wheel include the tire, the rim, the bolts, the inner tube, the pressure sensor, and the hubcap.
Assembly	Two or more components acting together to generate several unit transformations. The tire and inner tube, for example, form the tire assembly. The rim assembly include the rim, the spokes, and the pressure sensor. The hubcap assembly includes the cap and the clips for securing it on the rim. When the assembly is the product, as defined above, it includes all primary and secondary assemblies.

System	Two or more assemblies acting together. The wheel system includes the above assemblies. When the system is the product, as defined above, it includes all primary and secondary assemblies.
Installation	Two or more systems acting together. The front-wheel drive installation on a car includes the wheel systems, the brake systems, and the command hardware to control them. When the installation is the product, as defined above, it includes all primary and secondary systems.
Plant	Set of all installations forming an operating asset. The plant includes all three levels (primary, secondary, tertiary) of the elements constituting it.
Performance	The sum of the revenues generated, expenses incurred, and profits garnered by the asset.
BL[1]	Boundary layer. The physical envelope of a system, installation, or plant. The envelope is a narrow band forming the perimeter (real or assigned) of the layer. The layer defines what lies inside and outside of it, and is used as an interface junction between what comes in and out of the envelope. The ins and outs include physical connections, control signals, and geometric alignment between adjoining systems/installations. The layer also establishes the accountability of the parties involved inside and outside of the layer.
IBL	Inside boundary layer. Delineates the scope assigned to the accountable party.
OBL	Outside boundary layer. That which *is not explicitly* comprised within the IBL.

[1]The allusion to a *layer* rather than a *limit* is intentional. It borrows from the notion of the boundary layer in fluid mechanics, which is a thin physical layer of a finite width inside a fluid adjacent to a physical boundary (such as a wall or another fluid).

Table 1.2 Work taxonomy

Output	The outcome of applied work and evidence of the work so performed.
Deliverable	An output that is bought.
Task	Time-limited work performed by one specialty or discipline and producing at least one output. Examples include doing a calculation, preparing a letter, and creating a drawing.
Activity	Group of related tasks required to produce at least one deliverable.
Work package	Group of activities resulting in a design.
Scope of work	Set of all related work packages that form at least one system.
Phase	A life-cycle phase is a group of two or more scopes of work.

Table 1.3 Labor taxonomy

Specialty	Specific expertise, by individual. Examples include electrical engineer, architect, lawyer, and project manager.
Discipline	Group of related specialties. Contracts, for example, could include the specialties of formation, administration, and billing.
Function	Group of related disciplines. Engineering, for example, could include mechanical, electrical, structural, civil, and chemical engineering disciplines.
Team	Group of functions.

process may be completed without the need for a formal pilot demonstration. On the other hand, large-scale complex systems and installation will require a pilot demonstration stage to gain credibility in buyers' eyes. Three examples of these possible situations are shown in Table 1.4.

A Remark About Software

Software is an integral part of the innovation process. It may arise as a functional component of the product (the control system algorithm, for example), as the product itself (an app, an application), or as a business function (i.e., a *schema* product) supporting the commercialization. While the ICIPM approach applies equally to bits as to bytes, the reader is cautioned about embarking unconditionally into software projects. An algorithm that is strictly limited to the inner workings of the product, called a *control algorithm* in ICIPM, is included in the scope of this book. If the algorithm extends beyond the product, (for example,

Table 1.4 Examples of products ranked by technology readiness level (TRL)

Product	Machine	Hybrid[1]	Software	Final design TRL
Component	Winding	Antenna	Signal capture subroutine	6
Assembly	Rotor	Input module	Signal processing algorithm	6
System	Electric motor	Data processor	Transmission application	6
Installation	Motor-pump powertrain	Orbiting satellite	Satellite control	7
Plant	Pumping station	Earth-based GPS network	GPS network control	7

[1]The hybrid column illustrates a product that combines physical and algorithmic attributes.

uploading the data measured by a sensor to a Cloud-based archive) it is said to be an *application algorithm* (which will usually mean a collection of them working in tandem) and is excluded from this book's scope. In the latter case, the software-as-product (i.e., the application software) entails a different set of business requirements than physical products. The interested reader is invited to consult the existing literature on the subject.[8] Once a piece of software is released into the wild, it will take an everlasting life of its own, and spawn a permanent need for overhead staffing to look after it. There is no evading such duties as version maintenance, debugging, customer support, data integrity, crash and disaster recovery, hacking defense, privacy protection, pirating, server security, and whatnot. The cost of these demands increases exponentially when the software is intended for end users. Consequently, the product development strategy should give preference to commercial off-the-shelf software solutions rather than custom designed. The reader will be best served by seeking to minimize customized code. Things like databases, Cloud computing, data storage, account management, and crash recovery are best served by existing solutions. Never forget:

Software never dies until your business does.

THE POINT—AGAIN

It is important to emphasize once again the very point of the innovation process:

The innovation process serves to realize a commercially successful business.

The product is the cornerstone of the business. The asset (the product and associated business activities) is the enabler of the business. Finally, profitability is the aim of the business. The resources marshaled throughout are the investment vehicle. It is imperative that the reader grasps the fact that investors will not invest money, time, and patience to empower the reader to believe in the power of his dream. They will do so in the expectation of getting an ROI that is commensurate with the risks taken. It is easy to fall prey to the allure of the creative process and to get lost in the design journey while in the pursuit of perfection. The journey is *essential*, obviously, but only as the means to the end, which is the commercially successful business. Investors will part with their money when they believe that the innovator will make money one day, and lots of it if in the not-too-distant future. If the sole intent of the reader is to tinker on an invention until he is happy with it, this book is not for you.

NOTES

1. See *The Nature of Technology: What It Is and How It Evolves* by W. Brian Arthur.
2. See *How to Kill a Unicorn: How the World's Hottest Innovation Factory Builds Bold Ideas That Make It to Market* by Mark Payne.
3. Ibid.
4. *Wired Magazine.*
5. See in particular *The Art of Innovation: Lessons in Creativity from IDEO, America's Leading Design Firm* by Tom Kelley and Jonathan Littman and *The Ten Faces of Innovation: IDEO's Strategies for Defeating the Devil's Advocate and Driving Creativity Throughout Your Organization* by Tom Kelley and Jonathan Littman.
6. See *Investment-Centric Project Management: Advanced Strategies for Developing and Executing Successful Capital Projects* by Steven J. Keays.
7. These definitions are borrowed from Chapter 11 of *Investment-Centric Project Management: Advanced Strategies for Developing and Executing Successful Capital Projects* by Steven J. Keays.
8. The books *Clean Code: A Handbook of Agile Software Craftsmanship* by Robert C. Martin and *Agile Project Management with Scrum* by Ken Schwaber are an excellent starting point. The consensus that has emerged out of Silicon Valley is that successful software development must progress quickly in small chunks to figure out what works and what doesn't—fast. The mantra *fail fast then move on* underscores the industry's approach to code development.

2

THE INNOVATION LANDSCAPE

"All warfare is based on deception. Hence to fight and conquer in all your battles is not supreme excellence; supreme excellence consists in breaking the enemy's resistance without fighting. If you know the enemy and know yourself you need not fear the results of a hundred battles."
— Sun Tsu, *The Art of War*

ABOUT THIS IDEA OF YOURS

The Marketplace Is a Foreign Land

A newcomer to the innovation game often starts with the premise that the idea is so novel, so powerful, so economical that buyers will queue outside his eventual store for the privilege of plunking down good money to buy the thing. It's a variant on the better mousetrap analogy, prevalent among the inventor set. So, let us disclose the unsettling truth about ideas: the better mousetrap rarely, if ever, sells because it is better—it will sell when it satisfies the need of a buyer. That is not to say that your idea is futile or that you should abandon the dream. What it means is this: in the innovation game, creativity and single-mindedness are not enough, and faith is irrelevant. In the grand scheme of things, the widget does not matter because it is the *need of the buyer* that it purports to solve that sits in the driver's seat. Before you commit time, money, other people's money, and your health into transforming your idea into a product, you owe it to yourself to know first of all if that product has a realistic shot at being commercially successful. For that, you must survey the hostile market landscape that awaits you. Make no mistake about this: the market is indeed a hostile, dishonest, belligerent, and foreboding place where entrenched interests will fight tooth and nail to stop you in your tracks. It is neither fair nor prone to equality of opportunity to you or to the playing field. You enter it as a challenger; as such, expect all kinds of resistance, friction, rejection, betrayals, and heavy-handed tactics from those who are already setting up camp on the beach head. You will have to overcome all obstacles on your own.

You must understand what it is that you are up against. The forces arrayed against you paint a scary picture. All odds are stacked against you until you have formulated a strategy to turn them in your favor. You can't afford to chase trends and beliefs to satisfy your fancy. Nobody will stop you from believing in the power of your dream; but nobody will give you money just to satisfy your belief either. You must be focused on the same end game that your financial backers embrace: the creation of a commercially successful business. You must be in it to make money, and to do so as soon as possible.

8Q—The Eight Critical Questions

In order to succeed, you must be able to answer these eight questions—known simply as the 8Q set:

1. What does the buyer currently buy?
2. Why?
3. What does the buyer not currently buy?
4. Why?
5. What does the buyer wish that he could buy?
6. Why?
7. What does the buyer not want to buy?
8. Why?

These questions are at the heart of this chapter, in which the aim is to lead the reader to the answers. The first two questions help the innovator establish the baseline for what is bought today—the reality baseline. The reasons uncovered by Question 2 may not reveal exactly why things are the way they are, which is the purpose of Questions 5 through 8. Questions 3 and 4 place a boundary around the reality baseline, explaining in part what is deemed futile or valueless to the buyer and, in part, what was tried unsuccessfully in the past. The answers to these questions translate into cautionary advice to the innovator for not embarking on a dead-end development trajectory. Questions 5 and 6 indicate the potential domain of opportunities that should be explored by the innovator. The answers effectively point the innovator in the general direction of where his innovation should head. Finally, Questions 7 and 8 circumscribe the opportunity domain by laying down a secondary boundary beyond which development dead-ends and rabbit holes fester. Note the distinction between Questions 3 and 7. The third question speaks to the choice that the buyer willfully makes today in selecting one product over the others. The seventh question deals with what else could be offered out there, now or in the future, but remains unappealing to the buyer.

The very fabric of the competitive landscape lies hidden in the answers to the 8Q set. That landscape is the terrain where the innovation will need to defeat the incumbents. The marketplace is truly a battleground in the literal sense. Newcomers have no choice but to engage competitors in a battle against entrenched interests. Understanding what those entrenched interests are must be the innovator's immediate priority—which calls for facing and accepting reality as it is, rather than for how it should be.

When You Are Shopping for an Idea

What happens if the reader's situation is reversed? In this case, the reader is a buyer looking for an innovation to solve a problem or need. In effect, the reader becomes a *champion*, a concept that is discussed in Chapter 3 and expounded on in Chapters 6 and 7. The reader has no interest in undertaking a development program; she is only interested in finding out who can solve her problem in the marketplace. In this instance, the process for the reader begins with the 8Q as well. The reader needs to understand his environment and the status quo underlying it (more on that in Chapter 7). The pain points, the hurdles, the frustrations, and the problems will be compiled in parallel, possibly independently of the 8Q answers. Armed with this knowledge, the reader will be in a good position to start querying the marketplace for alternative solutions, or enlist the help of third parties to develop the required innovations.

MARKETS ARE BATTLEGROUNDS

It's a Big Boy's Game

Facing reality starts with the marketplace you intend to penetrate. Let us cast aside niceties and political correctness and frame the discussion bluntly: you are nobody and are worth nothing to the market—until you are worth more. Your idea makes no difference; nobody cares if it can change the world if it doesn't assuage someone's pain, nor is it worth anything until someone is willing to spend money to get it. This reality also belies a crippling paradox: in a world carried forth on the strength of innovations, its aversion to risk paints *your* innovation as futile. Like it or not, the marketplace is terribly unfair, biased, intolerant, and indifferent to your aspirations. If you are small or new to the market space that you intend to penetrate, you are stranded on the outside, looking in. This is the harsh reality that confronts innovators—big and small, far and wide. The game is skewed in favor of big, established players who have no qualms about squashing you to protect their interests. By itself, the novelty of your innovation makes no difference from the get-go; the would-be buyer has seen others like you before and has, in all likelihood, neither the time nor money to send your way.

> *In the buyer's eyes, your innovation is, first and foremost, an attack on his status quo, a threat to his modus operandi, and a risk to his bottom line.*

The wizardry of your innovation is meaningless if it is presented as the salient feature. Your claims of cost savings will be summarily dismissed unless you can back them up with hard, cold facts and metrics. Heed the words of Oscar Wilde: "A thing is not necessarily true because a man dies for it." So no, a better mouse-trap isn't going to sell itself after its big reveal. If you fail to confirm the need (see *proof of need* in Chapter 1), your chances of commercial success are remote, at best.

Fear Factors

Accepting the reality of the marketplace is not an option or a task that can be wished away by belief, conviction, or unbridled optimism. Doing so will only result in wasting time, money, patience, and goodwill. You must understand the sources of resistance existing in the market, which come in six types:

- *Sunk costs*—All industries can be characterized by the costs that are sunk into their business models over long periods of time. The car industry, for example, has over a century of investment in the internal combustion engine. If your innovation purports to replace this engine design with a novel approach (still based on internal combustion), you have effectively zero chance of getting a hearing. You must change the paradigm completely to have any chance of presenting your idea. That is what Tesla Motors did, for example, to gain traction and buyers.
- *Entrenched supply chains*—This is a corollary to the sunk costs. Businesses cherish their supply chains, if only for the sake of certainty of delivery. If your innovation is a fantastically different microchip that is intended for use in smartphones, it must first displace an existing supplier's offering. The relationship between maker and supplier may be far more valuable than the putative benefits of your widget, given its unproven performance, unproven production capacity, and threat to the other parts of the relationship. Displacing an entrenched vendor is hard and often impervious to cost competition from an unknown

source. Ask yourself if Apple would consider dumping Corning in favor of your new touch screen glass material because you claim it to be better and cheaper.

- *Fear of risks*—This is also known colloquially as the devil you know. Even when the supplier relationship is wobbly, at least the buyer knows what to expect and can plan accordingly. The risk of replacing this vendor with you, an unknown, unproven new-kid-on-the-block, is immensely greater than a wobbly *status quo*. The relationship between risk and *status quo* lies at the heart of all commercial and financial decisions. It can be a futile task to prove the superiority of the upside in comparison with the stability of the downside (keeping the *status quo*). If your innovation cannot unequivocally squash the risks that are perceived by your would-be buyer, forget about it; you will not sell it.

- *Regulatory exigencies*—Virtually all products in any market (those with high margins especially) are subject to a cornucopia of regulatory obligations, certifications, reporting, permitting, and the like. Your design must meet all applicable regulatory directives. As if this was not enough, your innovation must also be able to satisfy whatever additional standards and requirements are imposed by the buyer or his pertinent industry and enforced with the existing *status quo*. To ignore the idiosyncrasies of a specific market imperils the success of any innovation.

- *Return on investment (ROI)-deaf*—Products that are intended for the owners of homes and buildings suffer from the deafness of ROI analysis. In other words, these buyers have no desire to spend *now* in order to realize savings *later*. Say the innovation is a geothermal system that can deliver an 80% cost savings on a yearly basis, but with a break-even period of nine years. Although the homeowner would save 80% in energy costs every year, the price tag to get that savings is a show stopper, especially if it involves borrowing money. The ROI analysis may be perfectly valid on a financial basis but it will not sway the homeowner, who is more interested in *not* spending now than in saving *later*.

- *Price sensitivity*—This one is self-evident. Price is always a factor in the buying decision, albeit not necessarily the only one. The total cost of ownership (TCO) is a big factor in industrial equipment purchases. If your innovation touts a lower price than the *status quo*, the would-be buyer will react with a fear of risk. If you offer a higher price, justified on other worthy benefits, the reaction is likely going to be influenced by ROI-deafness. Whatever is the case, it behooves you to quantify your pricing and justify it in relation to the competition *in terms of the needs and pains of the buyer.*

Know Thy Enemy, Then Thyself

The reader, at this point, will be forgiven for feeling intimidated by the preceding discussion. The picture was painted in bleak hews specifically to drive the point home about the genuine reality on the ground. Once again, the marketplace will not care about an innovation until it can be made to care about its own bottom line. Getting there requires the innovator to know what lies beneath the surface rather than jumping in blindly. Only then can a potent innovation strategy be engineered. When reality is faced head-on unflinchingly, a strategy can be devised to manage the development risks in a controlled, proactive manner. The notion that these things are *nice problems to have* to be *dealt with when you get to them* is a recipe for failure—a costly failure.

Knowing the market is the starting point; but knowing yourself is the segue. Understanding the marketplace gives you the understanding of the *external propensities* that are acting upon your innovation project. What of the *internal* ones? The motivations of the innovator play an equally influential role in shaping the outlook of the project. He must understand, in equal measures, what these motivations are in order to marshal them unto the path leading to the end game: a commercially successful business.

INVENTOR VERSUS INVESTOR

A Critical Distinction

The inventor syndrome describes the propensity of a person or organization to become enamored with an invention. The lone wolf will gleefully spend untold hours in the garage tinkering on his beloved idea. He will obsess over every minuscule feature of the widget in the pursuit of the ideal in his mind. Fundamentally, the inventor believes that the design reigns supreme and lords it over the needs of an eventual buyer. He remains steadfastly convinced that the better mousetrap will drive sales *on its own merits*. Some will even go further with notions of game-changing paradigm shifts. History tells a different story. Genuine game changers are rare; and rarer still by lone inventors. A company like Apple was a genuine game changer, as was Microsoft with software licensing. Sir Tim Berners-Lee invented the worldwide web. Boole invented the mathematics of computer logic. William Shockley, of Bell Labs, led the team that built the first transistor. Someone in India in the sixth century invented the decimal positional number system. These inventions were game changers for the ages. Everybody else falls in the *me-too* category of inventions, be it Uber, Airbnb, Facebook, or Fortnite. James Watts' genius was to integrate several independent systems into a single steam-powered engine. Gutenberg did the same with the bits and pieces that made up the printing press. Tesla Motors packaged battery packs and electric motors into a slick design. Even Edison, master inventor par excellence, came to his light bulb on the strength of others' patents that he purchased and developed. Seminal inventions, in the sense of historical markers between the past and future, are the exceptions.

In all likelihood, your invention is not one of them.

Diametrically Opposed Motivations

The problem with inventor syndrome is to see the widget as the end game. All his efforts are placed on making the product a thing of creative beauty. In other words, the inventor starts with *proof of physics* (discussed in Chapter 1) and ends with the intention to convince the market that its needs are already met by it. By contrast, the innovator sees the widget as a means to an end, which is to realize a commercially successful business. The innovator starts with the needs and pains of the market and comes up with a solution that addresses them. He behaves like an investor with his eyes always trained on the end game. The contrast between the two is dramatic, as seen in Table 2.1.

Table 2.1   A comparison between inventor and investor

Feature	Inventor	Investor
Method	Tinker, tweak, ad hoc progress	Structured execution
Aim	Best product features possible	Best market solution possible
Schedule	Driven by tinkering; take as long as it takes	Speed to market governs
Progress	Fiddle with the design until all of it works	Version 1 meets essential market needs
Design	All in from the get-go	Incremental design evolution
Collaboration	Non-existent; introvert, secretive, not interested if not invented here	Extrovert, seeks knowledge far and wide to speed things up, involves future buyers
Obsession	The widget	Market needs
Funding	Self-funded, families and friends, conditional to full control by inventor	All sources welcome as long as it fits the strategic objectives
Control	Micromanagement	Formal framework
End game	A patent	A business

CHARACTERIZING THE OPPORTUNITY

Most Bang for the Investment Buck

Every problem is an opportunity potentially waiting to be monetized. The question is whether or not the opportunity is worth pursuing. This is a dilemma that plagues inventors and investors alike. The literature is replete with books and academic papers on the nature, forms, and categorizations of innovations. A thorough review is beyond the scope of this text.[1] For our purpose, the opportunity can be distilled down to three categories that are anchored to their competitive advantage: disruptive, diffusive, and dissipative.

The *disruptive category* is comprised of applications with the potential to change the *status quo* and carry 50% or more gains in efficiency or cost savings or both. This is the category of the genuine game changers. Very few innovations possess the caliber to belong in this category. They are big bets and moon shots necessitating a scale of resources that is the province of large, established enterprises. At the opposite end lies the *dissipative category*, germane to existing companies that are pursuing incremental changes to their product lines and yielding less than 30% gains to efficiency or cost reductions. The third category is populated by well-established incumbents who pursue their own improvement programs. This is the *me-too* group whose ROI require large sale volumes from the get-go. Outside innovations face the highest barriers to entry in this category. The risk-to-reward ratio is too great to justify the investment and is rarely worth the effort.

The worthwhile effort lies with the *diffusive category*, which is comprised of solutions that modify or expand the *status quo* with gains of 30 to 50%. This is the sweet spot for the vast majority of innovations, and the one with the highest probability of commercial success. Nimble outsiders have the upper hand over existing players whose decision frameworks are unable to cope with rapid market changes.

Reinventing the Wheel

A great, some would say tragic, source of opportunity dilapidation stems from the *not-invented here* mindset. This will be a familiar subject to readers who have been through the innovation process already and have encountered the wasteful pursuit of reinventing the wheel by the development team. The behavior manifests itself throughout the project's life, whereby the people working knee-deep in the research and development (R&D) weeds tend to approach every design requirement as a unique, proprietary feature that can only be obtained from a custom-fitted solution. The behavior can spring from a number of visceral emotions: obsession with secrecy, need for absolute control, fear of leaks to the outside world, enthrallment with the creative process, and belief in the exceptional nature of the product. Whatever the proclivity, it will produce the same harmful effects on the budget, the schedule, and the scope of work. Such behavior may suit the inventor stereotype but has no place in an investment-centric innovation project management scheme. Development must be limited to what is genuinely novel to the product (i.e., patentable and/or trademark worthy). Everything else must rely on readily available commercial solutions. For example, when designing a new electric motor, buy the bearings rather than design them. On a data gathering system, focus on user interfaces and buy the database application.

What goes for bits and bytes goes for knowledge and expertise.

Don't try to do everything in-house. It's best to go for just-in-time and call up the expertise piecemeal on a contract basis. The hourly rates will be higher, that's a given, but their cumulative hit to your investment budget will be less than paying someone full time to ramp up and catch up while working. Hire only the expertise that you deem critical over the long haul and which will give your business a competitive edge.

When seeking out an expert, beware the curse of the academic authority. The world of academia is swarming with experts in supremely narrow fields. These experts may possess the knowledge that you need, but may not share your urgency. Regardless of the expertise, never forget that the prime directive of academia is research, while the prime motivator is funding for doctoral student programs. Literature reviews, *invent-here-first*, and mathematical models are academic dogma. Things like *done beats perfect*, make it work, speed to market, and profitability run counter to academic research. When given the choice, pick industrial players by default and academic professionals by exception.

Essential versus All-In

Speed is an essential ingredient of a successful opportunity. Although technology development is more marathon than sprint, the pace of that development cannot afford inertia, if for any other reason than the investment budget is limited. The challenge for the innovator is to do the right things for the right reasons. That requires methodical patience, but also haste to get to the answers. Such a balance calls for a concise product development strategy, a proficient project execution plan, and the avoidance of wheel reinventing. These are the cornerstones of an investment-centric approach to the development process.

The mortar binding them allays judicious feature selection, state-of-the-art, and *go/no-go* decision making. A go/no-go approach is characterized by:

- *Feature selection to define the scope of work*—The latent tendency of the innovator's mindset is to aim for a comprehensive, all-inclusive configuration of features, options, and variants to make sure that all angles are covered. The *all-in* approach is held by many to be essential to the eventual success of the product's commercial rollout. However, the opposite is true. Buyers focus on a limited number of features that they deem unconditional, but are only vaguely aware of what else they could want. Hence, the critical task of the innovator is to decide from the outset what is mandatory (rules, regulations, codes), what is essential (what is bought by buyers), and what is most likely to be adopted first (the novelty of the product). All other features and options need to be put in the *future versions* basket. *Success will accrue from market credibility that is achieved by meeting the essential needs of the buyers.*

- *Built-in state-of-the-art*—The state-of-the-art must be embedded into the DNA of the innovation from the get-go. No product can afford outdated bits and bytes because the development team is not up to speed with the times. If the market expects blue-tooth capability, include that function. If the market demands a metallic casing, don't even think of going plastic. Whatever programming language is the norm must be the mother tongue of your product. It does not matter if your motivation to deviate from the state-of-the-art is rooted in the desire to cut costs; your product will be cast aside without further ado by those buyers whom you wish to convince.

- *Decision gates*—The *go/no-go* decision process is the gatekeeper of the budget. It serves three equivalent objectives: maintains the development focus on the essential features, prevents wheel spinning and wasteful digressions, and enforces the pace of the progress. The latter is best described by Sheryl Sandberg's maxim (of Facebook fame) that *done is better than perfect*. Once a feature meets the stated requirements, it is done. Move on to the next feature.

Cheap versus Valunomic

The drive for cost control is integral to the *go/no-go* decision process. But cost control is too often taken to mean doing things on the cheap—a mantra encapsulated by the ubiquitous *cost effectiveness*. But cost effectiveness will have the opposite effect if it is pursued in the name of cost savings *now* at the expense of the profitability of the business *later*. This dichotomy is solved by the *investment-centric project management* philosophy and the introduction of *valunomy*, described as follows:[2]

> "Valunomy shifts the emphasis of a buying design toward the maximization of future investment returns, and always includes total cost of ownership in the analysis. The highest valunomy is the one that achieves the highest sustained profitability over an asset's economic life."

In terms of product development, the concept of *valunomy* requires the innovator to make *all design and business decisions* based on what will maximize the investors' future ROI. Going cheap on components, labor, and processes may achieve cost savings to the business and price savings to would-be buyers, but if the result is a product that fails more than the competition or inflates warranty costs, the true cost of these so-called *savings* will be a destroyed reputation (for the product and the business) and a derelict financial performance for investors.

FUNDING SOURCES

A Permanent State of Want

Inventors and innovators possess a phenomenal capacity to make do with what they have. Resourcefulness, creativity, risk tolerance, and near mystical devotion to their pursuits set them apart from everyone else. These traits mold the innovator's personality into a can-do attitude that morphs into a stalwart willingness to overcome financial duress. Unfortunately, money is a cold-hearted master. In the end, faith and devotion are not enough. As money thrives, so will development; but when it dries up, all withers away. If you happen to work for a corporate behemoth, money problems are of a different order. Otherwise, money will always be a daily want.

Fortunately, innovators face an embarrassment of riches when it comes to funding sources, starting with governments. Yes, governments. There is indeed such a positive thing as *we're from the government and we're here to help*. National, provincial, state, and municipal programs flourish everywhere, perhaps on a broader canvas than may be realized by the innovation community. Governments caught on long ago to the value of innovations as engines of growth (meaning tax revenues) and have become willing partners to promising innovation proposals. As a bonus, many jurisdictions sponsor programs targeting the riskiest stages of the innovation process, often without any expectation of immediate investment recovery. If the R&D case is rational and the business case is sound, the innovator can find a receptive audience with one government body or another to get the ball rolling. Always look to these funding sources first when fishing for development capital. They are, after all, the most willing partners early on. Remember that doling out money to grow the economy is a potent motivator of the political establishment.

> *Look upon government funding as a reality check on your idea. If none is offered, something is wrong with the idea, the approach, or the business case. Don't criticize the funding programs or accuse their people of not understanding your vision. They've seen it all. If their answer is no, it's you, not them. Take it as a warning not to waste your and others' time and money.*

Spend versus Invest

Your funding is akin to the air in a scuba tank. Once it's gone, you're dead in the water. Never lose sight of the fact that this funding is the investment vehicle to realize the business. Weigh the merits of any spending in those terms. Is the expense aligned with the investment objectives? Is it essential to the progress of the development work? Is there another way to achieve the same results with less (in other words, are there more valunomic options)? These are the kinds of questions that must be asked each time. Do not confuse, however, the *merit* and the value of an expense. Going with the cheapest option (merit) is not always in the best interest of the project (value). For instance, the project will be better served by hiring a high-priced expert who can get you the answer you need quickly, rather than trying to *save* money on a neophyte who will take twenty times longer to come close to the same answer.

> *Approach all expenses as investments into the project and choose the option that offers the highest valunomy to the future business.*

Scaling the Expectations

The innovation project does not require from the outset a funding commitment for the entire development journey. The journey is one of many steps that are described in Chapter 4. It is better to progress incrementally and seek funding as needed. It is impossible to rationalize the funding required one or two years hence. The innovator who comes up from the get-go with a multi-million-dollar estimate for the entire endeavor will have little credibility in the eyes of would-be investors.

> *If the innovator hopes to become a unicorn, the discussion has effectively left the innovation realm to join the venture capital arena, which lies beyond the scope of this book.*

The Importance of the Oral Presentation

Presenting the innovation to potential clients, funders, and investors is supremely influential to the success of the innovator. Early on in the development journey and then later when commercialization must begin, the innovator will be required to stand up in front of a group of strangers to convince them to put their money into the endeavor. When the audience is a client or a partner, the point of the whole affair is to convince the audience that it would be a costly mistake to ignore the benefits of the innovation. When pitching to an investment crowd, the point is to convince the audience that *not* investing in the venture would be a costly mistake. The ultimate message must always convey to the audience what kind of ROI can be expected, and why. The innovator must keep in mind that the audience is motivated above all else by what's in it for them, which will always include the profits to be made. People will not accept an invitation to your presentation to discover the power of your dream, the wizardry of the innovation, or your mission to change the world. These aspects may matter to some of them, but will be meaningless if there is no money in it. The audience is there for the possibility of enriching themselves. That is the only perspective that matters in the presentation.

The most bang for the expense buck will come from delivering professional presentations to would-be investors (be they government, venture capitalists, or other). It is sad, and brutally unfair, that the presentation weighs so heavily in comparison to the message, but it is true. A skilled public speaker can deliver a message with immediate positive results, while a poor speaker can wreck the goodwill of the audience in a matter of minutes, regardless of the merit of the idea presented. Unfortunately, most people are not versed in the fine arts of marketing and public speaking. Fortunately, there are simple techniques that can go a long way toward mitigating your inexperience:

- Hire a marketing professional to develop the slide presentation. Keep the presentation short, concise, and to the point. Wherever possible, make it tell a story. At the front end, have a slide stating clearly what you seek to accomplish with the presentation (things like funding level, looking for expertise or referral, getting the audience to buy into the vision).
- Rehearse that presentation until you know it by heart.
- Come up with a list of possible questions that could arise before the presentation takes place. If you don't know the answer, don't try to baffle the audience with useless information. Just admit to your ignorance and move on to the next question.
- Before the presentation:
  - Turn off your and your team's cell phones and put them away. Nobody on your team is to have the phone in hand during the presentation.

- Run the presentation on your laptop at least once.
- Show up well ahead of the appointed time to connect things, test connectivity, and understand how the remote control for the project works.
- Have the power cables, extra batteries, chargers, and spare light bulbs at the ready.
- Bring with you a portable projector (as a backup), a cordless mouse, a laser pointer, and two flash drives containing the slide show (just in case, and make sure that they only contain the presentation).
- Bring enough paper copies of the presentation to distribute to the audience, and attach your business card with a paper clip (no staple) on each one.
- Forget knickknacks with your logo on them: they are wasted expenses.
- Run an attendance sheet or canvas for business cards (but never insist).
- When you deliver it:
  - Start on time.
  - Stick to the script. Don't improvise and don't read off the slides. Just speak to them or better yet, be a storyteller.
  - Never make promises.
  - Only make claims that you can substantiate with proven facts.
  - Don't speak about costs and cost savings. Let the audience arrive at their own conclusions while listening to you.
  - Never make statements that denigrate yourself ("I'm not too bright, it's not my field of expertise"), the competition ("their product is worthless, it's made in a sweatshop"), or the audience. When asked to voice an opinion, always set yourself apart by highlighting your positives (rather than harping on the other guy's negatives).
- After the presentation, sit down and wait for questions.
- Wait until the audience leaves before packing your things.
- If you have team members with you, do not make *any* comment on the presentation as you make your exit from the building (in the washrooms, in the corridors, in the elevator, in the lobby, or in the parking lot). Wait until you are shielded from prying ears to have this discussion with your people.
- Once you are out of the building, and only then, turn your phones back on.
- Back at the office, send an e-mail to all audience members to thank them for their time, and offer to make yourself available to follow up with any one of them as they require.

- Send a second e-mail to the person who facilitated the presentation to offer your thanks, and then request a follow-up meeting with her/him to discuss the next steps.
- Don't pester people.

PITCHING TO THE CUSTOMER

The Motivation

A customer will be motivated to invest in the innovator's project for reasons that go beyond the needs of the buyer that were captured in the 8Q answers. In a sense, the customer is being asked to invest in you, rather than to merely buy. Why would he want to buy? The easiest way to fathom the motivations is to put yourself in the customer's shoes and engage the customer in a discussion at his strategic level. Perhaps he is keen to gain a competitive edge through technology. Perhaps he wishes to have a permanent cost advantage over the competition. Perhaps he is thinking of future expansion by buying you out (which could be a highly lucrative deal for you). Perhaps he recognizes the need to take a preemptive move to prevent the competition from getting to you first. Certainty of supply and priority of service may be deemed critical (if the marketplace is already tight, for instance). Perhaps the customer is genuinely curious about your innovation. Or, perhaps he is under pressure by regulators to fix a problem and you're his best hope. Whatever the case may be, it behooves the innovator to listen attentively to what the customer says, and to what he does not say, without making any attempt to pitch your own needs.

The Pitch

These questions will be best posed within a setting that is meant to explore the needs of the customer. This could be simply a conversation over coffee, or it could be a group discussion that is mediated by the innovator. *It cannot be done by e-mail, by text, or by phone.* The process is fundamentally about establishing a personal relationship between the innovator and the customer *with the focus placed squarely on the needs of the customer*. You are not there to get money for your project; you are there to determine if your project can satisfy the strategic objectives of the customer. The exchange should be structured in three parts: discovery, presentation, and feedback.

- Discovery will occupy the first 50% of the exchange. The dialogue is entirely about uncovering the motivations of the customer, his strategic objectives, and his thoughts about how they can be realized. The last question to be asked should be about whether or not the customer has been involved in the past in similar development projects, and to find out what that experience was like. Get as much feedback as you can.

- The presentation—your presentation—will follow *if and only if you honestly believe that what you have to say will accord with the motivations of the customer*. This is absolutely critical at this point. Do not waste the customer's time if your idea does not converge with his; it is better to tell the client that your idea may not be the solution that he needs at this time. The customer will be grateful for the honesty and, perhaps, may even suggest introducing you to someone else who might be better placed to take advantage of the opportunity. If you proceed knowing that there is no fit, you will simply anger the customer and possibly burn a bridge permanently.
- Your presentation should take no more than 25% of the remaining time. Remember that this is not a sales pitch; it is an honest description of your company, of the innovation that you propose to develop, and the reasons why you think it is worth developing. Then, you should mention what kind of money you require to proceed with the *immediate* development—not the whole technology readiness level (TRL) sequence.
- The last 25% of the exchange is called the feedback stage. Here, the goal is to ask the customer about his impressions of your company, your innovation plan, and the potential for doing business together. Listen carefully to what is said and what is not said. If the customer sees an opportunity to work together, ask him for the best way to proceed. If he concludes that this is not for him, thank him for his time and offer to keep him apprised of your progress if he so desires. Do *not* ask him for a recommendation for someone else to pitch to. Such a recommendation will come naturally from him, or not at all. At all times, be polite, gracious, and respectful of the customer's willingness to listen to you.
- Finally, if he wants to continue the dialogue, do whatever is necessary to make the next step!

PITCHING FOR GRANTS AND VOUCHERS

The Motivations

The motivation of government and foundation programs is only partly influenced by investment return concerns. Of greater import to them are targets like social improvements. What they get in exchange for the money granted are job creation, tax revenues, reduction in inequity, and other like-minded social targets. It is probably fair to say that a majority of citizens and business leaders have no appreciation for the sheer number of funding programs across the TRL spectrum that are offered by municipal, provincial, state, and national governments. In many instances, the financial support is offered with little or no direct payback conditions, which should immediately appeal to all would-be innovators. These programs get their money back through future job creations and increased tax revenues. Their beauty is in their ability to take the long view for their investments while remaining intentionally hands-off over the day-to-day work of the innovator's development team. They are by far the easiest, least stressful funding sources to innovators (better even than family and friends, whose support adds an unnerving emotional baggage). The message is abundantly clear: the innovator should pursue these funding programs far and wide, with alacrity. This is as close to free money as you will get! And do not delude yourself into thinking that the paperwork will be burdensome; compared to what angel investors (described in a later section) and venture capital firms expect, the paperwork is a breeze.

The Art of the Proposal

All government programs require the submission of a proposal. The guidelines for contents and presentation will, of course, vary from one program to the other. The important thing to remember is that the proposal *must* be written explicitly and precisely in accordance with the objectives of a given program. The prohibitions against empty promises and specious sales pitches remain in full force. A proposal must never be a glitzy sales pitch or a flashy marketing brochure; nor is literary proficiency important. What matters, always, are the merits of the proposal *in relation to the stated objectives of the funding program*. For example, if the program focuses on front-end R&D to help innovators address the unknowns, uncertainties, and risks of an early-stage innovation idea, the contents of the proposal must address *specifically* those objectives in the description of the work to be done. If the program instead focuses on early commercialization, the emphasis of the proposal must be on the market research, results, analysis, and pricing strategy that was contemplated by the innovator. If the funding program targets production expansion, the text of the proposal must be anchored to issues of manufacturing techniques, quality requirements, supply chain capabilities, staffing needs, operating concepts, etc.

> *The probability of success of a proposal is tied directly to its ability to tailor the contents to the objective of the program.*

Always remember that *the program objectives govern*; hence, satisfying them rules the contents. Page count matters inasmuch as it maximizes contents in the fewest pages. When you consider the volume of proposals that any program will receive, it stands to reason that the proposal should also aim at easing the evaluator's task. Fewer words making a point are better than wordy documents that create the illusion of completeness. Bullet points are better than paragraphs. The active voice is superior to the passive. Short sentences constructed on the simple *subject-verb-object* structure carry more meaning more efficiently than rambling phrases spanning two or more lines.

> *If the innovator is unclear about the program objectives or the assessment criteria, get clarity from a representative of the program before writing the first word.*

Always remember that *order matters*. The proposal must adhere unconditionally with the content structure of the template that was supplied by the funding program. If the template specifies presentation requirements (fonts, text styles, table sizes, margins, line spacing, etc.), follow them to the letter. *Always ask for a stalwart example of a past successful proposal* and study its preparation. Additionally:

- Do not repeat information. State it once and refer to it afterwards.
- Avoid non-textual elements (figures, images, charts, graphics, audio/video files, organization charts).
- Never include hyperlinks.
- If required, complement the proposal with appendices that contain supplementary information (patent certificates, financial statements, marketing brochures, scope of work, schedules, costing details, test reports, marketing research reports, etc.).
- Answer every question.
- Answer only what is asked. Do not volunteer superfluous information.
- Keep the contents simple.

Getting Help

If writing is not a strength of the innovator, he or she will be better served by seeking the help of someone who is familiar with the process of writing. The better help will be from someone who is familiar with that specific funding program. On the other hand, be more careful when considering hiring a consultancy to do this work. That firm may be cognizant of the content requirements, but might not possess the technological insights of the innovator. Always keep in mind that the proposal will be required to provide a detailed work schedule. This is really an execution plan that will be expected to be implemented once the project gets going, which means that the innovator will have to live with it. Such a plan must be developed by the innovator, not an outside contractor.

Write Once and Reuse

It is always a good idea to develop the contents as *copy-and-paste blocks*. These blocks are exceedingly helpful when the innovator intends to pursue multiple funding programs. Although the program objectives will vary, a good portion of the questions asked will be the same for many distinct programs. For example, the members of the management team will always be asked about and is a perfect candidate for a copy-and-paste block. It is also a good idea to obtain proposal templates from several programs right off the bat. Together, they will reveal what information is requested repeatedly and perfect for copy-and-paste block creation.

The Hockey Stick Delusion

Every funding program will ask for financial statements, budget estimates, and future sales revenues—usually in the first five years following product roll-out. Many innovators make the mistake of assuming that the proposal will look better if sales figures are shown to explode in years four and five, illustrated on a revenue projection chart as a near horizontal line in the first three years followed by an abrupt upward ramp in year four—the so-called hockey stick profile seen in Figure 2.1.

For all intents and purposes, this scenario *never happens*. The proposal assessor will immediately recoil at the sight of this chart and conclude on the spot

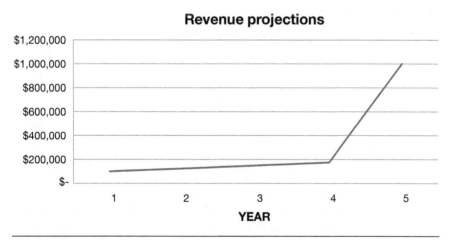

Figure 2.1   The hockey stick delusion: this scenario follows the false premise that the better mousetrap will sell on its own merits once people realize that it is available. In reality, it never happens this way. Portraying these projections as legitimate simply illustrates that the innovator is clueless about the marketplace that he or she wishes to enter.

that the innovator has zero understanding of the marketplace. That conclusion would be correct. A more realistic and therefore more credible projection of sales would look something like this:

- By the end of year one, the gross revenues will cover the operating expenses
- By the end of year two, the revenues *per employee* will exceed the average employee salary by 5 to 10%
- By year three, the ratio will exceed the average employee salary by 20 to 40%
- By year four, it should be above 70%
- By year five, it should reach 100%

Got Your Money?

This is the final point and a real kicker to boot: get your money as soon as you can! The typical funding program will require the innovator to file a claim report, a progress report, or both, as a minimum. The filing procedure, and in particular, the timing and deadlines, will be specified by the program. Whatever they are, follow them verbatim and file *as soon as you are allowed to do so*. This is money owed to you. Why on earth would you want to get it later?

PITCHING TO A SINGLE ANGEL INVESTOR

The Motivations

Angel investors are wealthy, successful individuals. They are, as a group, highly idiosyncratic and motivated by the freedom to pursue their passions. They are not interested in running anyone's company or taking over the day-to-day operations of a troubled business. They are willing to put their time, money, and connections to work on causes that matter to them. They may be very curious about a particular promise of technology (say, zero-emission power generation). They may be inspired to give back to society through charity. They may be keen on finding a cure to a disease or to prevent the spread of one. They may harbor a strong impulse to look after the welfare of the destitute. Their motivation is not primarily about making money out of their investment, but about advancing a cause that they embrace. Angels like to move in packs: when they invest, they often bring along their own network of friends and associates to pitch in. This is not to say, however, that they are careless about their investments. On the contrary, they will expect an uncompromising level of discipline from those in whom they put their trust.

The Pitch

The first challenge for the innovator is to find the angels. Angels usually don't go around advertising their wealth (contrary to the impression created by reality TV shows). Most are discrete, shun publicity, and are too busy taking care of their own business to frolic around like moneybag peacocks. Finding an angel investor requires time, patience, and constant networking. Government funding program people are likely plugged in to the angel investor scene and may be willing to pass along the innovator's message. What they will not do, however, is give out names and numbers. One simply does not cold call a potential angel to pitch an idea: one is invited by a said angel to come and present. It's a one-way street.

What happens then when the invitation has been received? First, do not accept to meet on short notice. You need time to do your own research on the individual. You need to understand his or her background, path to success, and track record with previous angel investments. Most of all, you must figure out what motivates this person. What is the passion beneath his or her willingness to extend the invitation to you. Then, and only then, should you pick a time, date, and location *that is suitable to the angel* to meet in person.

> *The sole purpose of the presentation is to determine if your project can satisfy the motivations of the angel.*

It is worth emphasizing the importance of your endeavor: you are not there to get money for your project. You will fail with that approach. This angel is a potential customer in every sense of the term. You are there to determine the angel's needs, expectations, and objections. In the grand scheme of things, his or her time is far more precious than yours. Don't waste it lest you are willing to burn a bridge (which will reverberate through the angel's own network by the way).

The presentation follows the structure that we previously spelled out for the pitch to the customer mentioned earlier—with one difference. The very first question that you should ask the angels is about their past experience with other similar investments. The answers will guide the remainder of the conversation. Like before, if you realize that your project does not align with the angels' motivation, don't waste their time further. Admit that you do not think that your project is a fit, express your thanks for their time, and offer to keep them apprised of your progress if they are interested.

PITCHING TO MONEY POOLS

The Motivations

Money pools are comprised of private equity, venture capital, and angel investor groups. These investors are typically solicited once the commercialization has started; not before. Conversely, these groups rarely get involved during technology development, except perhaps at TRL 8 and 9 (see Table 3.1 in the next chapter). They are essentially motivated in an investment deal that can be cashed in within three to five years at ten times the initial outlay. They are not interested in the innovation, only the commercial potential to increase the firm's valuation by tenfold or more. They have no time or patience for anything else. Aggressive growth coupled with rapid market share expansion is the name of the game. The price for their participation is a majority stake in the firm and running the business day to day. Innovators who cannot fathom not running the show would be well advised to not go down this route.

The Pitch

The pitch, in this instance, is a 12 to 15 minute presentation. That's it. The audience has little or no interest in the intricacies of the innovation, the insights of the presenter, or the vision of the firm's founder. The audience wants to know immediately whether or not the opportunity is worth investing in. Remember that you are but a single pitcher among hundreds of supplicants at any given time. Those in the audience have seen it all and have no time to waste on your project or on anybody else's, for that matter.

You have one shot at making your case.

The audience expects a concise, clear, and direct delivery, almost always through the medium of a slide presentation. The time constraint implies 12 to 14 slides to state your case. If you cannot boil your message down to fit this limit, you will lose the audience. If the audience begins to argue or push back, you will have lost. Ditto if the audience begins to read everything on the slides.

Airy compactness matters most. Airy implies the fewest words and maximum visuals. Compactness implies the most information conveyed over the shortest "distance."

Here are a few tips on the general look and feel of the slides:

- Visually clean and airy with a consistent visual look and feel (see also Chapter 9 under the heading *The Presentation*)
- Each slide must have the firm's logo, the marketing tag line, and the slide title

- Three to five bullets per slide and three to seven words per bullet
- One image or graph with *legible* labels per slide
- Keep animations, shape effects, and text effects to a minimum

The order of presentation is crucial. The contents developed by Linda Plano, Ph.D., founder of www.planoandsimple.com, is particularly effective.[3] A generic template of a presentation designed in accordance with the following guidelines can be found in the Web Added Value™ Download Resource Center located at jrosspub.com/wav. An overview is contained here:

- *Slide 1*: Introduction—This slide must answer the question why should the audience care? The answer must be focused on the principal pains of the existing marketplace, juxtaposed to the merits of your proposed solution.
- *Slide 2*: The Problem—This slide demonstrates that you understand your customer's problems and why the customer buys what he or she buys. Summarize with the 8Q (discussed earlier in the chapter). If the presentation is intended for customers or partners, include a bullet that will describe how your solution can expand their current markets.
- *Slide 3*: The Solution—This slide presents your answer to these problems. It also answers the question *what do you do?* Include a bullet on what your innovation does (but *not* how it works), another one about your secret sauce, then one about the overall vision, and a last one on which early markets you will focus on. Avoid jargon, complicated words, and obscure language. Keep the text *simple* and to the point.
- *Slides 4–5*: The Market—Two slides are permitted for this topic. They characterize the attractiveness of the market. How big is it? What is the growth potential? How is it segmented?
- *Slide 6*: The Competition—This slide is an honest summary of solutions that are alternative to yours; list them by name along with their vendors. The slide should also reveal to the audience why the market will choose you over the competition.
- *Slide 7*: The Differentiation—This slide explains what sets you apart from the rest, and the ease or difficulty for others to copy or reverse engineer your solution. Bullets should include: what demonstrable strengths you have, what resources you can deploy, and what intellectual property (IP) you possess or will possess.
- *Slide 8*: The Market Approach—This slide lays out your strategy and tactics to find and sign customers. Mention names if they are realistic. Include the parties that can constrain your effort (regulators, licensing, government departments, etc.).
- *Slide 9*: The Business Model—This slide tells the audience how money will flow to and from you. This is best shown as a flowchart of the various

commercial entities that will play a part in the firm's revenue generation process.

- *Slides 10–11*: The Forecast—Two slides are permitted for this one. They are meant to convey your plan to execute. It is a road map showing the liquidity events (when new capital raises will occur), the value-added markers to support the liquidity events, and the investment required for each phase.
- *Slide 12*: The Team—This slide identifies the key people who will be making up the top line (discussed in Chapter 10). The focus should be on expertise and experience, not degrees. Highlight the innovation track record of individuals, when applicable. Do *not* show an organization chart.
- *Slide 13*: The Ask—This final slide states what kind of help you need and how much money you need to move forward. By this time, the audience members should be realizing, on their own, that it would be folly to *not* invest in the innovator's journey.

The Backup Data

It is a very difficult challenge to put together these twelve slides. The necessity to keep things short and sweet goes against the grain of most innovators, who would rather wax lyrical about their vision. But there is salvation around the corner! Indeed, while this presentation will be the main item on the agenda, it is prudent to prepare a second presentation which is comprised of all the details necessary to corroborate the statements made to the audience. This is where anticipating the questions that might arise comes in handy. The answers to these questions are baked into the second presentation. While it is not critical to abide by the airy compactness imperative, it is always good practice to keep slides clutter-free and word-light. Images, animations, and videos can do a great job of conveying, at a glance, the answer sought. The look and feel of the second presentation must be identical to the first one, nevertheless. Such visual consistency goes a great way toward forging an impression in the audience's mind that the innovator has his act together. These recommendations go hand in hand with the additional advice provided in Chapter 7.

SLAYING THE IDEA SLAYERS

Sizing up the Competition

One unifying thread running through this book is the need to pay attention to the competition. Sizing up the competition is often taken lightly by the innovator and his team. Perfunctory efforts will be made to identify the immediate competitors and the obvious competing solutions on offer. Pricing data can be readily obtained and tallied into a competitive report. In most instances, that will be the end of it; which, as a result, could very well spell out the end of the innovator. Understanding the nature, heft, and breadth of the competition is absolutely critical to the innovation's success. Its importance becomes prominent in the later stages of development, when the desired innovative product has effectively reached the end of development.

Moving beyond product development and into commercialization planning brings the issue of competition back into focus—front and center. The aspects of competition that matter most to the plan are all money-driven. Some of these aspects are obvious: pricing, warranty clauses, sales volume (by competing product), and number of competing solutions on offer are relatively straightforward to compile. But there are equally important aspects that require more digging, more diligence, and more patience. Things like manufacturing times (how long it takes to get to the finished product), production logistics (which suppliers sell what to whom), component costs, volume discounts, buyer preferences, and after-sale support strategies come to mind. Finally, there are hidden aspects that must be uncovered as best as possible, such as competitors' gross margins (more on this in Chapter 11), competitors' R&D and innovation programs, market trends, customer trends, underlying technology trends, and the nefarious black swans (unsuspected competitors and/or unforeseen solutions from other markets that could cross over). The bulk of this information can be gathered through competitive intelligence activities, usually through third-party consulting experts. The costs are (surprise, surprise) significant but warranted. This kind of expense falls in the same category as the expense to quantify the IP landscape (who owns what patents, trademarks, and the like—more on this in Chapter 3). Be warned about skimping on them—the price of avoiding these costs could be to kill the commercial success of the innovation.

Why should this be so? In one single word—profitability. Competitors make money from selling their wares. Clearly, their production setups are such that they turn a profit on each unit sold. Or maybe they do not, and are continuously threatened economically. It is imperative that the innovator understands the extents to which the competition can counter the threat presented by the innovator's offering. What is the margin by which the innovator can withstand a price war? Can the innovator react with increased production volumes if the competition decides to flood the market? Can the innovator maintain his own gross margins throughout the conflict? Make no mistake about this, rolling out a new product into a given market is tantamount to a declaration of war upon the competition. Competitive hostilities will follow soon after. Can the innovator head off the reaction's onslaught? Can the innovator resist and overcome the wrath of competitors? Answers to these questions cannot be assumed nonchalantly, or dismissed out of hand. They can be inferred from the market research that will have been conducted well before the battlefield is overrun by opposing forces.

> *Understanding the competition has nothing to do with the wizardry of one's innovation and everything to do with the capabilities of competitors to wage mercantile war upon a new entrant. There is no glory in it, except for sweat, tears, toil, and blood—and the assurance that one will prevail in the end.*

The Luck Factor

Readers of a certain gilded age will remember, with a sardonic smile, a time harking back to the 1980s when the gloried business mantras of the day put greed on a pedestal and corporate raiders in the pantheon of capitalist daemons. Names like "Chainsaw" Al Dunlap (cost-cutter-par-excellence), the junk bond king Michael Milkens, and the prince of ballsy hostile takeovers, Robert Campeau, were everywhere in the news. Innumerable business books were written on how to join the party and cash in on these phenomenal opportunities. The unbridled passions of greed would not last long; in its stead came the great captains of global conglomerates, personified by the indefatigable Jack Welch, CEO, General Electric. A whole new category of business books, written by industry leaders, were rightfully commissioned to enlighten a new readership of would-be corporate managers on the right and wrong recipes to integrate vertically. Once again, the harsh and unforgiving quarterly earnings master came knocking on the doors of faltering behemoths that couldn't keep making the money to justify the vertical erection. Wouldn't you know it; conglomerates went from darlings to pariahs in the first decade of the 21st century. Getting back to one's knitting became the new mantra and the internet craze became its new enabling paradigm. Predictably, the leading books of old would not do anymore. A new crop of internet leaders came to the rescue and offered their own insights into what it took to succeed. The dot-com bubble came and burst, the banking crisis leveled business paradigms everywhere, and entire new corporate strategies had to be imagined. At which point, the second decade of this century arrived in great digital fanfare and with it, a brand new slate of business sages who offered readers yet another crop of tactics and strategies to take over the corporate world.

The pattern of business success followed by book writing by success leaders followed by wholesale rejection of the state-of-the-management art is readily discerned. One could go back further in time to witness this pattern repeating itself almost like clockwork every decade or so. Each new heralded paradigm shift was portrayed by its standard bearers as the right way to conquer markets.

Oddly, no one seems to have questioned the absence of continuity from one paradigm shift to another, as if the past had nothing to bequeath to the future. The reason should be obvious: this perpetual replacement of business paradigms was driven by those people among the C-suite set who had the luck to be at the right place at the right time and the foresight to recognize the opportunities presented to them. Pick up any business book by any business leader in any era; what transpires from them is the genius of their authors and the rewards they deserved from the hard work they put in. The corollary of these books was a tacit promise made to their readers about their own pursuits of a seat at the executive table. Follow the insights, keep the faith, and work hard—and the rewards will follow. At least, this is the putative outcome that should ensue.

The problem with this approach is that the method of the genius—whether that genius is a Caesar, an Elizabeth, a Newton, a Curie, an Einstein, a Noether, a Churchill, a Golda Meir, a Feynman, a Thatcher, a Jack Welch, a Sharapova, a Gates, a Jobs, or a Ginni Rometty—is that one cannot replicate the genius of their performances. One can admire and strive to emulate them, but the outcome will never be the same. The sad truth is that the method to the madness of the genius is integral to the outcome realized, *and hence unique to the individual.* That is why there will never be a school of preordained Nobel prize winners, nor a school for prescreened future rock stars. You could spend decades reading everything that Einstein ever wrote, yet you would still be utterly unable to even hope to approach his contributions. Welch, Gove, et al. published wonderful books on their respective stories and how they achieved what they did. But these were their own recipes, sprinkled with dashes of their own genius, served on their own luck-plated platter. They cannot be applied as road maps for the general public. They are, in the end, one-way travel plans to done-and-gone destinations.

What is not usually found in these books is a frank admission on the part of their authors about the seminal role that luck played in their successes. Everyone knows about Steve Jobs and Steve Wozniak, the founders of Apple. Far fewer people know about the third founder, Ronald Wayne. He sold his shares too early to partake in the fame that would accrue for his partners. Talk about bad luck. Luck, it turns out, played a huge part in Apple's early success. It was Steve Jobs who grasped the true potential of a device invented by Xerox researchers: the mouse. Unbelievably, Xerox failed to see what Jobs understood right away. The mouse became a keystone of the personal computer experience offered by Apple. Jobs benefited from an extraordinary stroke of luck in (1) being invited to visit Xerox's Palo Alto facilities and (2) getting a glimpse of this mouse thingy that was hopelessly stagnating in the labs.[4]

Luck, in other words, plays a huge part in the success of people and the companies they lead. It also plays a terrible part in the failure of many more people and businesses who, despite being equally competent, did not get the lucky breaks to join the rarefied ranks of the successful ones. Talent is not enough (ask Dean Kamen of Segway fame); faith is not enough (as William C. Durant, founder of General Motors, would find out during the Great Depression); hard work is not enough (ask John DeLorean of the famed car that bore his name). These people worked as hard and as diligently as any successful corporate chieftains, yet still suffered failures, sometimes shameful ones. They ran out of luck. Luck, therefore, is an integral part of a person's *individual* success and the reason why the histories of famous people are, ultimately, not replicable. These histories will contain valuable insights, lessons, guidance, wisdom, and advice that can serve anyone who becomes acquainted with them. The arc of those histories is where the connection is permanently severed—you will not succeed by following in the footsteps of someone else.

> *You will succeed by tracing your own path through time, space, and events—and by applying the hard-learned lessons of predecessors to your circumstances.*

Note that the reverse conclusion, inferred from the role of luck, does not follow automatically: success is not wholly dependent on luck to materialize. While business literature offers a surfeit of success stories that quietly rode the sinews of luck, it does a woeful job with its silence on those millions of untold, unheard, unsung success stories of companies, small and large, who have succeeded with their innovative contributions to the marketplace. By analogy, the business literature is to business what living species are to evolution: 99.9% of what came before is hidden from view. If you, the reader, are employed at the moment, chances are that your employer is one who goes about their daily business making money without making the news. Hard work, faith in one's vision, and talent will be as intense as anywhere at Google, Ferrari, and Vodacom. They make up for the lack of gross luck with process formalism, attention to details, and alertness to an ever-changing landscape. Those who succeed over the long run do so on the strength of repeatable execution mechanics and mechanisms. In other words, they help displace luck with disciplined frameworks.

> *A silent disciplined framework is the key success ingredient to a business recipe that isn't decided by luck (acknowledged or not). It confers, coincidentally, the same benefit to the innovation journey detailed in this book.*

A Hint of the Hinterland

By now, the reader should have gained an appreciation for the major obstacles inherent to the innovation journey. The picture may seem bleak at first, but that is only temporary. This chapter intentionally sought to open the reader's eyes to the reality of the landscape, echoing Richard Feynman's caution to scientists searching for truth: "The first principle is that you must not fool yourself, and you are the easiest person to fool." With eyes wide open, the reader can set about surveying the lay of the land, discern the danger zones, highlight the obstacles, and identify the belligerents. A thorough survey that is quantified objectively rather than through the distortions of one's fancy will reveal the nature of the risks and threats. What is involved in this survey is the subject of the next chapter.

NOTES

1. Readers interested in the topic will gain useful insights from *Ten Types of Innovation: The Discipline of Building Breakthroughs* by Keeley, Pikkel, Quinn, and Walters and *The Ten Faces of Innovation: IDEO's Strategies for Defeating the Devil's Advocate and Driving Creativity Throughout Your Organization* by Tom Kelley and Jonathan Littman.
2. See Chapter 2 of *Investment-Centric Project Management*, by Steven J. Keays.
3. The core features in this section were inspired by the work of Linda Plano, Ph.D., founder of the consultancy Plano & Simple (see www.plano andsimple.com). Plano's ten-question approach was taken as a starting point for the twelve questions implied by the presentation slides in the text.
4. Let us not forget that by the mid-eighties Apple teetered on the verge of collapse with Steve Jobs fired by then-CEO John Sculley. Decades later, Jobs would acknowledge the hidden luck that laid in this firing in helping him get back on track.

3

SUCCESS FACTORS

Patience, hard work, a sprinkle of serendipity, and a generous supply of money are always in good taste; they do wonders when seasoned with hard-won lessons from predecessors.

THE LIFE AND TIMES OF AN IDEA

The Adoption Cycle

The perspective in Chapter 2 was meant to jolt the reader out of whatever illusions or fancies he or she might have harbored about the innovation world. Confronted with this somber reality, the reader now understands what must be overcome. Fortunately, this chapter espouses a more positive tone, in order to offer the reader the tricks, lessons, suggestions, and advice—borne of experience—to aid the success of an innovation project.

The discussion begins with the *adoption cycle* that frames the perspective needed to devise a potent execution strategy. New market entrants follow a pattern of adoption that is reminiscent of the familiar bell curve. Moore, in his seminal book *Crossing the Chasm*,[1] divided the curve into five adopter types (*innovators, early adopters, early majority, late majority,* and *laggards*) that are depicted in Figure 3.1. Moore's original nomenclature appears in parentheses on the chart. An alternate terminology appears in the figure to avoid any confusion in the text. This new terminology includes *champions, enthusiasts, pragmatists, realists,* and *fatalists*.

The *champions* represent the intrepid buyers of whatever new product comes on the market. This group makes up about 2% of the buyers and is the principal diffuser of the merits of the innovation (or lack thereof). The second group, the *enthusiasts*, makes up about 15% of the buyers. These buyers validate the commercial merits of the innovation in the public's mind. The enthusiast group is motivated by the desire to get the benefits of the innovation without being

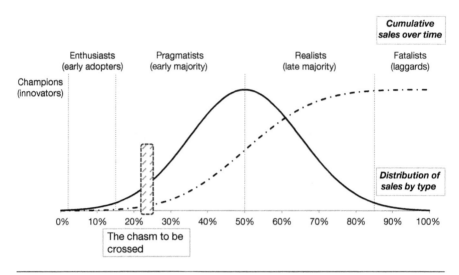

Figure 3.1   The adoption cycle: the cycle maps out the dissemination of an innovation throughout a market over time and across revenues; it is divided into five segments characterized by the motivations of the specific buyers for the innovation in each segment

guinea pigs. The third group is comprised of the *pragmatists* and makes up the early majority of the buyers (about 35%). It contributes the most to the increase in profitability of the innovation and helps establish the brand in the marketplace. *Pragmatists* are motivated to adopt the innovation once it has proven itself. Somewhere between the second and third groups lies the fearsome commercial *chasm* posited by Moore. This is the point in time when the innovation moves from niche to mainstream status. It is also the barrier that is the most difficult to overcome by the innovation's predecessor. The next group, called the *realists*, includes the *me-too* people who are late adopters (about 35% as well). *Realists* do not want to be left too far behind their competitors. The profitability of the innovation has plateaued by this time. Gains in market share are costlier and prone to diminishing returns. The *fatalists* finish out the buyer range. They are the laggards, encompassing the remaining 10 to 15% of the buyers. This group has no choice by that time because the innovation has essentially become the only alternative. Or, they could simply choose to skip the generation entirely and wait for the next big thing to come around (think of the cell phone's adoption in Africa). For the innovator, this last group is a lost cause and a waste of time.

The adoption cycle is important to our discussion for two reasons. First, it informs the would-be innovator of the expected growth in income over time and highlights the importance of getting things right with the first two groups.

If you fail to excite them, you have no hope of commercial success. Second, the adoption cycle informs the innovator about the maturity of the marketplace relative to the features and benefits of the dominant *status quo*. The proposed innovation must convey a differential advantage over the existing competition. In other words, *me-too* products that mimic what's out there are unlikely to gain much traction. The new product will compare favorably to the competition when its features and benefits place it on the left of the maturity cycle.

The Maturity Cycle

Figure 3.1 can be interpreted as the trajectory described by revenues over time. A second interpretation describes the impact of the innovation's technological prowess on the commercial success of the business over time, as shown in Figure 3.2. The vertical divisions do not line up with those of Figure 3.1; they are representative of possible financial milestones for the business.

Again, we have five divisions into this so-called *maturity cycle*. The *genesis* stage spans, effectively, Part 1 of this book. It is the inception stage—where the innovation idea is transformed into a commercially viable product from which the business is launched. The *genesis* stage ends at the 0% mark, when the *champions* in Figure 3.1 show up. During this stage, cash flow is always negative as are investment returns.

The *viability* stage is associated with Part 2 of this book. It covers a period of time that is marked by product rollout (at 0%) on the left, and the attainment of commercial break-even point (BEP) on the right. The BEP also marks the critical moment when sales have covered the development investment, cash flow has become positive, and investment returns begin to materialize. This point will

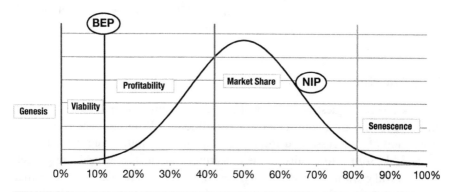

Figure 3.2   The maturity cycle: the technical progression of the innovation, in terms of market acceptance and competitive differentiation, is mapped by the maturity cycle which can be overlaid with Figure 3.1

usually occur at about the transition from enthusiasts to pragmatists in Figure 3.1. At the end of the stage, the product has achieved broad market acceptance. The *viability* stage proves out the idea's concepts in monetary terms and makes the shareholders whole again. The end of the second stage often corresponds to the point in time when large competitors have noticed the innovation and take an interest in possibly buying out the innovator (a suitable exit strategy if the innovator wishes to move on to other things).

The third stage is named *profitability* for obvious reasons: it marks a longer time period during which the business experiences the highest levels of profit margins from sales of the innovation. The end of the *profitability* stage usually occurs before maximum market penetration has taken place. It is also the ultimate time for getting the best deal to merge or sell to a competitor. If ever there was a time to cash out, it is at the end of this stage. If, on the other hand, the innovator prefers to stay in the game, then the next stage awaits. The *market share* stage implies a change of business strategy from profit maximization to market share expansion. Profits are still essential, obviously, but the name of the game is sales volume. The fourth stage will also be the time when minor upgrades, changes, revisions, and updates to the product are released (to keep an edge over the competition). The fifth and final stage is called *senescence*. In the absence of major design improvements, new product features, or product line expansion, the business is bound to wither away. The product enters a period of dramatic reductions in sales, market share, revenues, and profits—either from increased competition or loss of technological edge or both. This stage is typically accelerated by trends and forces external to the business, especially under the guise of novel innovations by competitors (think typewriters, film cameras, fax machines, rolodex, little black books, and paper maps). The correct strategy for avoiding this fate is to become proactive during the *market share* stage by putting in place the *next innovation program* (NIP), indicated by the circle *NIP* in Figure 3.2. This topic is discussed at length in Chapter 7 under the heading *Product Evolution Strategy*.

The Priority

We ask a simple question: what will the idea become when it grows up? The answer depends on the development methodology. When the objective is the realization of a successful business, the idea will grow into a commercial interest and blossom into profits. If the objective is to create a whizzbang gadget, the idea will grow into a concentrated technological marvel. Clearly, the former is the preferred path in the context of investment-centric innovation project management (ICIPM). Of course, the growth of the idea into profits must be palatable to would-be buyers. The idea must become a product that will succeed in convincing the *buyer* to part with his cash. That's *your* future cash, by the way. Hence, from the outset, the priority must be to find out who will be that *buyer*, in order to figure out what he will wish to buy from you. This seemingly self-evident truth is often missed by novice innovators and nearly always by inventors. Never make the mistake of assuming that buyers will somehow materialize through the magic of your game-changing (...! ...) product—cue the warnings about the better mousetrap! You are not Apple or Tesla or Baidu. The idea is only the means to an end, which is to get money from a buyer via a successfully commercial business. *In most instances, you only get one shot at this,* hence the importance of aiming correctly from the get-go. Your aim is the buyer, not the wizardry of the widget, as we will explore at length in Chapter 4.

THE DEVELOPMENT CYCLE

What Development Means

The word *development* takes on a specific meaning within the ICIPM framework. It signifies the ordered set of tasks and activities for transforming an idea into a commercial product. The technical objectives are motivated by the buyer priorities discussed previously. The process adopts an incremental evolution of its constitutive elements (as defined in Table 1.2). It is a specialized adaption of project management that is designed to corral risks, control budgets and schedules, and realize the commercially successful business. It is also a methodology that forces the innovator to proceed methodically to avoid the pitfalls of relying on preconceived notions of what the outcome should be. It is inherently flexible in the sequencing of the work, depending on the progress of the work, but always within a formal management structure that emphasizes discipline and facts over whims and wishes.

The overall outlook of the development process is illustrated by the mapping of Table 3.1. The map can be divided according to three different perspectives: by types of development, by types of acquired knowledge, and by types of evolutionary states—the technology readiness level (TRL) row. Each one of these perspectives is discussed in turn.

First Perspective: Types of Development

This is the first management perspective, embraced by the innovator's senior management team. The nature of the work varies as a function of the outcomes

Table 3.1 The perspectives of the development process

Development Types	Type I: Research to Prove Feasibility					Type II: Technology Demonstration		Type III: Asset	
Knowledge	Basic technology research		Technology development			System development		Product development	
TRL	1	2	3	4	5	6	7	8	9
	Basic principles	Concept formulation	Proof of concept	Element validation	Element verification	System design	Installation design	Pilot test (full scale)	Monetize
Risks	Extreme	Gamble	Worrisome	Tolerable	Tolerable	Acceptable	Acceptable	Worrisome	Enviable

sought, and is categorized into three types: (I) feasibility research, (II) technology demonstration, and (III) asset.

- Type I, as the name suggests, seeks to demonstrate theoretically and empirically the feasibility of the idea's elements. The inputs to the work comprise the scientific insights obtained from prior research (pure and applied). These inputs are translated into functions and conceptual processes from which arise the outputs at the heart of the value proposition to the buyer. The innovation is explored for novel features, worthy potential inventions, creative solutions, and unique characteristics that will differentiate it from the competition in the marketplace. The work is *research* and *development* (R&D) dominant with secondary emphasis on engineering and design.
- Type II switches the emphasis to engineering and design, and rapidly winds down the research aspects of the work. The objective is to aggregate the components, assemblies, and systems that make up the envisioned product into working, fully integrated prototypes. The first prototypes are usually small scale; they are strictly functional for laboratory and bench testing. The final prototype is designed as a full-scale version of the anticipated final product and is tested against actual operating conditions (dictated by the buyer).
- Type III takes the full-scale prototype into final validation by embedding directly into the potential buyer's operations. The results of this validation are used to complete the final, sales-ready version of the product. Pre-commercialization is conducted in parallel to get the business ready for business.

Second Perspective: Types of Acquired Knowledge

This perspective is oriented toward an aggregate understanding of the inner workings of an innovation under the purview of the technical development team. The objective of this understanding is to assist the commercialization team in putting together the production pieces needed to assemble the final product *bereft of quality issues, buried risks, or operational* unknowns. The work underscoring the knowledge-acquisition process is divided into four groups called *knowledge blocks*: (A) basic technology research, (B) technology development, (C) system development, and (D) product development.

- The first block, basic technology research, figures out the science involved and makes the corresponding physics/chemistry/biology work. This type is the largest employer of Ph.D.s, scientists, and academic professionals. The level of ignorance and unknowns (about the nature of the innovation) is highest, while the prospects of discoveries and novelty (in the patent sense) are the greatest. This type is nearly all research (pure and applied).

- The second block, technology development, converts the discoveries and findings of the basic research into functions and makes the corresponding physical elements work individually. The idea is mapped out as a collection of critical functions. Possible means of executing these functions are explored and, if absent, invented. The level of ignorance has gone down significantly. Creativity is at its highest. The potential for identifying meaningful inventions is at its greatest. The essence of the innovative features of the idea is gestated through the work. The research is mainly applied and development (in the R&D sense) is undertaken.
- The third block, system development, makes the physical elements work together and manifest the product's purpose (why it will be bought). We move beyond innovation and invention, toward the integration of elements into a working product. There are almost no R&D aspects to speak of; the activities having mutated into engineering and design. The elements (components, assemblies, and systems) are engineered, modeled, and specified by drawings, datasheets, calculations, and material selections.
- The fourth block, product development, makes the business work and engineers the commercialization of the final product. Production engineering is pursued. Supply chains, logistics, manufacturing, sales and marketing, and business services are planned, rolled out, and activated. The business is activated. The nature of the knowledge has migrated from technical to commercial.

The four knowledge blocks can be regarded as islands of risk. One does not choose the island for the idea; it is the idea that chooses the island, which in turn lays out what's in store for the innovator. Risks, uncertainties, costs, and timelines are greatest for the first block and become gradually smaller as the knowledge increases across the remaining three knowledge blocks. What's more, there may be instances when a particular element occupies a different island than the rest of the product. For example, the idea may be a portable sensor that measures the concentration of a chemical in a fluid. The sensor itself may rely on a new scientific technique, putting it in the first block, whereas the rest of the elements (electronics, displays, battery, buttons, casing, Bluetooth emitter) are off-the-shelf components that are typical for the fourth knowledge block.

The innovator should strive to minimize the number of inventions required by a given product. There must be at least one, however, to endow the product with intellectual property (IP) value (discussed in upcoming text) but no more than absolutely necessary. The reason should be obvious: inventions start as either Block 1 or 2 endeavors, and carry the greatest funding challenges owing to the highest level of uncertainty and adjoining risks. The ideal scenario is a product that requires no invented elements, but which is itself in the end a patentable invention.

> *The innovation development process is always better served by engineering rather than inventing a product's constituent elements.*

Another way to picture the knowledge blocks is to associate them with the burden of proof described in Chapter 1. Recall that the burden of proof is borne by the innovation according to the sequence:

> *Proof of need > proof of physics > proof of system > proof of installation > proof of economics >>> make money.*

The *proof of physics* falls naturally under the aegis of the first knowledge block. The *proof of system* belongs to the second block. The third block is the province of the *proof of installation*. Finally, the *proof of economics* lies with the fourth block.

Third Perspective: Types of Evolutionary States

This last perspective is the domain of the designers, engineers, and programmers who tinker with the nuts and bolts of the innovation. At this level, managing occurs directly at the physical, algorithmic, and operational level, where decisions are made on the reality of the innovation. The third perspective is, in fact, the foundation of the development process from which costs, budgets, timelines, and resources are compiled into project management and execution governance. It is where money is actually spent. Consequently, the description of this perspective warrants a section of its own next.

TECHNOLOGY READINESS LEVEL (TRL)

Managing Evolution over Time

The most extensive development process is the one that will aggregate the three work categories that were previously mentioned—I, II, and III. The product itself need not be complex or large in scale. The driving factor is always anchored to the amount of knowledge underlying the critical functions. For example, devising a smokeless flame for a humble match could entail significant chemical research of the kind associated with Type I. Whenever possible, the innovator should endeavor to find alternate means of achieving the required functions without needing the Type I work; but if not, so be it.

The three development types form a development continuum. The latter is encapsulated by the systematic R&D methodology called TRL. The roots of TRL can be traced back to the 1970s at NASA and its search for a predictable and manageable procurement process of large, complex systems.[2] The TRL methodology would later be adopted in several variants by the U.S. Department of Defense,[3] the U.S. Department of Energy, the European Space Agency, the European Commission,[4] and the Government of Canada, among others. The methodology consists in nine levels of increasing technical maturity, illustrated in Figure 3.3.

The TRL methodology instills in organizations an operational framework for evaluating different types of technologies (products, processes, and software). For large procurement programs, the framework is procedurally dense, but its principles can be readily migrated to smaller scale projects with a much reduced administrative burden. The TRL classification schema, in fact, is the foundation of ICIPM.

TRL 1: Basic Principles

The nature of the work is purely theoretical. Scientific research begins to be translated into applied R&D. The emphasis is on research, not development (we say Big R, small d). Examples might include paper studies of a technology's basic properties. Lab experiments could be conducted to test out various assumptions. TRL 1 is useful as a check against physical impossibilities (perpetual motion machines, water running up hill, Star Trek transporter) and against unrealistic expectations (a solar panel with 95% efficiency, transparent aluminum). TRL 1 invariably involves Ph.D.s, academics, and research professionals. Surveys of competitors' IP (patents, trademarks, logos, copyrights) are initiated.

TRL 2: Concept Formulation

The theoretical musings are translated into corresponding practical applications. The applications are speculative; and there may be no proof or detailed analysis to support the assumptions. The purpose of the innovation is defined, as is the landscape basis and the product objectives (discussed in Chapter 4). Compliance requirements and regulatory/certification obligations are identified. Performance targets are proposed. Analytical predictions are posited.

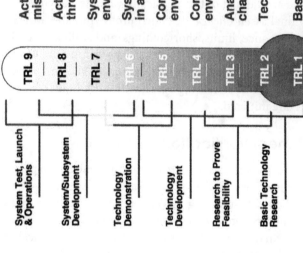

Figure 3.3 TRL: the original maturity mapping developed by NASA.
Source: https://steveblank.com/2013/11/25/its-time-to-play-moneyball-the-investment-readiness-level/

TRL 3: Proof of Concept

Active R&D is initiated on the primary functions of the innovation. This includes analytical studies and laboratory studies to physically validate the analytical predictions of separate elements of the innovation. These studies and experiments should constitute *proof-of-concept* validation of the applications/concepts formulated at TRL 2. Possible configurations of components and arrangements are devised. Analytical and laboratory studies are carried out to physically validate the analytical predictions of the individual components. Ugly bench prototypes are fabricated and tested to assess performance, limits, shortcomings, and scaling potential. The innovation's concept is validated and shown to be able to meet the product objectives.

TRL 4: Element Validation

The basic components and assemblies are integrated to establish that they will work together in a laboratory environment. The working model is purely functional without aesthetics or concerns with scalability. Performance targets and analytical predictions are posited for each assembly. Analytical and laboratory studies are carried out to physically validate the analytical predictions of the individual assemblies. Ugly bench prototypes are fabricated and tested to assess performance, limits, shortcomings, and scaling potential. Functional requirements for the secondary functions are defined. Find out what works realistically, what might work with additional R&D, and what must be discarded. On the IP front, licensing agreements with holders of existing patents plus other IP are initiated.

TRL 5: Element Verification

The scope of work splits into two streams that are pursued in parallel. In the first stream, the primary assemblies are integrated into primary systems to form the alpha prototype (corresponding to Version A), including primitive secondary components and assemblies. The alpha prototype is a reduced-scale version of the anticipated final product. Performance targets and analytical predictions are posited for each system. Laboratory studies are carried out to physically validate the performance of the systems under simulated operating conditions. In the second stream, the work for TRL 3 and 4 commences on the secondary functions. The basic technological components are integrated with reasonably realistic supporting elements so they can be tested in a simulated environment. The *permit plan* is compiled to address all regulatory, licensing, permit, and code certification requirements.

TRL 6: System Design

The work on the second stream continues until TRL 5 is achieved. The primary stream is developed into a beta prototype (corresponding to Version B), which is a small-scale version of the anticipated final product, and incorporates the secondary functions. Performance targets are formalized (instead of merely posited) and a testing protocol is developed, complete with pass/fail criteria. The beta prototype is tested in a laboratory environment against real operating conditions. Examples include testing a prototype in a high-fidelity laboratory environment or in a simulated operational environment. Patent applications are filed. Regulatory, licensing, and permit applications are initiated.

TRL 7: Installation Design

The beta prototype is developed into the full-scale gamma prototype (Version C), representing the final product form. The testing protocol is updated for laboratory testing under actual operating conditions. The test is conducted. Material lists and costing are compiled. Reliability and maintainability metrics are derived. Functional requirements for the tertiary functions are identified (TRL 4 and up are initiated). Note that it is possible to go through more iterations of the design during TRL 7, which could lead to additional versions, numbered sequentially: delta (Version D), epsilon (Version E), zeta (Version F), etc. Code certifications are initiated. Regulatory, licensing, and permit applications continue.

TRL 8: Pilot Test

The full-scale prototype is readied for field testing in an actual operational setting offered by a would-be buyer. This final prototype becomes the installation product (Version 0) that will be installed on site for the operational validation test (integrated into the client's plant design). The tertiary functions are developed in parallel from TRL 4 through 7 and then integrated into the installation's design. The installation is brought online and validated in the operational setting. The end of TRL 8 marks the end of the development process. Other IP applications are filed (industrial design, trade secrets, trademarks, and copyrights). Regulatory, licensing, and permit applications are obtained. Code certifications are obtained.

TRL 9: Monetize

The results of the pilot test are incorporated into the Version 0 design and released in its sales-ready, Version 1 form. Production planning, manufacturing setup, supply chain contracts, and marketing plans are put in place. Product literature is developed. The website is built. A sales force is trained. A service group is formed. The business is activated. Sales are generated. Planning of Version 2 development commences.

IMPLEMENTING THE THREE DEVELOPMENT PERSPECTIVES

Pick a Starting Point

It stands to reason that not all innovation projects will span the full TRL spectrum. In many instances, TRL 1 is not necessary and TRL 2 is limited to the purpose, landscape basis, and product objectives. For small products without complex assemblies or multiple functions, TRL 3, 4, and 5 could be combined into one. For innovators whose businesses are already established, TRL 8 and 9 may be already built-in, or at the very least whittled down to a few specific marketing and publication activities. It is up to the innovator to determine the proper TRL starting point and to gauge what level of effort will really be required in the latter stages. But this flexibility does not extend to the specifics of the development process that must go into each TRL. This process is mandatory, as we will now see.

Risk Profiles

When looking through the eyes of investors, the last row of Table 3.1 becomes paramount. It conveys the spectrum of risks involved at each TRL stage, ranging from extreme to enviable. The intensity of the risks mirrors the intensity of the funding requirements and the duration of this investment. Indeed, the level of risk (technical, financial, and commercial) is inversely proportional to the TRL level. The lower the TRL, the higher the risks, costs, time, and patience. Notice the jump in the risk profile at the junction between TRL 7 and TRL 8. This risk is mainly associated with the significant jump in the funding required to execute the pilot test. The bulk of this funding does not go to the product but to what must be done to embed the product into a live plant. These costs can be orders of magnitude larger than what has been spent from the start. Indeed, considerations for construction, for regulatory filing, for interruption of operations, for in situ labor during the test, and for possibly costing monitoring equipment add up to a pretty penny. At this stage, the risk is not so much in the performance of the installation as it is in the cash-flow demands necessary to set up and run the pilot test.

Overall, the technological risk inherent to any innovation program resembles Figure 3.4.

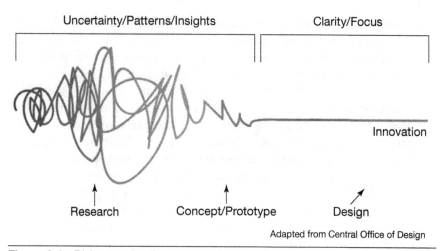

Uncertainty/Patterns/Insights   Clarity/Focus

Innovation

Research   Concept/Prototype   Design

Adapted from Central Office of Design

Figure 3.4 Risk emerging from uncertainty: the inverse relationship between risk and accrued knowledge

Managing According to Perspective Types

The four rows that make up Table 3.1 are instructive with regard to management priorities. The first row—development types—is concerned with financial management and involves the interface between the innovator and the investors. The investor is concerned with capital protection and probability of success. Risk tolerance drives the investment decision, while ownership issues dominate the innovator's engagement priorities. Exchanges between the innovator and the investors will emphasize risk management, financial management, funding models, returns on investment (ROI), timelines, and market analysis. The inner workings of the development process are incidental to the discussions. The investor wears the mantle of *investment manager*; his prime objective is to make the case for the commercial opportunity, not the wizardry of the idea.

The second row comprises the knowledge blocks and falls under the purview of *project management*. The interfaces arise within the project team and with the external entities involved. The innovator becomes the project manager and is concerned with developing the scopes of work, the execution plans, the budgets and schedules, the contract documents, the deliverable lists, etc. The priority is to align the resources with the plans and expectations. Add to it selecting the means of measuring performance and outputs. The resources, for their parts, pay attention to the convergence of the work definition and the allocations (budget, timeline, mechanics, and mechanisms) assigned to enable that work. In the case of external entities (funding agencies, third-party contractors, regulators, etc.), their attention is directed toward the contractual terms, conditions, and obligations set out upon the contracting parties. The inner workings of the innovation continue to remain incidental. The prime objective of the innovator is to create and implement the management framework that will govern the execution of the development process—right up to product rollout.

The third row places the inner workings of the innovation front and center. The interfaces become conceptual or physical or both. The innovator becomes the development leader, concerned purely with the transformation of the idea into bits and pieces and assemblies, systems, and control software. The physics is uncovered. The relationships between the components are quantified. Component and technology selections are made. The prime objective of the innovator is to evolve the idea from concept to function to physical manifestation, and to do so incrementally while documenting everything in the process.

The last row characterizes the severity of the risks over time across the three rows. For the first row, the risk is financial. In the second, it is organizational (the project may end up dying if the physics doesn't pan out). In the third row, the risk is technical (if the physics doesn't work, the idea is stillborn). Finally, in the fourth row, the risk is commercial. This row, incidentally, also helps to set the priorities of the risk management strategy as a function of the nature of the work.

Taking a Different Turn

We now leave the realm of innovation life cycles and development sequencing to explore a different set of project management concerns where success is equally important to the overall success of the innovation journey. These concerns pertain to patents, money, and tricks of the trade.

THE PATENT

Why It Matters

The patent is a powerful tool of exclusivity that is conferred upon the holder to its rights. The patented product is effectively granted a legal monopoly in the marketplace for a fixed duration. It is the primary source of protection available to the innovator for his costs of development, his investment returns, and against copycats. A patent makes the innovation a tradeable investment. By contrast, an innovation that is not or cannot be covered by a patent will be less likely to attract outside investments. The patent is the innovator's competitive bulwark against market threats.

What Is Patentable?

An invention is patentable when it is a new and useful process, machine, manufacture, or composition of matter—or any new and useful improvement thereof. Patentability comes with four caveats:

- The subject matter must be patentable
- The invention must be novel
- The invention must not be obvious
- The invention must have some utility or usefulness

A patent cannot protect an idea such as a scientific principle or theory ($E = mc^2$) or an abstract theorem. Instead, the idea must be embodied in one or more of the following:

- A process or method (such as a new way to manufacture concrete)
- A machine (something with moving parts or circuitry)
- A manufactured article (such as a tool or another object that accomplishes a result with few or no moving parts, such as a pencil)
- A new composition (such as a new pharmaceutical)
- An asexually reproduced and new variety of plant

The reader should note that satisfying any one of these categories does not automatically imply that the embodied idea is patentable. Some subject matters simply cannot be patented, such as mathematical equations, naturally occurring substances, physical laws, and processes that are inherent to the human body. For example, one cannot patent a technique for tight turns in downhill skiing.

The Requirement of Novelty

Novelty simply means the invention must be new. New implies a difference with what is known in the public domain under the expression *prior art* (which includes active and inactive patents, published applications, publications available to the public, and items on sale). Keep in mind that if the innovator publishes a magazine article about his purported invention, or starts to sell it, that information becomes *prior art* twelve months after its first public appearance (at which time it becomes prior art to everyone else right away). In other words, once in the public domain, the innovator has twelve months to file for patent protection.

The Requirement of Utility

Utility implies physically accomplishing something. If an invention produces a result, it has utility. It is hard to fail this test, which happens when the invention's logic is materially flawed (for example, a perpetual motion machine or a net energy-creation process). A utility patent protects how the object is used and how it works. When the invention relates to an object's ornamental design, the utility requirement does not apply.

The Requirement of Non-Obviousness

This requirement stipulates that people who are skilled in the field specific to the invention would not deem the invention evident. If, for example, the proposed invention swaps one color for another, it fails the non-obviousness test. Or, combining two current inventions in an intuitive way does not yield a patentable invention. In other words, the invention must exhibit creativity and inventive steps beyond what is common knowledge to be patentable.

The Timing

Patents are expensive and must be filed for each country where protection is sought. There is no such thing as an international patent; only a patent filed in multiple countries *at the same time*. That is why the innovator must choose the target markets judiciously. At $10K to $20K a filing, doing so across multiple countries carries a hefty price tag. Trying to cut costs by cutting out the lawyer is not a viable avenue—the filing process is fraught with difficulties known only to legal aficionados. One can, however, reduce the expense by eliminating unnecessary changes and reworks during the preparation for filing the documents. This suggests that one should not initiate the patent process too early in order to minimize back and forth amendments and corrections (usually stemming from new technical information coming to the fore) and maximize the impermeability of the claims. For the inventor (the terminology used in patent lingo) based in North America, two strategies are worth considering:

- *Strategy 1: U.S. provisional patent application*—The provisional application is unique to the United States. It grants priority of claim over the twelve months following the application for a large number of countries. The date of this filing becomes the *earliest priority date*. A provisional patent is comprised of the full description of the invention developed to date and further modifications and changes that the inventor has contemplated. The provisional patent is not released into the public domain during the twelve-month period during which the inventor compiles the full application. If other jurisdictions are considered, filing in those jurisdictions *must occur at the same time as the full application in the United States is made*. Filing in Canada should be a must. Adding Mexico achieves continental coverage (only if your invention is going to be made and/or sold therein as filing and prosecution in Mexico involves translation costs as well). A patent application is published 18 months after the filing date.

The release of a patent in the public domain nullifies any possibility of filing in other jurisdictions from that point forward. If the full application cannot be filed by the 12-month deadline, let the provisional application expire and submit a new provisional one.

- *Strategy 2: Patent Cooperation Treaty (PCT)*—This treaty encompasses a large number of signatory countries, including the United States, Canada, and European states. The treaty was established to help applicants obtain patent protection internationally for their inventions. The process begins with the filing of a single application in any country that is signatory to the treaty, typically as a provisional patent in the United States. Twelve months hence, the inventor submits a PCT application. About three months later, the PCT office will issue the inventor an international search report and a written opinion on the merits of the proposed application. The inventor has another ten months to respond to the written opinion if he so desires. The deadline for requesting an international patent examination (IPE) occurs 19 months after the original filing (i.e., provisional filing). The same deadline applies for requesting a supplementary international search report. Note that both of these requests are optional for the inventor. If the IPE is not requested, the inventor must submit the full patent application in those countries that require it. For those that do not, the full application must be submitted no later than 30 months after the earliest priority date.

Other IP

The expression IP pertains to an intangible creation of the mind that can be legally protected. It includes several categories of legal protection that should be secured when applicable. One can never have too much IP protection:

- Patents protect an invention against outright theft
- Trademarks, such as brand names, confer sole ownership and rights to use to their owners
- Copyrights shield an artistic expression from copying (songs, books, movies, video clips, marketing animations, etc.)
- Industrial design, when registered, protects the nonfunctional features of a product

- Trade secrets are meant as safeguards to keep a formula or manufacturing process confidential—they are not subject to registration, however, but are still recognized by the courts as IP, when so proven
- Contractual rights pertain to the licensing of a right that is granted to another to use your IP

In all cases, the prudent innovator should consult an IP professional to strategize the best way to use IP rights to his advantage. A summary of the IP domain is illustrated in Table 3.2.

The Illusion of Protection

An IP is only as strong as the owner's capacity to defend it in court. A patent, for example, gives its owner the right to sue for infringement. That's fine in theory; but in practice, things are a tad more delicate. Defending a patent in the courts is a hundred times more expensive than filing for one in the first place. A commercially successful patent always runs the risk of predatory behavior from the competition. A small firm has very little realistic chances of enforcing its property rights if the predator has deep pockets and is willing to drag the legal proceedings. This venal abuse of the legal system is, unfortunately, tolerated and leads to exhaustion by attrition. The question for the innovator boils down to this: how much is it really worth to defend one's rights?

- If you are able to allocate $3M to $5M to the cause, go for it. Since the law is on your side, your chances of prevailing are excellent (but check with a reputable patent lawyer first, just to be sure).
- If you do not have a large bank account and the predator is a small fry, try the intimidation game. Have your patent lawyer issue a cease-and-desist letter—or other like-minded ultimatum. It may just be enough to get things settled quickly, in which case, you should then approach the defeated party to discuss a licensing deal. (Why not? After all, it's an extra source of potential revenue for you.)
- If you do not have the $3M, the predator is bigger, and the intimidation letter did not work, your best bet is to sell your IP rights to a comparatively sized competitor of the predator. Or enter into some kind of business deal that will bring you the protection that is necessary to defend your rights.

It is, sadly, what reality looks like in the real world of business competition. It is not right, it is not fair, and often, it is not even legal but, in the end, it is what it is. Pursuing legal challenges is prohibitively expensive without any certainty of positive outcome in the end. Stressing out about the unfairness of it all will get you nowhere—the predator couldn't care one bit about you. The choice is yours

Table 3.2 The intellectual property landscape

	Patent	Industrial Design	Trademark	Copyright	Trade Secret
What is protected	Functional aspects of an invention	Aesthetic features (the look and feel) of a product	Word, phrase, symbol, or design that identifies and distinguishes a product or service	Original work of authorship (literary, dramatic, musical, and artistic)	Business secret like a formula or a pattern
Example	Mousetrap	Smartphone case	A company logo	A movie	The coke formula
Eligibility	New Useful Non-obvious	Must be filed within one year of first publication (publication means making the design available to the public).	Must be clearly descriptive. Cannot be generic or poorly described. Be distinguishable from others.	Originality	Used in business Not generally known Has economic value Efforts are made to keep it confidential
Term	20 years from filing date—not renewable	5 years—renewable for an additional 5 years	15 years—renewable in perpetuity	Life of the author + 50 years	As long as kept confidential
Fee range	Prior art search: $2K Drafting/filing: $6K–10K Prosecution: $4K–7K	$1.5K to 2K	$2K	$400	None
Average registration time frame	2.5 years	1 year	1–2 years	1–2 weeks	Not applicable

to make; but you must make it as soon as you are confronted with it. Things will not sort themselves out on their own. The legal challenge is akin to a grenade in your hand with the pin pulled out. You don't know how long you have before it blows, but you know that it will. It's best to toss it while you are still safe.

Here is a quick checklist to determine if a patent is worth the time and effort to acquire. The patent is essential when one or more of the followings conditions are met:

- The future revenue and business model will include licensing or royalty payments from third parties
- The innovator is certain to seek out external sources of financing to reach commercialization (banks, angel investors, private equity, and venture capital)
- The realistic size of the market offers a 10 times return on investment within two years of the patent being granted *and* the innovation can be reverse engineered by a competitor within that two-year window
- The exit strategy for the firm includes a buyout by a competitor or merger with a bigger player
- The manufacturing strategy can only be met by a network of suppliers and fabricators
- The rate of change of the innovation will be less than one new release per year
- The economic life cycle of the innovation (from roll out to obsolescence) is a year or less

The patent should *not* be pursued when one or more of the following conditions pertain:

- Licensing and royalty schemes will not be pursued
- The export strategy includes patent-feeble jurisdictions (whereby it is inevitable that the IP will be stolen by domestic competitors—with a meaningful chance of legal redress)
- External sources of financing will not be needed from angel investors, private equity, and venture capital
- The known size of the firm's market is too small to interest larger competitors
- Reverse engineering will be difficult or near impossible within a two-year window *and* the rate of change of the innovation will be more than one new release per year
- Contract manufacturing will not be a critical component of the supply chain
- The secret sauce for the innovation can be equally protected, at lesser costs, through trade secret mechanics

The other types of IP—industrial design, copyright, trademarks, contractual rights—are usually worth the money and effort in all instances.

MONEY IS TIME

It's a Marathon

Newcomers to the innovation race are often surprised to discover how long is the road from idea to product launch. The journey starts out with an idea. The innovator imagines that the idea will lend itself to a quick product implementation resulting in a prototype ready to be shown to prospective clients or be introduced at trade shows to drum up interest. As familiar as this sounds, it never works out that way (refer back to Chapters 1 and 2 if you need a refresher). The prototype never works the first time out—and never works quickly either. Enthusiasm turns to discouragement when the reality of the situation finally dawns on the innovator. Rather than making a quick buck, the innovator is forced to stop, cringe, and go back to zero.

The inconvenient truth is indubitable: product development is a marathon. Even when the technology proceeds rapidly, the pace of commercialization won't. It takes time to convince the marketplace to second guess its own *status quo*. It takes time to build up the corporate functions that are necessary to enable the sale of the product. It takes time to get the patents. And it takes even longer for a successful product to cross the chasm that is illustrated in Figure 3.1. Everything takes time and patience.

But It Is Also a Race

The marathon is the correct analogy from a project management perspective. The process, however, remains a seriously competitive race from an investor's standpoint. The innovation journey is a championship marathon where speed and stamina matter. Do not delude yourself into thinking that you are the only one to have sensed the opportunity. Some competitors might already have seen it. Others might have already solved it. Patents—yours and theirs—may be expiring soon. Regulatory changes may be afoot. Different innovative solutions may already be appearing in the market. All that you do and don't do costs money. Recall that money is to the innovator what air is to a scuba diver: the supply is limited. When it's gone, you're dead in the water, literally. In other words, you need to be imbued with a sense of urgency. Put yourself in the investor's shoes. You buy into the merit of the idea *but* before you give away a cent, you'll want to know a few things. Things like how much money the innovator wants? How much does he really need? What will he spend it on? How long will it take to get to market? The investor is concerned about making his capital work for him. He is not so interested in the features, the gadgets, or the buttons that the innovator wants to develop. He wants to know whether his money will be spent efficiently, on the right things, at the right time, and for the explicit purpose of maximizing the profitability of the product once it hits the marketplace. And, he will want to get a sense of the investment risk involved with the development process. That is why very few investors are prepared to get into TRL 1 and 2, given the magnitude of the risks.

This is the source of the urgency underlying the development process. Do not view yourself as an innovator—fearless and inspiring. See yourself, first and foremost, as an investment manager. Your ultimate objective is to cause your innovation to make money. Your second objective is to waste as little of it as possible in the process. Your job is to deploy the investment capital on what matters first. Because each development stage requires different skill sets, there is always a risk of wasting valuable time and resources in trying to master each area of the innovation. There is also the risk of falling in love with the wizardry of the innovation and spending endless hours trying to refine everything or add more and more features. The prime directive must always be the shortest time to complete the marathon.

Speed to Market Demands Real Expertise

The fear of spending with wanton abandon is naturally countered by the willful minimization of expenses, especially in matters of labor. Ironically, the low-cost reflex can work *against* the efficient deployment of investor capital. The prime directive pushes the innovator to reach commercialization as soon as possible—it is not to save costs discretely at every stage. This need for speed will always be satiated by marshaling the proven expertise pertinent to the development requirements. In other words, *it pays to pay more, not less, to accelerate development times.* The genuine expert may cost $200 an hour (which implies a truly clever technical expertise), whereas three competent technical people on your team only cost you $60 each per hour. At first glance, $180 is cheaper than $200 per hour. But the no-brainer decision is still $200 an hour: the odds are that the expert will solve your problem faster, better, and more realistically than whatever options your three-man team would sprout. *Going cheap at the outset always costs more in the long run.*

Done Beats Better

A corollary of the need for speed is the need to get things done. The reader who is acquainted with software development will surely relate with the obsession that is driving some programmers to continuously tweak, expand, and broaden the scope of a subroutine so that it can handle ever more inputs and transformation processes. This never-ending cycle of tweak/expand/ broaden is counteractive to efficient capital deployment. Speed to market is possible when:

- The development work is limited to those functions and features that are deemed essential and critical to the *initial configuration of the product being introduced in the market.* Forget the extra bells, whistles, buttons, options, color finishes, and the rest.
- You engineer by default, invent by necessity. Maximize the use of what's already available in the marketplace to solve your design. In plain words, buy the screw rather than invent a new one. Invent only what is *absolutely necessary* to the innovative features of the product.
- You fail fast and move on. This is the key insight bestowed upon us all by Silicon Valley. In the thick of development things, it is easy to get sidetracked by a desire to make something work at all costs. This mantra makes sense if you work on bleeding-edge technology, on fundamental research, or on profusely funded projects. In all other cases, it works against speed to market. It is better to try something, learn from its failure, then move on to a different solution, rather than persist on the same futile path. Fail fast, dump, move on, and repeat.

Looking Through the Buyer's Eye

Another aspect of effective capital deployment is to know what to spend it on. The initial obligation is defined by the state of the art. Whatever is the state of the art *in the marketplace* for a product, a process, or a service, that state of the art becomes the starting point of the development process. This self-evident truth may not be palatable at times. For example, if your product idea is meant to compete with an existing solution imbued with nanotechnology or quantum-mechanical effects, you cannot avoid these characteristics simply because they scare you (especially if they imply Ph.D.-level mathematical physics knowledge). The state-of-the art cannot be avoided—*ever.*

After figuring out what the buyer wants, your attention should turn to the matter of what will he or she want to buy *from you.* Once again, notice that the question starts from the buyer's perspective, not the innovator's. We do not ask what you should sell; we ask what the buyer wants to buy. Do not forget that your buyer is already buying what they need to meet their needs from the marketplace. *Your future offering can only succeed if it displaces a competing offering.* This buyer is not purchasing features, buttons, or glitzy design. He does not buy a widget to save money or to save time. People and organizations ultimately buy one thing: a *purpose.*

The Purpose

Buyers buy a product or a service to fulfill a purpose. The purpose of a toaster is to make toast. The purpose of a car is transportation (or investment, in rare cases). The purpose of a smartphone is communication (with others, with the web). When the purchase is by a business, that purpose is always associated with profits. Airlines buy airplanes to generate revenue from travelers. They will buy fuel to power the airplanes in order to generate the revenue. They buy insurance to protect their future earnings in the event of a crash. Airlines do not buy a sophisticated aircraft because it is shinier or faster or bigger than the competition. They buy that aircraft when those features (shinier, faster, bigger) make them more money in the end.

The purpose *is the* why *of the innovation.*

The purpose of your idea is the starting point of the development process. You must strip the idea down to its essence and toss aside all other nifty things for the time being. The *purpose* of your idea will be the basis of its sales in the future. The *purpose* is distinct from its embodiment (i.e., its physical manifestation). Take the simplest example of a door key. Its *purpose* is to activate and deactivate a locking mechanism. Its embodiment could be made of metal, it could be a key fob, or it could even come as a plastic card. The embodiment varies in each case but their purpose is the same.

Parsimony

The innovator must spend the money necessary to advance the development process along the shortest timeline. This approach is investment-centric and capital-preserving. On the other hand, the innovator must justify cash flow outlays as a function of the ultimate objective—the successful commercialization of the product. This imperative implies a tight control of expenditures to stretch the funding as far out into the future as possible. To buy or to rent is a decision that is best made through valunomic arguments (valunomy was explained in Chapter 2). You should always buy:

- Expertise, specialized services, and quality parts
- What is deemed critical to the business and integral to IP
- Key trade secrets and industrial know-how
- What is essential to your competitive advantage
- Specialized training for key personnel

You should share, rent, or lease everything else—for example:

- Office buildings, photocopiers, printers, plotters, 3-D printers
- Administration services (receptionist duties, video-conference, webinars, cleaning, travel, web and e-mail hosting)
- Marketing, market research, IP searches, legal, regulatory support
- Large information technology components (servers, Cloud storage, databases, specialized software, networks)

Last, but not least, you should never buy:

- What is routinely or already commercially available (machine shops, printing services, legal services, buildings, business condominiums, testing equipment)
- Photocopiers, plotters, 3-D printers, cars, trucks
- Specialized tools and software that requires acute individual expertise to operate
- Expensive office furniture, art work, or Tier One office space
- Antique coke bottle distributors, pool and foosball tables, health memberships, marketing knickknacks, free food, strategic retreats, club box at the stadium, golf memberships, fancy clothes, exotic pets, art work, etc.

KEY HEURISTICS

The Project as an Investment Vehicle

We close this chapter with a short list of key ingredients that will benefit any development process. The first ingredient, which reigns supreme over the rest, is the *investment mindset*. The innovator must look upon the innovation project as an investment vehicle first and a journey of discovery second, in that order. The gestation of the idea into the commercial product is powered by money. It is not powered by dreams or one's belief in the truth of the idea—or even the promises of riches at the end of the road. The innovation can only succeed when funded adequately. That statement means investors and government programs that imply prudent capital management.

The Patient Investor

We have already detailed on the fact that the innovation game is a long race akin to a marathon. There are no quick ways to turn an idea into a successful product, and no quick path from market introduction to mainstream acceptance.

The innovator needs at least one patient investor. Both innovator and investor must understand the timelines in play and agree on the necessity of not cutting corners in order to speed things up. No time can ever be meaningfully saved by setting arbitrary milestones and false deadlines. The worst possible thing that an innovator can do is to promise the would-be investor a quick development and a rapid ROI period. The promise will be broken soon enough and the investor, burnt and poorer, will lose all faith in the innovator. Funding will vanish, and with it, the death of the idea will be hastened.

Get Your Money!

The reader may be surprised at the number of assistance programs that are offered by all levels of government to promote innovations. Whether you are in the United States, Canada, or Europe, the challenge is usually one of finding the right assistance program rather than convincing someone to fund your project. It behooves you to seek out new sources of funding and new government organizations—to boldly go where others have gone before. In many cases, you will find money that is already there for the taking with no strings attached other than an expectation of growing a business and generating jobs (which, to governments, equate to tax revenues). Do not let the paperwork scare you into thinking that the burden isn't worth the effort—it is nothing compared to what you will have to go through to convince independent investors to give you their money.

Do not make the mistake of securing government assistance, then not following through on the reporting requirements. Yes, this is paperwork, and yes, this paperwork will take some time that you may feel could be better spent elsewhere. But this paperwork that you so loath is also your ticket to getting your money! If your terms of engagement require you to file a monthly report by a given date, for crying out loud, file the damn thing by that date! This is your money that is just waiting to be approved! Don't delay! Don't complain! Where else can you get money with no other demands?

A Patent Is Neither a Product nor a Business

Being granted a patent is an essential element of commercial success. But a patent is not a product and it also is not a business. Many innovators believe that having a patent is proof that the idea is commercially viable: it is not. As a matter of fact, there are more patents out there that will never see the light of day than those that will. The patent says absolutely nothing about the value of the idea in the *eyes of the market*. It says *nothing* about the means of fabricating the product *profitably*. It is silent on the competitive advantages of the product, and it is utterly meaningless in terms of marketing and the sales pitch needed to make inroads into the marketplace.

Disciplined Project Management

At first glance, the reader may struggle to reconcile the seeming contradiction between the emphasis on the long-distance nature of the development process and the relentless call for speed. One natural reflex would be to embrace the latter because it appeals to our craving for gratification. It is easy to translate this urge into cutting corners, skipping steps, and running things in parallel to save time. As we said before, no time can ever be meaningfully saved by pursuing time-saving measures. The safest, quickest path to successful commercialization is through ordered, incremental progress. Such a path requires disciplined project management—the kind that is impervious to whims and artificial milestones (the kind discussed in Chapter 7). Always stick to the development plan. Do not improvise, do not jump the sequence, just follow the path laid out at the outset. Modify if you must, but always do so within the decision framework that is embodied by your project execution strategy.

The Champion

The successful execution strategy must be complemented with a direct connection to the market that the innovator intends to pursue. This connection is provided by a *champion*. This is a person (in most instances) or a company who understands the value proposition from the get-go and is willing to help you succeed, pursuant to the tacit expectation that he too will achieve success from your innovation. This champion is crucial to your race to market and to get that all-important first sale. The champion provides you a window into the soul of your future client base. She will help you uncover the design drivers that matter to a buyer (rather than your preconceived whims). She will educate you on the pros and cons of the *status quo*, the pains and frustrations that keep her awake at night, and the features and functions that she must have. You will quickly discover that price, while always a concern, is usually not the primary concern. Your champion will give you precious insights on what is hidden from you: the source of resistance to change, the ulterior motives, and the unsung requirements. Bring her on as soon as the product idea has been formulated (sometimes in TRL 2). The earlier you get her onboard, the better.

The champion must remain involved throughout the development process. She is also the best person to help you garner continual intelligence from the marketplace by setting up roundtables with her own employer to assess the merits of the development's progress. Let the champion handle the event logistics (but you should cover the costs), and let her figure out who needs to attend (the decision influencers). The roundtable is the perfect venue in which to ask:

- Why the attendees would *not* buy your solution (which helps define a baseline of needs)
- What would entice them to try your solution (which suggests the purpose of the idea)
- What would compel them to buy your solution (which defines the success criteria)

On the other hand, *never ask* what these people can do for you, or why they should like your idea better. These roundtables serve two purposes: to acquire intelligence within an intelligent setting and to allow your future would-be clients to see what you can do for them.

Your Idea, Your Lingo

This is the easiest heuristic to implement. Develop a comprehensive list of acronyms, abbreviations, and definitions. Never assume that your audience, be it internal or external, is fully versed in this taxonomy. It is best to compile this list from the outset and distribute it to whomever will be in contact with you (the champion, the investors, government agencies, patent lawyers, website designers, contractors, and supply chain partners, to name but a few). Finally, put this list up on the website as soon as it goes live—assume nothing; cover everything.

YOU ONLY GET ONE SHOT AT THIS

Take the Easy Road

The dirt road to success is paved with bumpy intentions, especially when it is the reader's first rodeo. The innovation journey is unlike a typical business where the main concerns are receivables, cash flow, and order backlogs. Its untrodden nature (as viewed by the innovator) adds to the intensity of the pace. It is more arduous and more unnerving—plain and simple. So, why not do everything possible to *lighten* the load and make things easier whenever one can? Driving the easy street is indeed one success factor that punches above its weight when it comes to its contribution to the innovation journey. There will never be a shortage of hard problems to face, but that does not mean that the working environment should be as strenuous as the problems it harbors.

The innovator owes it to himself and his team to seek out the opportunities to make life simpler, easier, and faster wherever they can be found. The search begins with the working environment proper, where the onus is on the innovator to implement. Things like culture, expectations, and priorities start and end with the innovator's direction. The workplace can be intense and focused while simultaneously carrying on with joy and levity—or it could be a hard-driving arena thriving on rabid internal competition (which will suit some personalities and repel many others). The shape of the workplace will ultimately come out of the culture promoted by the innovator, a topic that is explored in detail in Chapters 8 and 11. The innovator should take time to think it through before the team is assembled. The goal is not to implement a culture that is thought to be the best by pundits and business studies. The goal is to put in place a culture that reflects the true nature, motivations, and aspirations of the innovator.

Going one step deeper brings us to the physical layout of the workplace. The primary thought leaders on this subject, often sprouting from Silicon Valley, have put the need for collaboration front and center in this discussion. The net effect has been a 180 degree swing in the pendulum from the office cubicle of the 1960s to the wide-open floor arrangements that are prized by software companies. The history of the cubicle is worth looking into for it holds precious lessons that have been lost on the coder brethren. The concept was imagined in 1964 by Robert Propst as a way to empower office people who were hitherto forced to work in open-space floors arranged with endless rows of work desks. Propst proposed a radical departure from the paper production-line setup: the *action office*. In this new approach to floor space management, each person was assigned a large desk, a filing system, and roaming space within a set of partitioned walls. The concept sought to give workers privacy, which is essential to good thinking and unimpeded productivity. Everything within the *action office* was adjustable to fit the ergonomic profile of its occupants. The design also called for walls at obtuse angles (greater than 90 degrees) to create a fluid working space. The whole point of the concept was to make workers more productive. People and businesses were not ready for that vision of the future. It flopped as soon as it came out in 1968. It was also deemed to be too costly, relative to the automaton-efficiency of the endless desk rows. Propst went back to work on a new design to address the issues. The result was a cheap design that could cram way more people than its predecessor into a given floor area. Gone were the adjustable features, the roaming space, the ample work space, and the fluidity of the volume. In came rigid dimensions, knee-busting spacing, and crammed desks. The modern-day cubicle was born and swept throughout office lands across the world to the everlasting detriment of workers everywhere. Privacy was obtained, but at the cost of lost productivity and narrow-mindedness. It also heralded the arrival of silo management as collateral damage.[5]

Today's buzzword is collaboration, which takes form in the physical realm as an absence of boundaries, as the theory goes. What the theory failed to recognize is that *no boundary* implies *no privacy*. When collaboration is forced on people as a management principle, it tramples over their need for isolation from constant collaborative interjections. It's one thing to bump into colleagues and bounce ideas off each other, but constant bouncing is utterly useless if people have no opportunity to reflect on these ideas and think them through. That requires privacy, which requires physical boundaries. That is the lesson offered to the innovator here. The workspace for your workers cannot be allowed to create a never-ending stream of disturbances and interferences upon them. People need space to think, to ponder, to analyze, and to produce. Unless they are working on an assembly line, where creativity and problem solving are not at the top of their priority lists, people will not be productive or efficient or even creative, for that matter, when they are forced into the open without any ability to find mental shelter. *By all means*, encourage collaboration, but do not lose sight of the more important act of *thought* to give form to those collaborative threads.

Tools of Ease

Ease of work flows from an efficient workspace, not the reverse. Hence, the workspace must be solved first. Afterward, the next opportunities to ease the work are found in the tools for doing the work, starting with collaboration. The marketplace is overflowing with potent and affordable applications to connect people in real time while simultaneously managing the information that flows among them. E-mails and texting are rudimentary methods to get the show on the road. But these should be augmented, if not outright replaced, with more effective solutions. There are hundreds of viable solutions being offered today that deserve the innovator's attention.[6]

There are also a plethora of applications that are tailored to specific tasks, such as: market research; translation; collaborative document editing; and finding on-demand contractors, expense reports, etc.[7] It is safe to say that there is an application available somewhere on the internet for every conceivable task and activity carried out in day-to-day work. These applications are often free or offered on an affordable subscription basis, for example, software as a service, usually deployed on the Cloud (which eliminates the need to buy dedicated hardware), and intuitively operated, which speeds employee ramp-up times. Again, it will be worth the time and effort to the innovator to look into the applications that can best automate, or at least streamline, the work of his team.

In the realm of recruitment and business relationships, the innovator would be remiss if he did not take full advantage of specialist social media platforms like LinkedIn (to name but one). These platforms offer the benefit of instantly reaching millions of potential answers for the innovator at no or little cost. Recruitment is especially well served by these platforms by making job ads *active* rather than passive website postings.

We now turn to the matter of managing the data that is produced on a daily basis by the team, which is code for generating spreadsheet documents, most likely using *Excel*. Spreadsheets are wonderful tools (and *Excel* is the king of spreadsheets, a wonderful program) for tracking data, compiling results, generating charts, and running what-if scenarios. They are also impossible to manage properly within a formal document management framework. Anybody with a laptop and even a smartphone can create one and e-mail it to untold recipients at the click of a button. In other words, spreadsheet files forever litter the management landscape with data whose origins, dates of release, revision numbers, and publication history are utterly unknown and unknowable. In Chapter 17 of *Investment-Centric Project Management*, the case was made to encourage organizations to abandon spreadsheets in favor of simple database applications (such as Microsoft's *Access*) to manage the so-called *dynamic data* produced continuously by a business. The term *dynamic* implies that the value of those data change over time (say, the number of units produced last month) rather than being static records (like a birth date). The innovator is encouraged to read the arguments posited for the case and adopt a database basis for managing dynamic information during the innovation journey.

Finally, the subject of internet security must be broached. As the innovator sets up the organization by deploying laptops, computers, and servers from the get-go, the question of datum integrity and cybersecurity must be addressed. *As a matter of fact, it should be addressed before all other IT concerns.* Ours is a world that is permanently and pervasively connected by digital networks. Hacker attacks, denial of service attacks, ransomware, and cyberespionage have entered the lexicon of business talks. The threats of nefarious cyber actions cannot be assumed to target only the largest organizations. *Anybody* and *everybody* have become potential targets. Commercial interests are, of course, prime targets to anonymous criminals with a view to acquire a quick buck. The innovator should start with the premise that his IT infrastructure will be hacked at some point in the future, and then proceed to determine which digital assets must be disconnected from the internet and which ones can be exposed to it on the condition that there are adequate protective measures and recovery plans. It is, unfortunately, an inevitable cost of doing business nowadays. The choice is a stark one: spend nothing now and live with the prospect of potential economic annihilation in the future, or spend some money now to build a bulwark against future intrusions, at least to provide some level of insurance against future losses.

Cybersecurity resembles the innovation journey in one respect: you only get one shot at succeeding in defeating attacks before they happen. Waiting for the attack to take place may leave you too weakened to survive the fallout.

Trying Again, for the First Time

We conclude this chapter with a few more success hints. At the human level, the innovation process is akin to meeting someone new. First impressions matter, failed first impressions are deadly, and continued impressions require nurturing. The development process will span months or years and will be replete with false starts, dead ends, going in circles, iterations, and missteps. Sardonically, none of that matters when crunch time comes during product rollout. At that point, there is no past, only the present. And the present is binary: either the product succeeds or it fails (sooner than success, in fact). In other words, you only get one shot at this. You get one shot at investors, at would-be buyers, at the patent, at the market, and at the money. Second acts are a rarity. You can improve your odds of success in two ways: never assume and never promise:

Never assume.

- Don't assume that costs drive all buying decisions
- Don't assume that you know better than the buyer (you don't and never will)
- Don't assume that your idea will sell by itself because it is so stunning—it never does
- Don't assume that you know what's best for the client or for his industry
- Don't assume that the buyer *should* understand what's at stake, or *should* get the importance of your message, or *should* see the big picture—*should* has no business in innovation; and if you can't make the case without relying on *should*, you have no case

Never promise.

It is easy to fall prey to the glorious future that is hinted at by your idea. From there, it's one step over the delusion's precipice. Until you have irrefutable proof (not evidence or whim or intent) of the claims you make, you must *never*:

- Make unsubstantiated claims
- Make claims that address the buyer's needs only (the love affair syndrome)
- Rely on something other than success at every step (bull-is-bull proclivity)
- Talk rather than listen to all feedback (good and bad, but especially the bad)

- Choose whims and desires over facing reality—faith is not a strategy
- Choose to justify a result, rather than live by performance—a failure acknowledged is a piece of knowledge gained and failure to admit failure is failure of success

NOTES

1. *Crossing the Chasm: Marketing and Selling Technology Project*, by Geoffrey A. Moore. Moore's seminal contribution to marketing was inspired by his tenure during Apple Computers' original heyday. It is a must read for anyone wishing to understand the art of successful marketing.
2. See John C. Watkins's white paper *Technology Readiness Levels*, published by NASA in 1995.
3. Source: *Technology Readiness Assessment (TRA) Guidance*, prepared by the Assistant Secretary of Defense for Research and Engineering (ASD(R&E)), May 13, 2011.
4. Source: The TRL Scale as a Research & Innovation Policy Tool, EARTO Recommendations, April 30, 2014.
5. Source: http://www.businessinsider.com/a-brief-history-of-how-the-cubicle-2014-4.
6. See, for example, the list at https://en.wikipedia.org/wiki/List_of_collaborative_software.
7. See, for example, moz.com, Google translator, bluebeam.com, upwork.com, receipt-ban.com and hubdoc.com.

4

SECRET SAUCE

"The world we live in is vastly different from the world we think we live in."
—Nassim Nicholas Taleb

THE BLUEPRINT BENEATH THE ROAD MAP

Leveling the Playing Field

Neophyte and seasoned innovators alike struggle to figure out how to get started on the development path. The innovation landscape (see Chapter 2) is a matter of time and unbiased effort, from which the *proof of need* from Chapter 1 is derived. The heavy-duty work required by technology readiness levels (TRL) 1 and 2 lies in the realm of academia and laboratories (see Table 3.1). The innovator is required to provide a simple statement of the problem, a pail of money, and a bucket of patience. The real challenge for the innovator and his investment cohort starts at TRL 3. The challenge is further intensified when the innovator does not come from a background in design, product development, or research and development (R&D). It is of little use to harp on the innovator to come up with a technology development plan—like the proverbial *don't work harder, work smarter*; such a diarrhetic[1] pronouncement gets nobody nowhere fast. The reader can take solace in the fact that even large companies struggle with it, as Figure 4.1 illustrates. In other words, TRL 3 acts as a great leveler of the playing field.

This chapter spells out how to create this technology development plan. The reader will find a step-by-step recipe to move from idea to concept to design to product to profits in a logical sequence that will corral, assuage, and mitigate risks—financial risks, investment risks, dead-end risks, commercial risks, and heart attacks. The recipe is the secret sauce of the book.

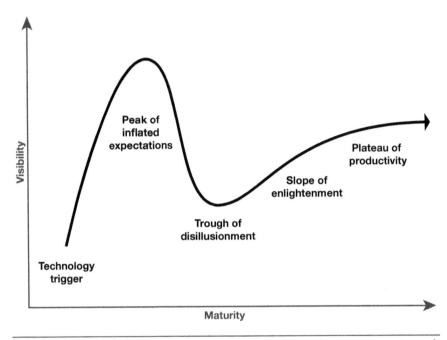

Figure 4.1   The vagaries of the innovation journey: in this illustration, courtesy of www.controldesign.com, the uncertainty of outcome is nearly universal and indiscriminate as to the firm's size or prowess. *Source: http://www.controldesign.com/ articles/2014/five-phases-in-the-adoption-of-a-technology/*

> *Readers beware: there are no quick paths to success, no royal shortcuts to the promised land. Slapping bits and pieces together to create a working prototype, making them work, and taking this mock "prototype" on to road to drum up customer interest (door-to-door, conferences, trade shows, and the like) does not work, wastes everyone's time, and burns your credibility.*

That was the meaning of the marathon race in Chapter 3. Per force, the process is stepwise incremental in the evolution of a feature, a design, and commercialization. The literature often refers to it as the *waterfall model*. There are other models out there (think lean, kaizen, and agile to name but a few) but they require an organizational maturity that lies beyond this book. They are best left to more experienced firms with proven track records.

There Are No Guarantees

Even with the secret sauce in hand, there is no guarantee that the outcome will be tasty. The development process is fraught with complexity, uncertainty, and risk. Over time, the work will hit dead ends, spin its wheels, go around in circles, get messy, or diverge from the plan. *This is business as usual in the innovation game.* You must accept that those issues will emerge, even if you start upon a solidly defined path. Inevitably, you will stumble upon a proliferation of ideas, what-if scenarios, and out-of-the-blue realizations, as illustrated in Figure 4.2. Salvation comes from the imperative to remain disciplined and avoid going off on a tangent. *Discipline* is the keystone of the investment-centric innovation project management (ICIPM) philosophy. The development road map is built along its strengths.

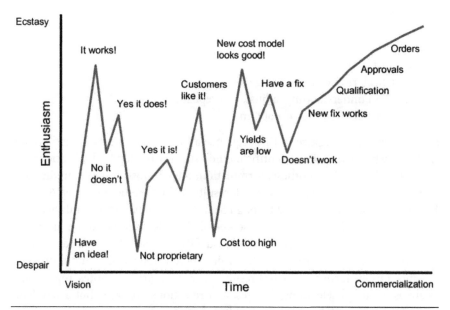

Figure 4.2 The inevitable issues of development: dead ends, wheel spinning, going around in circles, getting messy, and diverging from the plan are normal evolutionary steps on the path to product development. *Source: https://www .researchgate.net/figure/303673139_fig1_Figure-3-Ups-and-Downs-during-an -Innovation-Journey*

THE MECHANICS OF DEVELOPMENT

Prime Directives

The greatest differentiator between an inventor and an innovator is the development process. The inventor dabbles and tinkers, laboring under a single goal of perfecting the widget work. The innovator plans the work, then executes it in accordance with a trio of overarching directives in order to govern the evolution, increase knowledge, and protect the investment. The impetus for governing the evolution of an idea into an asset is given by the other two directives. The evolution will consume money, time, resources, and patience. It must be governed firmly and be kept on the straight and narrow. Managing it requires a repeatable and measurable set of activities to be carried out in this controlled sequence:

1. Plan
2. Set targets
3. Experiment
4. Test
5. Check results against targets
6. Gain understanding, adjust, and repeat until
7. Final configuration is obtained.

The reader may recognize in this sequence a hint of the scientific method and that would be correct. The scientific method starts with Step 1: observations and follows with Step 2: hypothesis formulation, Step 3: posit testable predictions, Step 4: run experiments, Step 5: check results against predictions, Step 6: adjust hypotheses and repeat Steps 2 through 5, and Step 7: develop general theories.

The second directive—to increase knowledge—is essential to the future beyond commercialization (what lies beyond TRL 9). The main byproduct of the evolution process is information; for which there will be an enormous quantity produced in the form of data, test results, drawings, sketches, notes, reports and analyses, material selections, failures, and rejections, to name but a few. This information is a rich treasure trove of knowledge:

- What was tried and why;
- What was not tried and why not;
- What worked and what did not;
- What could have worked but was not checked;
- Why behaviors and reactions to stimuli turned out the way they did;
- What else could be done to get different results; and
- Why choose some components but not others.

This knowledge helps limit the possible paths for the next development steps. It informs future employees about the reasons why the product became what it is and why other features and configurations were not pursued. Of greater importance to the immediate development process, this knowledge enables the innovator to create the mathematical and algorithmic models that are necessary to assess the product's design envelope, performance limits, failure containment, operational characteristics (reliability, maintenance, troubleshooting, overhaul periods, spares, life-cycle costs), commercial metrics (costs, revenues, profitability), and scalability.

> *Without knowledge, the product is technologically orphaned and condemned to costly re-invention cycles when future versions are planned.*

The third directive is derived from the objective of the development process, to create a profitable business that will generate revenues from the developed asset. It is not—let us emphasize once again—to come up with a fancy product imbued with technological wizardry. The best innovation is the one that sells best and the one that generates the most investment returns *in the long run*. Everything costs money during development; thus, everything must be justified on the sole basis of the commercial objective. For a refresher on what this entails, refer to the section called *Money* in Chapter 2.

The Pitfalls of Preconceived Notions

Recall the importance of the *purpose* of the innovation, which is the reason why a consumer buys your product. Knowing what the purpose is and knowing how to execute it are two different things. Innovators and inventors alike instinctively assume that they already know the features of the innovation. They proceed from preconceived notions to solve a particular problem. These assumptions may cause them to miss out on truly novel ways to evolve the original idea. Take the simplest of examples: the humble door key. The would-be innovator might readily assume that its shape must be similar to the keys in his pocket—or he may wish to embed in it a programmable radio-frequency identification and assume that the software language must be such and such (Pearl, for example). These preconceived notions are detrimental to the innovation process and must be violently banished. A successful innovation process avoids all preconceptions in order to free itself to go beyond the *status quo*. Once the purpose is articulated, the innovator starts with a blank slate and implements the *W5H approach*.

The W5H Approach

The W5H approach is derived from the *esemplastic key* mechanics that were introduced in *Investment-Centric Project Management*.[2] The acronym W5H stands for Why, What, Where, When, Who, and How. The method emphasizes a serialized evolution sequence. At the start, nearly all ideas, suggestions, and thoughts are welcome, specifically to deny preconceptions that may intrude on the creative process. The physical nature of the elements that make up the idea is likewise kept unclear and undefined:

- The first W stands for *why* and represents the purpose of the product. The *why* speaks *specifically to* the reasons that will motivate a future buyer to choose the product over all other options that are available in the marketplace. The *why* defines the purpose of the innovation *from the perspective of the prospective buyer.*
- The second W stands for *what*—whereby the *purpose* is translated into one or more elementary functions. A function is a process (physical or algorithmic) that transforms a set of inputs into another set of outputs. The outputs are the manifestation of the purpose of the product. Nothing is said about how these functions should work. They are described only in terms of the nature of the transformation of inputs into outputs. This is where the prohibition against preconceptions is strongest. The innovator must resist the temptation to imagine the physical, the procedural, and the algorithmic. Do not dwell on things like buttons, color schemes, metal specifications, control subroutine codes, voltage limits, dimensions, user interfaces, etc. The lack of physical description (the embodiment) is necessary to avoid the creation of unnecessary limitations. If a limitation must be established from the outset, it must be essential. As a rule, limitations are avoided by default and adopted by exception.
- The H stands for *how* and is where a function is explored for possible means of effecting the transformation. The *how* effectively embodies the function (either physically or algorithmically). For example, say the purpose is the transmission of a mechanical power by rotating motion (in other words, an electrical motor). One function for this purpose is a rotating shaft acting as a power transmitting element. This shaft must be kept rigidly in place. The potential means of doing this (the *how*) include a variety of mechanical bearings (sealed, self-lubricating, ball, cone, magnetic—to name but a few). All of these solutions are retained for consideration at this time.
- The third and fourth Ws stand for *where and when.* Here, the various solutions are translated into specific methods (sizing, materials, types,

power and control, etc.). Then each method is evaluated against the performance expectations of the function. Design sketches, schematic drawings, control diagrams, and other types of interface management documents are developed to integrate these methods into a working model.

- The fifth W stands for *who*—addressing the matter of choosing the vendors from which to buy the parts and labor. The emphasis on the *who* is intentional: it also helps the innovator determine what gets built in-house versus what should be outsourced or bought off the shelf.

The W5H sequence satisfies the first two prime directives. Starting at TRL 3, the sequence is applied to go from functions to testing. At each TRL, the test reveals what works best, what doesn't, and what improvements should be investigated immediately. This recursive process is sketched in Figure 4.3.

The benefits of the procedural discipline that is implied by the W5H method become clear when numerous tests of several model configurations are required prior to making a final selection. The results may reveal incongruences between what is physically possible versus what was initially expected and may require an adjustment to the purpose, to the functions, or even to the product objectives.

The essence of the innovative features of the product will be discovered through the creativity unleashed in the "why," "what," and "how" activities.

This statement cannot be overemphasized. The opportunity to truly innovate begins with the judicious selection of the purpose of the product (the *why*). The opportunity becomes tangible when the *what* options are formulated without preconceived notions or arbitrary fixations. It materializes when the *how* explorations are conducted with an open mind that is unshackled by personal biases, idiosyncrasies, rigid adherence to past experiences, or nefarious impulses that are characteristic of the inventor mindset. There can be other innovating opportunities later on—particularly in the manufacturing methods.

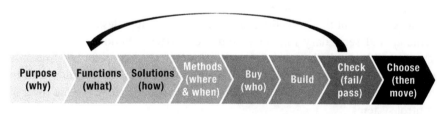

Figure 4.3   The W5H sequence: the stepwise process of evolving an idea into a product is recursively iterative

Classification of Functions

From a functionality perspective, all products, from the simplest component to a complex industrial plant, can be divided into three classes of functions: primary, secondary, and tertiary.[3] The classification matters to the innovator because the various functions are developed in distinct timelines that are staggered across the development process. The primary functions—those associated with the *purpose* of the product (why it gets bought)—are developed first (TRL 3 through 5). The secondary functions are *enablers* of the primary functions and are almost exclusively internal to the product. They appear as outputs of TRL 5 and are subsequently developed concurrently with the primary functions in TRL 6 and 7. Note that from the buyer's standpoint, what is bought is the combined primary and secondary functions working symbiotically. Finally, tertiary functions act as a bridge between the product and its usage/operation. They appear on the scene as an output of TRL 6 and are developed in parallel with the product in TRL 7 and 8. The process is illustrated in Table 4.1. Tertiary functions exist independently of the product but are nonetheless necessary to its operation. Simple products (a door key, a stapler) may not involve tertiary functions. Most do, however, if only to be powered up from an electrical outlet on the wall.

To illustrate, consider the previous example of the electric motor. Its purpose (why) is the transmission of mechanical power. The corresponding primary function (what) is the generation of a torque in rotation. One possible embodiment of this function is a solid round shaft (how). The length, diameter, geometric features, dimensions, and material selection make up the design (where and when). It will be bought with the use of a procurement datasheet (who). The shaft will be fabricated and installed into the prototype rotor-stator assembly (build). Then the whole thing will be tested to validate the design (check). Once the design is chosen, its installation requirements are identified—yielding the secondary functions, which could include features like power input leads and a manual control for on/off—and visual presentation of the power and speed delivered. Each of these features is, in turn, subjected to the same W5H sequence, until all final selections are made. The product design integrates the primary and secondary functions, and the tertiary functions are identified. These would include the supply of electrical power, the motor's installation base (or foundation, if large enough), the coupling to connect the motor's shaft to the intended equipment, and the control signals to be relayed to the site's overall control system.

Table 4.1 The innovation map: the development of interdependent elements (primary, secondary, and tertiary) is seen to occur at different times, each at different stages of development

Development Types	Type I: Research to Prove Feasibility			Type II: Technology Demonstration				Type III: Asset	
Knowledge	*Basic technology research*		*Technology development*			*System development*		*Product development*	
TRL	**1**	**2**	**3**	**4**	**5**	**6**	**7**	**8**	**9**
Primary	Basic principles	Concept formulation	Proof of concept	Element validation	Element verification	System design	Installation design	Pilot test (full scale)	Monetize
	Landscape	*Purpose (why)*	*Functions (what)*	*Component selection*	*Assemblies (how)*	*Systems (where & when)*	*Installation (who)*	*Presale*	*Asset*
Secondary					*Functions (what)*	*Assemblies (how)*	*Systems (where & when)*		
Tertiary						*Functions (what)*	*Assemblies (how)*	*Systems (where & when)*	
Prototype					*Alpha (vA)*	*Beta (vB)*	*Gamma (vC)*	*v0*	*v1*

The Unit Transformation

Functions are best articulated through the use of the *unit transformation* mechanic.[4] As the name implies, the transformation is a process that converts a set of inputs into a set of outputs. A component (as defined in Table 1.1) is a physical embodiment of a unit transformation. So it can be an assembly, a system, or an installation. The installation is the level at which the *purpose* of the innovation is manifested. Hence, the installation acts as a unit transformation for the *purpose*.

The unit transformation models a function as a black box into which flow various inputs that are transformed into outputs, as illustrated in Figure 4.4. The process is the *action* that converts inputs into outputs. The outputs, finally, are the purpose of the function (i.e., that which is bought).

When a single input is transformed into a single output (flicking a light switch on or off), the transformation is said to be one-to-one. If two or more inputs are required to produce a single output, the transformation is said to be many-to-one (the three-way light switch). Conversely, if one input is transformed into two or more outputs, the transformation is one-to-many (say, the light bulb is turned on and a status signal is sent to a control panel). The *constraints* in Figure 4.4 define the limits on the inputs, the outputs, and the *action*. They can be externally imposed (regulations, legal, operating conditions) or internally motivated (accessible only by an adult, be insulated, operate only on 115 volts).

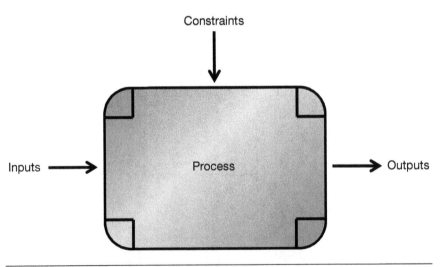

Figure 4.4   The unit transformation: abstracts the input-process-output relationship into a conceptual information flow without regard to the inner workings of the transformation process

Note finally that the nature of the *action* has not been defined in any way, shape, or form at this stage. The only thing that we assume is the *requirement* for an action to be able to manifest the transformation of the inputs into the outputs. Analogously, the inputs and outputs have not been defined in physical terms. We do not say, for example, that the input for the light switch is a lever type, a push button, or a rotary knob. The only description that we want to posit now is that the input must be supplied manually.

LAYING THE PURPOSE'S GROUND WORK

Step 1: The Landscape Basis

The *purpose* of the innovation exists in relation to the environment in which the product will be bought and operated—what we call the *market ecosystem*. Consequently, one must first understand what this ecosystem entails before suggesting the features of the *purpose*. This is the all-important first step that must be carried out in TRL 1 before spending any money and time on development activities. The goal is a compilation of the *landscape basis* to capture the many shades, the many nuances of would-be buyers. The document expounds the reasons why buyers buy what they buy, what is not bought and why, and what might possibly change their minds. The *landscape basis* does not address the issue of what new things would appeal to them. In the majority of cases, people and firms simply have no idea, nor do they have the time to ponder the question. The *landscape basis* is divided into six sections:

1. Current environment
2. Application driver
3. Compliance
4. Metrics
5. Intellectual property (IP)
6. SWOT (strengths, weaknesses, opportunities, and threats) analysis

Section 1—Current Environment

The first section captures the idiosyncrasies of the market's *status quo* from the perspective of both buyers and users. The contents are derived from the findings of the landscape survey (see Chapter 2 *Markets Are Battlegrounds*). The section addresses such questions as:

- What are the commercial solutions currently favored?
- Who uses what? Why?
- What are the pain points? The frustrations?

- What is the cost of that pain to the user? To the buyer?
- What are clients currently paying? Are they willing to pay more for more?
- What are the compliance obligations (legal, regulatory, commercial, financial, etc.)?
- What are the acceptance criteria for choosing one solution over the others?

Section 2—Application Drivers

The second section identifies the constraints, real or perceived, that are placed on the solutions chosen by buyers and users. The findings are also taken from the *landscape survey* from Chapter 2. These constraints can be externally imposed (a regulation) or internally enforced (a corporate standard) and originate from a multitude of sources that include:

- Design (input/output (I/O)), data collection, portability, power, etc., W5H)
- Operational requirements, modes of operations (the environment in which the buyer or user will operate the product)
- Commercial terms and conditions
- Accepted limits on operations, performance, and warranty coverage
- Health and safety regulations
- Data and information concerns (storage, ownership, security, access, recovery)

Section 2 must be detailed, specific, and numbers-driven. Opinions and wishful thinking are *persona non grata*. Vapid statements such as *must be compliant with applicable regulations* are utterly useless. If a regulation must be met, it must be described quantitatively so that verification can be measured. These quantified drivers will be necessary to the development process later on; hence, the importance of measurable specifics.

Section 3—Compliance

The third section documents the codes, standards, regulations, and industry practices that are imposed on the current market offerings. This can be difficult to an innovator who is new to the market segment. It is doubly treacherous when the innovator possesses no working knowledge of the industry from which the all-important industry practices are learned. These practices may not be codified or embraced ubiquitously, but they play an outsized role in the acceptance of a new offering by the marketplace. Some of the practices can be inferred from the answers that were documented in the first section;

most, however, are neither evident nor intuitive. The only way to uncover them is to consult with industry veterans—which is also good advice regarding all other codes, standards, and regulations. When capturing any one of these constraints, the innovator should identify the specific name and version, including pertinent articles within the constraint. The need for specificity is driven by the design process itself down the road. It is not enough to record, for example, that the product must be designed to contain pressure in accordance with ASME B31.3. You must also extract from that code every single article that is deemed applicable (for example, ASME B31.3, article 301.3.5b).

Section 4—Metrics

The fourth section compiles the comparison numbers that are typically found in a given market segment to quantify the expectations surrounding a product. Cost is the obvious standard-bearer of these numbers. So is price, warranty, maintenance and installation, and license fees. Regulatory fees and any other unavoidable cost drivers must be identified and quantified. Other metrics refer to the product's operations (up time, serviceability, staffing needs, training, certification, calibration). Metrics also include performance-type specifications (standard sizes, weight, throughput, installed footprint, output per unit area, electrical charge density, load and stress limits, etc.). For example, if the product is a new kind of solar panel that is intended to be mounted on roofs, one important metric would be the power produced by a unit of covered area.

Section 5—IP

The IP section seeks to discover what patents and trademarks permeate the current marketplace. The IP section is divided into two parts: prior art and commerce.

- Prior art is concerned with competitors' patents (extant and expired) as they relate to the innovator's own IP objectives. This section is critical to the development process. Its objective is to stop you in your tracks in case your idea is not so new after all and to avoid unnecessary litigation. It is also useful in identifying possible licensing agreements that can accelerate the development process.
- The commerce part deals with trademarks and copyrights in a manner similar to the prior art and for the same reasons.

Section 6—SWOT Analysis

The sixth and final section provides a SWOT analysis of the existing commercial landscape. This section informs the innovator about the pros and cons of what's already out there making money for the competition, what works and why, what doesn't work and why not, and what opportunities lie beyond the status quo. It is crucial that the text be written in blunt terms without trying to dismiss competitive concerns to prop up the innovation's own prospects. The SWOT analysis yields the insights into what features of the innovation are most likely to lead to commercial success. The tone, in fact, should borrow the harshness that was embraced in the innovation landscape analysis. The reader is doubly warned: either face reality head on or face the reality of failure dead on.

Step 2: The Purpose

The outcome of TRL 1 is twofold: validate the theoretical basis of the idea (if such scientific knowledge must be derived) and quantify the character and expectations of the marketplace. Both validations must be confirmed before spending money on TRL 2 when the purpose of the innovation is delineated. The TRL 1 knowledge is *essential* to this process—without it, the process would devolve into a game of guessing based on the innovator's whims, preconceptions, and biases. This process of purpose definition culminates in the formulation of the *product objectives*, which set out the product and commercial targets to be realized during the product's development process. The *product objectives* form a controlled document that is divided into the following sections:

- *Purpose statement*—What the product purports to accomplish for its buyer. The description should remain high level and introduce the reader to the *purpose* of the innovation in terms of needs (extant and unmet) of the market. *This is not a sales pitch!*
- *Constraints*—What the internal and external constraints are that will be imposed on the innovation and what the metrics are by which compliance is verified.
- *Buyer's conditions*—List of the *known* terms and conditions that must be satisfied to justify the buyer's purchase decision.
- *Modus operandi*—Description of the ways and the environment in which the buyer or user will operate the product. Includes the conditions for which it will work and the conditions that are excluded.
- *Metrics*—Compilation of the target metrics underwriting the commercialization of the product.

Some readers may be conflicted by the effort required to produce the *landscape basis* and the *product objectives*. This is where the third prime directive, to protect the investment, comes into play. If the innovator requires financial support from external sources, be they angel investors, venture capitalists, government programs, or family and friends (and especially them), she will be expected to prove that the innovation has a chance to succeed. The investment case will be made when the two documents are in hand and congruent. Make no mistake about what you are about to do. The innovation game is akin to a battlefield fought with mercantile ammunitions—something that *money people* understand instinctively. Your product can only succeed if it displaces someone else's offering, which implies lost revenues, which means war to the competition. The *landscape basis* is your battle plan before engaging the enemy, useful insofar as it paints the correct picture of the terrain, the combatants, and their weaknesses. The *product objectives* spell out why the product must be *this* way and not *that* way to win the battle.

The reader should note as well what is *not* included in the *product objectives*. This document purposely avoids saying anything about the *what* and the *how* of the innovation. Nothing is said about the bits and pieces; the mechanical, electrical, and control interface requirements; the modes of operation; the size of the equipment; or even the materials chosen. Nothing physical is prescribed, nothing functional is preconceived, and nothing is said about the price of the product. It is not yet your concern. For all you know, the product may sell for more than the competition and still be embraced by buyers!

FROM PURPOSE TO FUNCTIONS

Step 3: The Wish List

In TRL 3, the *purpose* is dissected into primary functions (the *what*); secondary functions are addressed in TRL 4 and 5 and tertiary functions in TRL 7 and 8. In all cases, the dissection utilizes the *unit transformation* to break down the *purpose* into the set of functions. The *purpose* helps define the inputs and outputs around the black box (i.e., the innovation). Then, additional functions are imagined to complement or supplement the purpose. All possible functions are compiled into a *wish list*. It is imperative that the innovator remain open to all possibilities and not discard suggestions that may appear wacky or irrational— throw everything at the wall, regardless of it sticking or not. As Linus Pauling, twice Nobel laureate (chemistry 1954, peace 1962) once quipped, "Your best shot at a great idea is to shoot a bunch of them first."

The *wish list* paints a utopian picture of what the innovation could be. It is a trove of possibilities of what is essential, what is desirable, and what must be discarded. As we saw in Chapter 2 (see *Essential versus All-In*), the initial thrust of the development process must hone in on what is essential to the initial success of the product—i.e., the essential functions. The second group includes the desirable functions that should be retained for future revisions. Finally, whatever function is left from this double parsing is chaff and assigned to the discarded group. Knowing what must be discarded is as important as what's essential for one reason: it stops the development process from wasting time and money on futile pursuits. The discarded functions would include the rest.

Step 4: Parsing

The compilation of the wish list and its parsing is best accomplished by a plurality of individuals with as broad a spectrum of experiences as possible. The most beneficial venue is the brainstorming session—or, more likely, a series of them. The method to the madness that is advocated by the product company IDEO[5] is a great starting point to any would-be parsing team. The process will be successful when the sessions are free-wheeling, creative discussions, circumscribed by razor-sharp focus, and are enforced by a facilitator. All opinions and ideas must be welcome without denigration or regards to the messenger. Nobody is allowed to pull rank, nor are they permitted to dominate the discussion. The sessions must be held as no-fly zones for phones and devices. Sessions should be set up to maximize the senses: everything is visual, tri-dimensional, physical, and tactile. Wheel spinning, beating-about-the-bush, and ego battles are banished. Consider, retain, or discard quickly; then move on to the next idea. Don't waste time writing everything down. Let the facilitator take pictures of white boards, sticky notes, mock-ups, doodles, and sketches. There will often be more than one brainstorming session to get to the final listing of essential, desirable, and superfluous functions. Between each session, participants are required to explore the retained ideas further. More insights are gained this way which are then reviewed at the next session. The process is iterative, rarely linear, and often forced to go backward before a final decision is made.

Step 5: Prioritize the Functions

From this point forward, the essential functions circumscribe the project. The development activities will be carried out exclusively on them while the desirable functions are set aside until after commercialization. A new parsing round is required to classify the essential functions into primary, secondary, and tertiary groups. Note that additional primary functions may come to light during the evolution of the work. The same applies to the secondary and tertiary functions. Most of these functions are unknown at the moment, and rightly so; having merely imagined the purpose of the innovation, we do not yet possess sufficient information to predict the future.

Step 6: Functional Requirements

The outcome of these multiple parsing sessions produces a final list with which to set the tone and pace of the development process. The list is the cornerstone of the project's foundation. It is captured into a document called the *functional requirements* (FR). The contents of the document are dynamic, that is, they will change continually over time as knowledge accrues. The FR document is divided into four sections: functional analysis, primary functions, secondary functions, and tertiary functions:

- The first section, functional analysis, captures the learnings from Steps 3, 4, and 5. It summarizes the decision process behind the compilation of the essential, desirable, and discarded functions.
- The second, third, and fourth sections will be developed at different times. Each section will follow the same script:
  - Document the development, decision, and selection process for each function;
  - Describe each function's inputs, transformation, and outputs— provide a narrative to complement the description, which includes a summary of the brainstorming details that led to its selection into this group;
  - If known and confirmed at this stage, list the external constraints for each function; and then
  - Describe the relationships across function classes.
- Note that nothing is said about *how* to embody the function.

FROM FUNCTIONS TO ACTIONS

Step 7: Functional Specifications

This step defines the *how* of each function that is described in the FR. The process consists of investigating the possible means of transforming a function's inputs into outputs. The investigation starts with the conceptualization of the elements involved in the unit transformation. This is usually done with a *throughput diagram* to schematically show the relationships between the interconnected elements. The diagram is a sketch or a drawing that records what flows into each function (the inputs) and what comes out (the outputs). The term *flow* is descriptive of the movement of the inputs and outputs.

The *throughput diagram* is a theoretical model of the anticipated elements that are required by each function. A second conceptual aid is the *network diagram*, which identifies the main control points surrounding each input, each output, and each transformation. A common name for this drawing is the *process flow diagram*. The *network diagram* represents a possible *configuration* of the arrangement of any number of elements. Each *configuration* is a different way to embody the function. In other words, this is the point in time when the true potential of the innovation is explored (and the reason for the admonition against preconceptions). The emphasis is to maximize the number of testable *configurations* to assess which will offer the best prospects to meet the objectives. Issues of costs, supply chains, quality control, and regulatory compliance are kept in the background.

> *The whole point of Step 7 is to throw the doors of creativity wide open to see what can really be done with the innovation to diverge from the market's status quo.*

Together, the two types of diagrams furnish the innovator with the starting point to select the actual components that will be assembled into the physical representation of the *network diagram*. Since any function can be modeled in several possible *configurations*, each *configuration* will give rise to its own *network diagram*. The selection of the components requires the innovator to *specify* their physical features, their intrinsic transformation processes, and their algorithmic aspects. Hardware bits, software algorithms, electrical wiring, primitive control devices, and other physical connections are selected. The information associated with each component, along with all configurations and diagrams are compiled into a new document called *functional specifications* (FS). The FS render each function measurable (in opposition to the requirement, which only qualifies it). The nature of a specification can take multiple forms:

- The nature of the unit transformation is defined
- The components are explicitly identified
- The numbers associated with the transformation are selected
- The types of usage, operation, and their limits are established
- Performance targets and operating ranges are stated
- A code compliance matrix is compiled
- Drawing schematics, design envelope sketches, datasheets, and interface diagrams are created

Step 8: Design Specifications

The next step in the development process is to transform the FS into design models. These models are comprised of several kinds of information that are folded under the name *design specifications* (DS). The goal of the DS is to develop the information that is required to buy, fabricate, manufacture, assemble, and operate the conceptual network configurations that were developed in Step 7. The DS effectively embodies the specifications into theoretically posited physical models. 3-D computer-aided design models are created. Spatial dimensions, proximity distances, and instrument positions are fixed. Fabrication drawings are generated. Inertial and dynamic loads are quantified. Material and consumable lists are compiled. The control logic and its algorithms are developed. I/O signals are tabulated. When safety requirements exist, the design is subjected to two analyses. The first one, *process safety analysis,* seeks to confirm the safety of the physical layout and the required warning and emergency devices—safety is assessed in terms of spacing requirements, failure prevention, failure containment, unplanned emissions and releases, and fire and explosion containment. The second analysis, *constructability and maintainability,* is conducted jointly between the project team, the vendor team, the owner's operations team, and hired construction specialists. The point of the exercise is to make sure that the layout of the equipment is ergonomically suitable to human interactions, and that the unit can be maintained, repaired, and upgraded with minimum access challenges.

The outcome of the DS is the creation of the design (this term was defined in Table 1.1). The design is the virtual representation of the physical bits and pieces that will be constructed in Step 10 and tested in Step 11.

Step 9: Procurement Specifications

The *procurement specifications* (PS) aggregate the documentation that was required in order to acquire the elements of the design that were achieved in Step 8. The extent of the specifications will vary according to the complexity of the element, but will generally include:

- Contract terms and conditions, including third-party terms and conditions (for procured items);
- Quality assurance (QA) records to be kept and delivered;
- Vendor data requirements (manuals, QA records, 3-D kernel data, budget and schedule updates, material inspections, material certifications, translations, training materials, as-built documents);

- Schedules (awards, inspections, testing, audits, final acceptance, shipment);
- Equipment preservation and storage;
- Shipping, transportation, and logistics specifications;
- Delivery timelines and vendor support requirements;
- Preferred and barred supplier lists;
- Configuration management and recommended spares;
- Maintenance program and cycles/data collection;
- Installation support requirements (commissioning, start-up, ops training, initial operations);
- After-sale services (warranty, field maintenance, depot maintenance, data collection during operations, reliability and maintainability analysis);
- Publication life-cycle programs; and
- Training programs for plant personnel (operations, monitoring, emergency, maintenance, troubleshooting, and data transmission to the vendor).

FROM ACTIONS TO VALIDATION

Step 10: Build Specifications

Step 10 is the moment in time when the design takes physical form. The work requires the creation of the *build specifications*, which includes the information necessary to inspect and accept vendor parts, then assemble, align, calibrate, commission, and start operating the design. Simultaneously, the design elements are procured, received, tested, and readied for assembly. Fabrication and construction activities are then initiated. Logistics, shipping, preservation, material handling, and acceptance issues are resolved. The documentation mandated in the PS (vendor data, QA records, test records, material certificates, permits, etc.) is chased and compiled. Vendor payments are triggered and testing protocols are developed.

Clearly, there will be as many physical designs as there were *configurations* defined in Step 7. Consequently, the volume of information being developed in Steps 8, 9, and 10 may become significant. This volume of documentation is a primary motivation for establishing a formal document management process (discussed in Chapter 7).

Step 11: Testing Protocols

These protocols define which tests are required, under what conditions, and what pass/fail criteria will be applied *for each design configuration to be tested.*

These protocols are essential to the *knowledge requirement* underlying the development process. Slapping things together and running them through ad hoc tests and checks only prove whether something works or not, but provide no insight into why that was so. Without the why, the evolution of the development is doomed to wasteful improvisation and tinkering.

Step 12: Test

This last step puts the physical design through its paces in accordance with the test protocols. Test results are gathered, performance parameters are measured, system responses are gauged against theoretical predictions, and element deficiencies are uncovered. The test results are analyzed by the development team to determine what works, what doesn't, and why or why not. Possible remediation solutions are devised and recycled back to the appropriate step as early as Step 3, if necessary. Once all design configurations have been tested, the innovator convenes at least one brainstorming session with the technical team (and only that team) to review the results, pick the viable options, and plan a new round of models to be tested again. One or more brainstorming sessions will take place iteratively until the best unit transformation is uncovered for each function. One final development document is required to close the knowledge gathering loop: the *test results* report. This report is compiled and aggregated by design configuration. Reviews, assessments, prognostics, diagnostics, observations, design decisions, and conclusions are included.

The probability of hitting dead ends and circular progress is highest in Step 12. The innovator should fully expect the work to advance slowly, even randomly. Progress can even move backward. Some elements will pass, some will fail, and some will leave you baffled. Some inputs may not be known and likewise for outputs.

ACCELERATORS

Getting to *Yes* Faster

Thus far, it has been assumed that the idea that was perceived in TRL 1 was sufficiently complex to warrant the full implementation of the TRL development process. While the first three TRLs are pertinent to every single innovation pursuit, some leeway exists to scale back the minutia of details that are documented in the requirements, specifications, and protocols that will be encountered in TRL 4 through 8. This flexibility is all the more pertinent when the product will not require the full-scale pilot integration test of TRL 8. In that instance, the development process will be better served by adopting the fast-prototype method advocated by IDEO[6] as a principal development tool (instead of the W5H method). The method actively encourages tinkering and tweaking and yields the so-called *minimum viable product*. The functions are embodied through trial and error by building simple, cheap mock-ups and simplistic prototypes with whatever elements can be bought off-the-shelf. There may still be a need to create sketches and drawings and other kinds of technical documentation when fabrication and assembly instructions are required, but the W5H specification documents are omitted entirely until such time as TRL 9 commences. Fast prototypes have a number of benefits: rapid development times, quick discovery of unforeseen problems, immediate resolution of critical problems, and organic growth of the design through multiple versions of the prototype. Speed is the ultimate driver of the process.

Getting to *No* First

How can we reconcile the methodical, incremental, and document-heavy character of the W5H method with the unbridled creative abandon of the fast prototype approach? In a word, knowledge! The W5H method is appropriate when any of the following are true:

- The development process hinges on understanding the underlying physics, chemistry, or algorithmic complexity of an idea;
- Mathematical models of that knowledge are required;
- The aggregate behavior of connected elements is nonlinear (in a mathematical sense), requiring mathematical models of the coupled physics;
- The final design must be validated in an operational setting through an integrated pilot test (TRL 8); or
- The design's complexity cannot be mastered in a fast-prototype approach.

The fast-prototype method should be preferred when:

- The end product is autonomous (i.e., not required to interact dynamically with other systems);
- The elements of the product can be connected and activated once in place; and
- The elements do not require R&D prior to being selected.

Take the example of a smartphone. The touch screen was developed on the W5H basis as were the battery, the microchips, the circuit board, and the antenna. The outer casing, on the other hand, would have been an ideal candidate for the fast-prototype basis; as would have been the addition of the audio jack component and the power supply connection. Virtually all industrial products, conversely, will see their primary functions developed according to the

W5H method (while their secondary and tertiary functions could be done in a fast-prototype regime).

> The development process will often combine both methods with the W5H used on primary functions as well as some secondary functions and the fast-prototype method used on most secondary functions and all tertiary functions.

KNOWLEDGE ACCRETION

Dynamic Documentation

The constant updating of the *specification documents* that were developed in Steps 2 through 12 stems from the iterative process that was illustrated in Figure 4.3 and from the staggered inclusion of the development work on the secondary and tertiary functions. They are updated at the end of each TRL when the test results reveal the need to modify the design and recycle the revisions through the test protocols.

> These specification documents are critical to the smooth management of the overall project.

They become repositories of knowledge, findings, discoveries, and assessments of what worked or not. This cache of knowledge will become an integral component of the business' trade secrets, industrial knowhow, and competitive differentiator in the future—acting, in other words, as a barrier to entry for would-be challengers. This reason alone imparts upon them a measure of importance that must not be underestimated by the innovator. The innovator must develop these documents meticulously.

Nucleation

The mechanics of nucleation was introduced in *Investment-Centric Project Management* as *the mechanics of modeling numerically the theoretical state of the asset.*[7] This model is altogether different from the engineering and manufacturing models developed in Steps 8 and 10. It also serves a distinct purpose. The nucleation model is rather like a computer simulation that predicts the behavior of the product operationally and financially. From these predictions, the innovator is able to determine the economics of the asset, which cover such disparate profitability concerns as warranty duration, after-sale support, spare inventories, reliability and maintainability performance, operating costs (incurred by the buyer from operating the product), liability from failure, failure containment, usage profiles, performance metrics, the product's design limits and operating envelope, the operating requirements, and the total costs of ownership (to the buyer). These asset matters form the essence of the work in TRL 9 regardless of the existence of this model or not. The profitability of the business depends on a thorough understanding—by the innovator acting as business manager—of the cost drivers that will define his commercial bottom line.

Nucleation must begin no later than TRL 8 and is carried out in parallel along three axes: the engineering axis, the information axis, and the operational axis. *Engineering nucleation* models the full-field physics of the product. *Information nucleation* models the entirety of the data associated with the product and the asset. *Operational nucleation* models the activities of the product throughout its economic life.

Engineering Nucleation

As the name implies, *engineering nucleation* seeks to model numerically the physical behavior of the *product* within and without its operational envelope. The model yields the limits of that envelope within which the product is deemed to be safe to operate. It also predicts the reaction of the product when subjected to operating conditions outside the envelope, up to the so-called *black swan* scenarios. The model includes several components such as: computer animations, physics simulations, behavioral limit tables, and fail/safe criteria under expected, abnormal, and extraordinary conditions. The physics simulations, in particular, will cover:

- Element-level full-field physics modeling that is used to quantify the spatial and temporal variables involved in the component, assembly, or system's reactions to the physical inputs.
- Installation-level, nonlinear behavior modeling that, this time, is used to assess the linear and nonlinear responses of an installation under expected, abnormal, and extraordinary operational conditions. The models help set the margins of safety.

The behavioral limits of the product are obtained through a series of studies:

- Quantitative risk assessments for systems and installations that may be subject to or exposed to explosions, losses of containment, pressure and temperature spikes, earthquakes and climate vagaries, fires, and power losses.
- Failure-containment studies that, in tandem with the quantitative risk assessments, quantify the ability of a system or an installation to continue to operate safely when subject to a partial or severe failure of one or more components; to what extent it can contain the results of a failure; and the risks of a cascading failure throughout an installation or plant.

- Life-cycle cost (LCC) modeling is used to discover the variables that will determine the profitable performance characteristics of the product. One such variable relates to the system or installation's reliability obtained by the installation-level nonlinear behavior modeling (mentioned previously). Reliability is quantified by mean time to failure, mean time between failure, failure modes, and probability density functions. The second LCC variable is maintainability and is modeled through maintainability vectors, recurring maintenance requirements, and plant-wide reliability management specifications. Note that the LCC parameters become the input variables to the operating nucleation described in the following section.

Information Nucleation

The engineering nucleation generates an *endogenous dataset* that is proprietary to the business. It should never reach the public domain. The *exogenous dataset* that is intended to be accessed by the product's buyer is generated by the information nucleation mechanism. In this case, the goal is twofold: (1) orchestrate into a single datum network the myriad information created during the development process in a multitude of file formats and media; and (2) connect the product user to this dataset. The process of nucleation occurs through three interwoven threads: model-centric architecture, access, and integrated maintenance management.

- *Model-centric architecture*—Create a virtual physical model of the product right down to the last screw. For each element of the product, create links to its associated set of technical data, drawings, 3-D models, manuals, and marketing materials. Enable these links to be accessed by the product buyer online by simply pointing and clicking.
- *Access*—The datum network must reside on the internet and be easily accessed by browser. The graphical user interface must be intuitive, clean, and efficient *for the user*.
- *Integrated maintenance management*—When the use of the product generates real-time data for its buyer, create a new web-based interface to capture this data automatically in real time as well. This information is critical to the innovator who is intent on validating the engineering nucleation models.

Operational Nucleation

This nucleation closes the loop for the asset model. Whereas the engineering and information nucleation are specific to the physical product, the operational nucleation predicts the *resources involved in its use by buyers*. The model will yield business parameters such as staffing requirements; training needs; regular maintenance plans and schedules; spares, consumables, and inventory levels; utility and power consumptions; effluents, emissions, and disposal rates; regulatory filing requirements; personnel and material movements; emergency responses; and economic performance estimates. The outcome of the nucleation process is a prediction of the profitability of the product *for its buyer*.

Complexity Management

Clearly, the development process is liable to explode in complexity when a product is a complex array of elements. Starting at TRL 3 and intensifying at TRL 4, the development work splits off in several parallel directions: continue the R&D on the primary functions, initiate the design work on the secondary functions, perhaps initiate R&D on some secondary functions, deepen the design work on the proven primary functions, and begin integrating the primary and secondary elements into assemblies and systems. That is a lot of moving parts evolving on their own sweet time—a situation that is conducive to the onset of chaos and loss of control. Keeping focused on the objective (a commercially successful product) becomes a mantra to the project manager and the development team. Getting sidetracked by curiosity and what-if scenarios beyond the *how* stage will be a constant danger. The project manager must remain steadfastly vigilant.

WHAT ABOUT SCHEMA PRODUCTS?

Ubiquity of the Development Model

Up to this point, the development discussion has tacitly assumed that the product could belong to any one of the three categories described in Chapter 1 (*integrated*, *ready*, and *schema* products). We now state explicitly that this is indeed the case. The applicability of this chapter is ubiquitous to the three categories, and can, in fact, be extended to the higher abstraction of designing a business or a corporate structure. The extents of the twelve development steps introduced before will, of course, vary in depth and resources as a function of the complexity of the idea under consideration. For the simplest of objects—say a door key, a clothespin, a protractor, or a nut—the time required to complete the twelve steps will be orders of magnitude shorter than complex systems like a computer, a novel water treatment chemistry, a radiative-voltaic power cell, or a hologram-rendering software. The steps should be applied as a whole regardless of the idea because the procedural discipline expected of the ICIPM methodology is an emergent feature of the sum of those steps.

Deviation from the Norm

Whereas both *integrated* and *ready* products should submit to the development model, the *schema product* can, nevertheless, be treated differently. Recall from Chapter 1 that the *schema* product is, at heart, a process through which information and interactions flow, one that does not generate revenues. On the other hand, the *schema* product determines the efficiency with which a unit transformation is performed, hence its impact on the profitability of the business. That is why Chapter 1 specified that this product constitutes the broadest source of internal innovations from which higher profits can be wrung out. Take, for example, the very simple approval process of an invoice. This process is a unit transformation with one input (the invoice) and several outputs (the set of signatures required to affirm the approval of the invoice). The approval process in this case is the *schema* product for which we ask the questions: how efficient must the process be? How many signatures are really required and in what order? Must the signatures be gathered on paper or can they be done digitally? And, is there a different way to obtain the approval that does not require multiple signatures? In this instance, the development model would be unnecessarily burdensome to implement. A faster approach would start with the W5H technique and the unit transformation mechanics in tandem, but expanded in the unit transformation process (UTP) discussed next.

The UTP

The UTP mechanics expand the unit transformation of Figure 4.4 into the analytical tool shown in Figure 4.5. The tool was introduced by the author in Chapter 4 of *Investment-Centric Project Management*. The *activity* is comprised of all of the features that appear in the figure. These features are grouped into three classes of mechanisms: inputs, process, and outputs.[8]

The input mechanisms include:

- The *inputs* that are processed into outputs and are supplied from one or more preceding activities
- The *attributes* that must be embedded into the output
- The *targets* that quantify the execution of the *activity*

The output mechanisms include:

- The *outputs* that are the outcome of the activity to be passed on to one or more subsequent activities
- The *characteristics* that are derived from the contents of the output
- The *metrics* that are achieved during execution (underwritten by the *targets*)

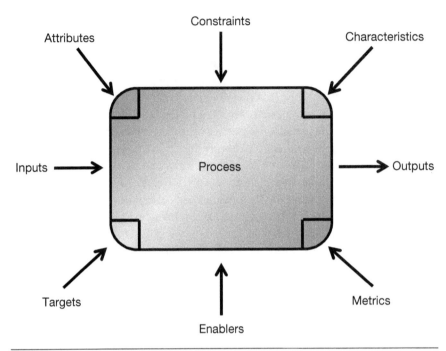

Figure 4.5   The UTP: the fundamental analytical tool for breaking down objects, procedures, processes, and relationships

The process mechanisms include:

- The *process* that derives, transforms, or creates outputs from inputs
- The *enablers* that are supplied by the organization to execute the activity
- The *constraints* that create the closed boundary within which the activity is executed

Inputs and Outputs

The inputs are independent variables that are supplied to the process to be transformed into outputs. Some inputs flow through the process unchanged and emerge as identical outputs. Others will be converted into a different form. Others, still, will be created as new outputs. The outputs are dependent variables that are transmitted to other unit transformations. In some cases, the outputs must be fed back into the process, when an iterative process is required.

Process

The process is the *action* that transforms the inputs. This action could be physical (convert electricity into a magnetic field to turn an electric motor), algorithmic (receive a radio transmission and trigger the ringer on the phone), procedural (send an approved invoice to the finance department for payment), or relational (issue an order to a subordinate). The process is internal to the activity and fully defined within it. The process is not beholden to external approval, only its outputs. The process is executed with the resources supplied as enablers, against the limits and specifications externally imposed as constraints, and measured for efficacy against targets and metrics obtained.

Attributes and Targets

These two input mechanisms differ from the process inputs in that they are *independent* of the process and essentially flow through the activity unchanged. The *attributes* pass through the process to end up as information embedded in the outputs. Instances of attributes include: a drawing number, a document title, a revision number, title block information, inspection requirements to appear in the notes of a drawing, a serial number, a part number, a price, weight and volume, owner of the activity, and reviewer of the outputs. *Targets* go around the process to end up on the accounting ledger associated with the activity. They are intimately associated with the output *metrics*. Examples of targets will typically be tied to time, money, and quality and will include things like: budget breakdown for each task of an activity, duration of the activity, schedule deadline, maximum number of errors, number of staff working on the activity, productivity, performance specifications on the output, and reliability rating of the output. Globally, the targets provide a baseline to quantify the actual execution of the activity (i.e., the metrics).

Characteristics and Metrics

These two output mechanisms are the counterparts of the attributes (characteristics) and targets (metrics). The first, *characteristics*, are sets of countable features extracted from the outputs, which may be subject to future activities. For example, a fabrication drawing will have a material list, showing the items, quantities, and part numbers. These items would be subject to procurement activities of their own. *Metrics* are linked to the *target*. They are the actual, measured values of those targets obtained during the execution of the activity. *Metrics* provide a measure of the efficiency with which the activity has been performed. An obvious example is a budget, specified at the outset as a target, and recorded as an accrued cost at the end of the activity.

Enablers

The resources required for the execution of a process are called the enablers. They include people, qualifications, training, systems, mechanics, mechanisms, methods, and protocols. Enablers also include the *internal* validation and verification mechanisms to check the results of the *process*.

Constraints

Constraints are *externally* imposed upon the project by the owner or a regulator, for instance (the building code is a classic example). *Constraints* establish the acceptance space within which the activity must take place. Some constraints are self-evident: budgets, timelines, physical location (such as land for example), tare weight (airplanes), and completion deadlines (Olympic facilities). Some are legislated: building codes, electrical codes, occupational health and safety, union collective agreements, practice of engineering, and foreign worker employment. Others are more subjective: community relationships, social development, environmental commitment, strategic positioning, and reputational situations. Constraints are divided into four types: *compliance, standards, criteria,* and *allocation*.

- *Compliance* pertains to the regulatory requirements applicable to the realization of the activity, to the individuals performing the work (qualifications, certifications), to the tools used for the work (approved welding equipment), and to the permits.
- *Standards* encompass the codes, standards, specifications, requirements definitions, templates, schemes, and other prescriptions upon the activity. Industry standards are usually adopted based on professional practice and acknowledged priority or on legislative standards. Standards also comprise those of the innovator's organization and are imposed upon on the project in equal force with the legislated ones.
- *Criteria* are the externally defined constraints imposed on the inputs and outputs. *Criteria do not apply to the process.*
- *Allocation* represents the budget, time, and physical limits allocated to the activity or project.

Back to W5H

The W5H method comes into play as the prime enquiry tool for identifying, quantifying, and circumscribing the features of the activity. The nature of the questions to be posed during the enquiry is guided by Steps 2, 3, and 4 of the development model. The *purpose* of the activity will ultimately clarify why an action is required (in our example, that would be who absolutely must sign off), why an action should be avoided (who really does not need to sign off), and how the activity is manifested (the signature is recorded in ink or in bytes). The outputs of the activity will also help identify the associated and follow-up activities that must be carried out in relation to the initial activity (where the approved invoice is stored, by whom, and who else needs to know that it is approved).

It should be evident that the efficacy of a *schema* product is inversely proportional to the number of interdependent activities involved. In our example, a single signature, applied digitally, is the most efficient way of approving the invoice. Having seven people sign off on a paper form accompanying the invoice is more complex (and therefore more costly, slower, and more prone to errors and delays).

THE TECHNOLOGY DEVELOPMENT PLAN

The Governance Road Map

The culmination of Chapters 3 and 4 is the creation of a *technology development plan* to govern the innovation journey. Its purpose is fourfold:

1. To align the innovator's organization on the execution strategy to develop the idea into a successful commercial business;
2. To prescribe how the execution will be carried at each TRL;
3. To convey the seriousness of the endeavor to past, present, and future investors; and
4. To secure the necessary funding for each TRL.

The *technology development plan* is not a ponderous, static document. It is a concise, prescriptive statement of what must be done, by whom, when, at what cost, in what time, and in relation to what targets. The text abides by the W5H methodology explained previously and must be written with the aim of getting to the point. The initial compilation of the plan commences once the *landscape basis* from Step 1 is done and the idea is deemed worthy of pursuit—occurring during TRL 1. The publication of the first version occurs *before* the work on Step 2 is started. The *purpose* document produced by Step 2 becomes the first deliverable of the plan and serves as a basis for scoping out the effort anticipated by the next phase of the innovation journey. After this scoping endeavor is completed, a new version of the plan is compiled and issued *for the next TRL phase only*. Afterwards, the sequence *deliverables, scoping, plan update, and publication* is repeated for each subsequent TRL. The process is illustrated in Figure 4.6.

The Contents

The stewardship of the technology development plan falls upon the innovator, whose responsibility it is to develop the contents and maintain the published versions to keep them current. The extent of the plan is tailored to the scale of

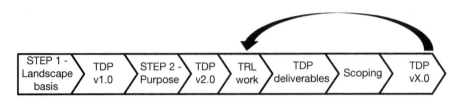

Figure 4.6   The technology development plan: the plan is seen to be a highly dynamic document that evolves over time with as many iterations as the development work requires

the development program. In the case of innovators who are new to the innovation journey, the plan provides a blueprint of the skeletal functions of the future business structure. In most instances, as a result, the innovator may not have any contents developed for Sections 2 and 3 of the plan. These sections need not be completed before the development works begin, but they should be developed in parallel to those works such that, by the time TRL 9 begins, they are on hand to support the commercialization effort—without which the profitability of the business will suffer.

An example of a technology development plan (less the overview) is part of the WAV™ material for this book found on the publisher's website at www.jrosspub.com/wav. The contents are divided into five sections: Overview, Technical Road Map, Execution Framework, Standard Operating Environment (SOE), and Scope of Work.

- The overview section is intended primarily for an external audience and the pursuit of funding sources. Its readers must get a sense of what the innovation is, what commercial potential it is believed to offer, what work has been done, what remains to be done, and what major hurdles and challenges are on hand.
- The second section outlines the overall technological road map that underpins the development journey. It describes the innovator's initial technical objectives that need to be created; the challenges, risks, and unknowns associated with each objective; and the set of possible solution approaches to resolve each challenge, risk, and unknown.
- The third section details the management structure of the innovator's firm and the resources that are either on hand or externally supplied to do the work. Attention is placed on the constraints that are external to the firm—in particular, the ones stemming from regulators.
- The fourth section establishes the mechanics and mechanisms that need to be adopted by the firm in order to standardize the execution of the work.

- The fifth and final section addresses the work details for the particular TRL stage under consideration. The details include the scope of work; the expected outcomes of the work; the resources required—mapped out across a schedule along with the attendant budget and the nature of the involvement of third-party contractors, vendors, and agencies.

The reader will note that the plan does not attempt to define the detailed work for the entire innovation journey. Those details are captured in the last section as the work progresses across the TRL spectrum. The first instance of this tailored approached will occur with the work associated with the *purpose* definition in Figure 4.6. Every TRL afterward will be planned in a like manner and published each time as a new revision to the plan.

Salient Features

The plan contains a limited number of features that require further explanation:

- *Article 1.4*—mentions the term *allocations*, which was introduced previously as a type of constraint put on a UTP.
- *Article 3.2.4*—refers to *champions*, the same ones that are discussed in Chapter 3.
- *Article 3.6*—introduces the concept of *accountability matrix*, which is explained later on in this chapter. The matrix establishes who's who in the approval process and is based on the *directrix* concept that was introduced in *Investment-Centric Project Management*.
- *Article 3.7*—highlights the gaps within the innovator's organization between what is on hand and what is missing from the items required to do the work. To each one of Articles 2.7.1 through 2.7.7, the gaps will be tabulated according to the template shown in Table 4.2 (with examples from 2.7.1 expertise).

Section 2, *Technical Road Map*, also warrants further expounding. The road map alludes strictly to the technical aspects of the technology development. The road map begins with a statement of the overall technical objectives for the innovation in Article 2.1. These objectives exclude things like pricing, development costing, marketing strategy, sales pitch, commercial goals, schedules, and business operations. The emphasis is on the technical reality that is implied by the proposed innovation, including issues of physics and chemistry, mathematics, engineering design, and performance requirements. For example, let's assume that the innovation is to be a system that can transmit electric current

Table 4.2   Example of an inventory gap table: in this instance, a partial list of expertise requirements illustrate the gap findings

Required	On-Hand	External Source	Training/Certification/ Validation Required
3-D modeling	George Michael, designer		Yes
3-D animation	George Lucas, video editor		No
Marketing	Missing	New hire	Conditional
Web marketing	Missing	Consultant 1 Consultant 2 Consultant 3	No
Code compliance	Alan Parsons, Engineer	Testing Lab ZYX	No

wirelessly to a device (a motor, a controller, a phone, a TV, etc.). Examples of valid technical objectives would include:

- Transmit the current over a distance ranging from 6 inches to 5 feet in air at room temperature
- Current levels to range between 1mA to 2A and voltage between 1.5V and 115V
- Transmission losses to be limited to 2% at maximum separation
- Power supply to be 115V at 15A
- Conversion efficiency from source to transmission to exceed 92%
- Zero electromagnetic leakage other than through the transmitter nozzle
- System weight limited to 32 lb. within a box not exceeding 18 × 12 × 12 inches

Observe in this list the absence of pricing, costing, material selection, or fabrication methods. Nor does the list address the issue of development costs, timelines, and resources needed to complete the program. These come out at later stages of the technology development journey. It is entirely possible at this early stage that some or all of those objectives could prove unrealistic or commercially impossible to achieve. It is an inevitable possibility of the R&D endeavor, in which case the objectives will have to be revised, altered, or abandoned altogether.

Article 2.2 follows up with an outline of the anticipated challenges, risks, and unknowns that are associated with each technical objective. Once again, the intent is to lay out what can be fathomed on the road ahead. *The objective is to dive into detailed descriptions of specific solutions that can be envisioned by the innovator.* It is essential that the list of items for each objective be as comprehensive as can be inferred. These items end up being the basis of the scope of work to be undertaken in the technology development journey. Take, for example, the last objective—the list of issues could include:

- The difficulty of generating a magnetic field of sufficient strength within the space and weight constraints
- The wireless current transmitter does not exist—it needs to be invented—its shape, weight, and performance are unknown and potentially impossible to achieve (the risk)
- The current will need to be focused into a coherent beam—you have no idea how to do this
- The current receiver will need to be connectable to the device—the interface details are entirely defined by its size and weight—it is not known if a compact design can be directly mounted into the electrical socket of a device

The third component of the technical objectives is covered in Article 2.3 as a compilation of possible solution approaches for each item listed in Article 2.2. At long last, the innovator is encouraged to lay out whatever solution that needs to be investigated, be it a known design or a potentially new method. The innovator should start with the solutions that are already known, then expand to other sources of resolution that can be either conceived, imagined, or borrowed from other fields. Each possible solution is further described in terms of the expected costs, timelines, and resources required to see it through. The resources include the expertise and skill sets (already within the team, available through training, or acquired from consultants), as well as the specialized processes, tools, and/or procedures implied by the solution.

Accountability Matrix

Investment-Centric Project Management dedicates an entire chapter to the subject of accountability; in Chapter 5, accountability is defined as the path of attribution of merit or blame for the outcome of an activity or task. Accountability is further characterized as an individual function; it is never assigned to a group or a functional department. This definition is embraced by the ICIPM philosophy. Chapter 5 goes on to spell out the three conditions that must be met for accountability to exist:

1. The decision of the accountable individual determines the success or failure of an outcome
2. The individual can be singled out for reward or punishment for an outcome
3. The individual will directly live with the consequences from the decision

In *Investment-Centric Project Management*, it is made clear that accountability, responsibility, and authority (to approve) are distinct individual functions that together form the *directrix*. Within the *directrix* framework, the accountable person or party (AP) is vested with the power to execute a UTP. The AP owns what goes on inside the boundary of the activity shown in Figure 4.4. The AP defines what outputs must be generated, specifies the transformation mechanisms required to produce the outputs, specifies the inputs needed by the transformation, and identifies the enablers required to execute the activity. The responsible party (RP) owns the mandate to make available to the AP the resources that are required to execute the unit transformation. The RP supplies the attributes, the targets, and the enablers (project information, tools, processes, procedures, and appropriately trained personnel). Finally, the probate party (PP) is granted the power and authority to approve the outputs of a unit transformation *that are meant to be utilized by others*. The PP defines the limits, the constraints, and the acceptance criteria for the outputs. The PP certifies the correctness of the outputs and UTP characteristics before moving on to the next UTP. This work includes the verification of the compliance of the outcome against the constraints being imposed upon the work.

It is in this interplay that the principle of checks-and-balances comes into force. The AP is the first among equals in one specific aspect: he is the one to take the lead to coordinate the timely participation of the PP and RP in the UTP. The interactions between the three individuals are illustrated in Figure 4.7.

When applied to the technology development plan (see Articles 2.6, 3.3.3, 3.4.8, 4.2.5, 4.3.5, and 4.4.5), the *directrix* assignments are presented in a matrix similar to the one shown in Table 4.3. The reader should notice the absence of duplication of the roles for any given deliverable. This stems from the exclusion principle enunciated in Chapter 5 of *Investment-Centric Project Management*, whereby the same person cannot be both AP and PP, AP and RP, or PP and RP at the same time, on the same UTP.

PUTTING IT ALL TOGETHER

The combination of Chapters 3 and 4 in this book yields a potent development strategy that is constructed upon the pillars supplied by the three prime directives of: governing the evolution of the works, increasing knowledge as time goes by, and protecting investors' capital. The reader may strain under the impression that the process is cumbersome, Guttenberg heavy, and procedurally constricting. However, this impression need not materialize; the many prescriptions found in this pair of chapters can be adopted as checklists by the innovator or as a road map of milestones to get the work planned. Nevertheless,

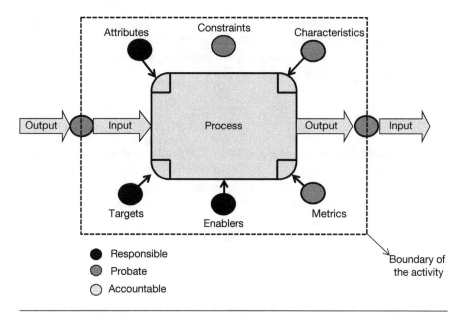

Figure 4.7 The *directrix*: the AP looks after the inner workings of the transformation, the RP supplies the resources to the AP to do the work, and the PP makes sure that what comes in and out of the activity can be relied upon to execute the work

Table 4.3 Example of an accountability matrix: the directrix for each deliverable is different as a consequence of the distinct skill sets involved with each directrix function

UTP	Deliverable	AP	PP	RP
10.1	Drawing	Arthur	Ernest	George
	Datasheet	Barbara	Ernest	George
	Characteristics	Charlie	Ernest	Arthur
10.2	Calculations	Diana	Francine	Barbara
	Load limits summary	Diana	Francine	Halley

there is no escaping the need to plan the work within a formal framework. Only through formality can risks be identified, corralled, and castrated before they have time to react. Furthermore, this level of formalism will convey to observers and would-be investors alike an impression of self-control and ordered mindset emanating from the innovator and his team. This impression will, in turn, aid the funding success of the innovator. There can be no freewheeling if outside money is involved; nor can the innovation journey be improvised as the primary means of traveling down the timeline if the ultimate destination is a successful commercial business, which begins, inevitably, with the first client—our next stop in the upcoming chapter.

NOTES

1. The word *diarrhetic* is a neologism by your author to describe a statement that has substance at first sight but none on closer inspection.
2. See *Investment-Centric Project Management*, Chapter 12.
3. Ibid. In systems engineering, the primary function is directly associated with a transformation process tied to revenue generation. The secondary function powers the primary function. The tertiary function enables the operation of the primary-secondary function tandem.
4. See *Investment-Centric Project Management*, Chapter 5. The UTP is the theoretical building block of the project management philosophy advocated in the book. It applies to products, services, processes, functionals, organizational structures, business functions, scope definition, work planning, and others.
5. See Chapter 4 of *The Art of Innovation* by Tom Kelley. The reader will also gain valuable insights from *The Net and the Butterfly* by Olivia Fox Cabane and Judah Pollack.
6. Ibid.
7. See *Investment-Centric Project Management*, Chapter 12.
8. Further details on the meaning and usage of the terms associated with this activity are provided in Chapter 4 of *Investment-Centric Project Management*. The theoretical construct of the activity is substantiated by seven axioms that are discussed in that chapter as well.

5

THE FIRST CUSTOMER

The road to commercialization starts from the end.

THE STARTING POINT

The Buyer Sets the Tone

The presentation of the material in the preceding chapters has hitherto followed the logical sequence of the development process. Chapter 2 was especially important to the sequence because of its emphasis on forcing a change
of perspective in the innovator's eyes from the widget to the market. Chapter 5
brings us back to the importance of a market-driven mindset to the success of
the commercialization effort. Our discussion changes the focus from procedure
to management. The heart of the chapter is framed by two questions: how to
pick the right buyer target and what to do with that buyer during development.

The reader may ponder the rationale for the first question. After all, it is
difficult to predict from the outset who will buy the innovation. Innovators and
inventors would rather start out with the presumption that the innovation, if
properly developed, will define the buyer in the future. Steve Jobs once famously
declared that Apple never did any market research before embarking on the
seminal development of the iPod. The key here should be obvious: neither you
nor anybody else is Apple—not even mighty Google is Apple. Apple is the exceptional exception to the rule. The number of companies that have successfully commercialized genuinely virgin markets are few and far between. More
of them have tried and failed. The point cannot be made clearer: you cannot
develop an innovation in a vacuum bereft of potential buyers' inputs.

The better mousetrap never succeeds on its own merits.

The gravest error is to fail to nail down a specific market for the initial product rollout. Worse still, this error is the easiest to make when the idea fools

the innovator into believing that it can spread across a multitude of markets and usages. Consider as an example the ubiquitous material nylon, which was discovered by Wallace Carothers in 1935 while employed by the Dupont company. The material is so ubiquitous today that it is easy to forget that it took Dupont five long years to figure out how to make it, and for what applications, back in the 1940s. Today, nylon is everywhere. Seventy years ago, it began life in women's stockings. That choice was driven by what the market was hiding in plain sight: before nylon, stockings were made from silk, which had become too onerous for most working women during the war years. The product rollout was a stupendous success. Notice how Dupont focused its commercialization on one very specific market. It did not try to be everything to every usage for everyone. Its eventual foray into industrial applications was forced by the onset of the Second World War, rather than a forward-looking management strategy. Dupont succeeded—beyond anyone's wildest expectations—because it chose one specific market at the expense of all others.

Pick a Winner

Choosing the buyer, and therefore the market, is not a matter of choice but an obligation. It becomes a question of life or debt when the product is potentially far-ranging, and the risk of a missed opportunity increases exponentially. The selection of that first customer must be motivated by two overarching concerns defined during technology readiness level (TRL) 5:

1. Will the product be successfully accepted by the buyer (the *acceptance criterion*)?
2. Will the buyer's market be large enough to break even on the innovator's investment in a reasonable amount of time (the *recovery criterion*)?

The answers must both be *yes*. It is not enough to succeed with the product rollout if there are not enough sales to make the commercial endeavor a success. And it does not matter that a market represents millions of potential buyers if the product has no chance of widespread acceptance. Remember that you only get one shot at this.

Let us explore the ramifications through a second example. Assume that the innovation is a newly discovered material that converts heat into electricity with an efficiency of 60% (versus 2–4% with the current state-of-the-art product). The application relies on a well-known process called thermoelectric generation (it's the thermometer in your oven). At first glance, the application potential for the material is absolutely huge. Aside from oven temperature sensing, the material could be used in waste heat recovery applications to produce useful electricity. The heat sources include the engine block or the muffler in a car, the exhaust pipe in a house's furnace or water heater tank, or the exhaust stream of flare stacks and incinerator chimneys in power generation plants. Waste heat is a universal by-product of physics-based unit transformations; as such, it represents a dream market that reaches into every corner of the world, regardless of politics, policies, industries, or cultures. To the neophyte innovator, it's the kind of market size that dreams are made of.

Of course, none of it will make any dent on the face of the market's indifference if one chases them all at once. To consider any one of the multitudinous choices, one must think through what the scale implies. The oven application requires the simplest design packaged into a compact little sensor with two electric leads. The car muffler requires a matrix that can be curved around the muffler within which is embedded the thermoelectric material, along with the cabling, voltage collection, phase inversion, and control unit. The power plant chimney requires costly piping to guide the exhaust down to a collection unit comprising banks of thermoelectric cells, as well as an electrical distribution network to make use of the electricity produced. Clearly, the development of the innovation cannot possibly produce such a broad variety of design configurations in one TRL program. And, lest the reader imagines the feat possible, recall that each design option will require its own innovation landscape survey, its landscape basis, and its product objectives. It is impossible for any innovator with limited resources to pursue these paths simultaneously. However, if the choice of a target market proves difficult, the innovator would do well to carry out the landscape survey as a first attempt at quantifying the pros and cons of each application option.

CONSEQUENCES OF THE CHOICE

The Champion Enters the Scene

This first target market is decided by the *acceptance* and *recovery criteria*, which was described earlier. The decision immediately sets the development requirements. In some instances, the development process will span the full TRL process and require a pilot test. In other instances, no pilot test will be required. The requirement for the pilot test enables us to classify products as *integrated* (requiring pilot test) or *ready* (no pilot test). The classification matters enormously to the innovator in terms of planning, timelines, and budgets (the usual expectations suspects). It matters especially to the recruitment of a champion (one of the key ingredients emphasized in Chapter 3). If a product requires a pilot test, more than anyone else, it will be the champion who will influence its outcome and bear witness to the merits of the product. Whereas in the absence of a pilot test, the champion will not be one but many who are enlisted by the innovator to validate the final design.

> *The champion personifies the target buyer of the initial product release and will indeed willingly buy the product at that time.*

When is a pilot test required? That would be when the operation/use of the product is integrated to the buyer's installation (or plant). The term *integration* implies that the behavior of the product is coupled to that of the framework. In other words, the product's behavior directly affects the behavior of the installation and vice versa. It is this coupling effect that mandates the pilot test. The integration of the product implies that there is a level of control and system interfaces that preclude a *plug-and-play* approach. Generally speaking, functional elements (see Chapter 4) limited to components and systems will not require a pilot test. Things like a screw, an electric motor, a sensor, a control panel, a clothespin, a button, a smartphone, a car, a light bulb, or a laptop is not behaviorally coupled to the buyer's installation. On the other hand, more complex functional elements like installations, plants, software, industrial processes, information technology (IT) networks, and fleet management operations are inherently coupled to the buyer's larger installation or plant, and will require a pilot test. Even the humble game app on a smartphone must be pilot tested to make sure that its underlying code is compatible with the phone's operating system, that its user interface commands are working, and the aggregate power demand upon the phone's battery is not excessive.

The Pilot Champion

The pilot-tested product lives and dies by the dictum *form follows function*. To its user, the value proposition is what it does rather than how it looks. It is bought first and foremost for its ability to perform its functions as advertised. The feel, look, color, surface finish, and pleasant user interface, to name but a few, are of secondary concern to the buyer unless these things perform a function as well. The color of a circuit breaker assembly is of no importance to a buyer, except when that color is tied to an amperage scale, for example. That is not to say that the presentation and packaging of the product is immaterial, however. On the contrary, no product can afford to create an impression that it is inferior, weak, unsafe, or unsuited to its purpose. The look and feel of a pilot-tested product comes into play once its purpose is functionally complete.

The role of the champion to the development of the *integrated product* is dramatically different than for the *ready* product scenario. The champion of an *integrated* product is invited to join the development team (in an informal capacity) as early as possible (preferably when the product's purpose is being defined). Starting with TRL 3, the champion's interaction with the development team will be mainly in an advisory capacity. The champion's opinions will be especially important to the innovator during the review of test results. Remember that the champion is hoped to become the first buyer which lends urgency to his feedback, which should be gathered no later than TRL 6. This feedback will take several forms:

- Suggest success criteria for product objectives, primary functions, and performance test targets
- Participate in design reviews and TRL tests
- Define the scope of the pilot test
- Clarify the physical, control, and algorithmic interface requirements at the pilot test site
- Identify the site's hazard and emergency response plans
- Specify the regulatory requirements that govern the conduct of the pilot test
- Lay out the commercial requirements of the product from the buyer's perspective (documentation, regulatory compliance, warranty coverage, after-sale support, naming and numbering convention, reliability and maintainability targets, total cost of ownership (TCO) targets, etc.)
- Assessment criteria for the pilot test results
- Final acceptance testing requirements
- Buy/no-buy decision criteria

The Ready Champion

The *ready* product differs from its *integrated* cousin in that the *form* is equal to the *function*—even superior in some cases. The *ready* product cannot succeed commercially on the strength of its purpose; it must appeal to the buyer's sensitivities in equal measures. Presentation and packaging play a dominant role. Take the smartphone market as an example. Before the entrance of Apple's iPhone, the market was dominated by Nokia and Blackberry. The iPhone was functionally and purposefully equal (even superior in some features) to the competition, but its presentation was in a class by itself—the smooth finishes, the pleasant feel in the hand, the crisp graphics, the sleek colors right from the first contact with its packaging. Everything that was intimate to the user's sensory experience was sublime to the user's mind. Compared to the competition, the first iPhone was technology made into art. It was the art that made money. Lots of money.

How does the champion fit into this picture? In a word, not. When *form equals function*, value becomes a matter of opinion. Hence, there can be no single champion, but many. As a group, however, these champions do not possess the same importance that the single champion bore upon the pilot-tested product. The group's principal role is to try out the design variations of the development team from which an aggregate picture of the user experience can be compiled. The reader should note that the starting point of any proposed design variation must be at least on par with the market's status quo (see *Looking through the Buyer's Eye* in Chapter 3). You cannot propose a design that is lacking or inferior in functionality when compared to the market's offering.

The true champion of a *ready* product is the innovator. It is his vision of how things could be that drives the development process. Champion groups are used to obtain independent feedback and suggest additional design variations. They should not be used as focus groups, however. Most people cannot envision needs that they do not have or fathom functions and usages out of thin air. They are best at trying things out and giving their opinions on what works or what doesn't.

PREPARING FOR FIRST SALE

The Path

The first customer is synonymous with commercialization. It also marks the beginning of the end of the development process with the start of TRL 8. By now, the design should have advanced sufficiently and resolved all technical unknowns and uncertainties. Certainly, there should no cause to contemplate a design change of any kind at this late stage of the game. The design should, in fact, have reached a state that is nearly final, except for the details associated with the tertiary functions (in the case of an *integrated* product). For the *integrated* product, the remaining work in TRL 8 is concerned with the fabrication of Version 0 of the product and the design work required to integrate it into the champion's or prospective first buyer's operating facility. For the *ready* product, the remaining work merges TRL 8 and 9 in terms of pre-commercialization. In TRL 9, the product is transformed into the commercial asset, able to generate the long sought revenues and return on investments (ROI).

Both product types follow the same path forward:

- Nail down the success criteria (technical and commercial) upheld by the would-be buyer to justify the purchase
- Put the product through its paces to validate and verify its ability to meet the criteria (at no cost to the first customer)
- Finalize the design up to Version 1.0
- Get the business ready to start manufacturing and selling the product to the first customer

- Monitor the customer's first impressions to address any and all issues that prop up to threaten the product's acceptance by the customer
- Get ready for full-on product rollout

Note as well what is not included in this list. There is no mention of marketing, website design, advertisement strategies, and selling topics. These omissions are intentional: the first customer should always precede the official product rollout event. As a matter of fact, the first customer offers the innovator the opportunity to covertly prove out the sales-ready product—without running the risks of having to deal publicly with unforeseen failures, shortcomings, deficiencies, or negative buyer reactions. The likelihood of these outcomes occurring will have been mitigated greatly by the implementation of the development process. Nevertheless, one can never be certain of unconditional success until success has been shown unconditionally. The covert approach also benefits the first customer. Should things really not work out, for whatever reasons, there will be no need to address the issue publicly. But if things succeed, the first customer gets the double glory of an instant leg up on the competition *and* positive publicity for filling the role as technological trailblazer.

First Things First

The aim of TRL 8 is to finish the development process by getting to Version 1. Cost and quality issues come to the fore, but do not yet occupy center stage. That honor goes to the success criteria advocated by the champion (or buyer if no champion exists). Notice the emphasis on the buyer's perspective. Success has nothing to do with how great the product performs or appears, per se. What matters is how *the buyer perceives the product*. The success criteria are divided into three groups: commercial, technical, and final acceptance.

- The commercial success factors pertain to the buying decision. They were initially posited in the landscape basis and the product objectives (see Chapter 3). Now, they must be nailed down to specifics. What is the buyer's price range? How sensitive is the buyer to price variations as a function of performance? What is the target TCO? How fast is the buyer expecting to take delivery of the product after ordering? What minimum warranty guarantees will be necessary? What factors are seen as deal breakers? How many products will the buyer want initially? How many later?
- The technical success factors pertain to the purpose of the product. What performance numbers must be achieved by the product to convince the buyer of the validity of the design? What should be the reliability and maintainability specifications? What are the tertiary functions to which

the product will interface? What kind of regular maintenance frequencies will be acceptable? What level of operator expertise will be mandated by the buyer? What are the regulatory compliance obligations that must be satisfied? What materials are mandatory, desirable, or banned?

- The final acceptance factors pertain to the results from the pilot test(s). In this instance, the buyer defines explicitly how the product will be assessed during the pilot test, against what criteria, and how success or failure will be determined. Presumably, a product that achieves final acceptance unconditionally will be hard to reject as a purchase option by the buyer.

Each category of success factors raises a number of questions. All of these questions must be resolved jointly by the innovator and the buyer before any work is started on the Version 0 design (pilot prototype or Version 1 of the *ready* product). The answers will furnish the development team with the list of external constraints that will govern, in part or in whole, the selection of the final configuration of the product.

Version 0 Product

TRL 8 continues on with the design and fabrication of the Version 0 product, against the backdrop of the success factors. In the case of the *integrated product*, the champion will also provide the development team the site information that is relevant to the design of the product (installation requirements, spacing, tertiary function interfaces, environmental protection, power supplies, control signals, etc.) and its installation within the facility (hazardous operation constraints, safety measures, emergency response plans, permits and licenses, construction windows, test times and duration, etc.). The development team prepares the *pilot test plan* (which could include several tests) to validate and verify the Version 0 design against the success factors. The test plan is implemented and the product put through its paces (whether as a pilot test for the *integrated product* or as a champion group test for the *ready product*).

> All costs incurred by the champion and the prospective buyer during TRL 8 are born by the innovator alone. Testing the product should always be free of charge to them.

The tests should be conducted with the champion and the prospective first buyer (likely different than the champion) in attendance. Transparency is crucial to the credibility of the results in the buyer's eye. *This is a beauty contest.* Test results are compiled and reviewed through a *postmortem* assessment conducted jointly between the development team, the champion, and the buyer. At this juncture, there should not be any unforeseen surprises, although one can never be sure. Minor modifications and alterations are to be expected. All potential changes are discussed by the participants; the corresponding design modifications are proposed. These changes are compiled into a *product completion plan*, complete with budget and schedule estimates.

The *product completion plan* leads to one of two paths: (1) incorporate the changes directly into the Version 1 product (sales-ready); or (2) revise the design of Version 0 with the changes and repeat the pilot test. With the first path, the work proceeds to TRL 9 as described in the following section and in the next chapter. With the second path, the Version 0 test is repeated.

With Your Permission

During TRL 6, the various application filing for permits, licenses, and code registration will have been initiated (refer to Chapter 3). The totality of attendant authorizations must be granted and on hand before the construction of the pilot test facilities can commence. The innovator must keep a close watch on the outstanding applications at all times; failure to do so could result in a nasty surprise on site, which could delay things severely at a high cost and at the price of lost confidence by the champion.

GETTING TO FIRST SALE

Version 1

The work on Version 1 marks the start of TRL 9. TRL 9 is a composite of three groups of activities that are conducted in parallel: complete the Version 1 product (*production readiness*), change the focus from product to asset (*asset readiness*), and sell the product to the first customer (*first sale*). TRL 9 is concluded with a fourth activity group called *monetization*, discussed later on under *First Sale*. The shared objectives of the first three groups are:

- Complete the development process
- Achieve a commercially viable product (able to generate a profit)
- Achieve product acceptance by the first customer

Version 1 of the product must be sales-ready. It cannot entertain further changes (in which case Version 0 must be recycled). Never release Version 1 with known deficiencies: inevitably, they will catch up with you and injure market acceptance. The same goes for software. You are neither Microsoft, Apple, nor SAP. These giants have the benefits of market dominance and a virtual monopsony over powerless buyers. When you are new to a market, a bug can easily turn into a lethal infection. Remember: you only get one shot at this.

Production Readiness

Production readiness refers to the ability of an organization to manufacture the product for sale. This means that whatever is required to make, assemble, install, test, store, ship, and service the product must be done profitably and repetitively. The game moves from single production (the prototype) to volume production (multiples of the same). Product research and development are done. Engineering and design are done. What is left to do is the creation of the information, data, procedures, processes, and material handling that will be necessary to sustain economic production. The effort is multidimensional:

- *Systems engineering*—technical datum set, issued for fabrication or construction comprised of everything that makes up the product, including testing equipment: drawings, 3-D models, component datasheets, material specifications, quantities, performance specifications, reliability and maintainability specifications, costing, acceptance criteria, testing protocols, calibration requirements, tolerances, part and numbering conventions, and product software and code
- *Product documentation*—manuals (assembly, installation, testing and troubleshooting, part lists, operations and maintenance), technical brochures, engineering guidelines, user interface guides, ordering forms, failure report templates, and code and standard compliance certificates
- *Production engineering*—processes and procedures (fabrication, assembly, dimensional checks, material testing), inventory control, material and component tracking, equipment and machining, equipment calibration, work sequencing, tools and techniques, labor qualifications and testing, material flow, labor loading factors, cost and time tracking shipping and receiving, equipment preservation and storage.
- *Configuration management*—version control of all parts, equipment, machinery and associated engineering data, and processes and procedures; and forward and backward retrofit compatibility
- *Documentation management*—version control of documentation (all of it) including quality assurance records
- *Quality assurance program*—processes, procedures, certification requirements, registration requirements, inspections and records, and vendor quality assurance
- *Supply chain strategy*—vendor selection, pricing schedules, pricing histories, logistics, and transportation records
- *Product data*—data derived from the product while in operation; including such sources as operator usage, field-reported failures, time-to-failure, failure modes, etc.

When the commercialization strategy calls for revenue streams from both product and service sales, it is important to establish a *product team* that is distinct from the *service team*. If client training is expected to become a third revenue stream, then a *training team* should be created as well. The justification for doing so stems from the nature of the work involved with each team; clearly, the skill sets, problem types, client expectations, and the mechanics and mechanisms will be different between the three teams. All three teams can be made to report to the head of sales. Alternatively, the *product and services teams* can report to the former, while the *training team* could be equally served by reporting to the head of marketing. Any structure will do as long as the independence of each team is functionally entrenched. Evidently, there will be a need for the three teams to be on the same page at all times and communicate with each other in real time through direct channels.

Asset Readiness

This group of activities lays down the foundation of the business. The revenue engine is the production group that was previously described. The profit engine is the asset framework, which will drive the ROI performance of commercial operations. The work is split between the following pillars:

- *Functional structures*—the organization of the departments needed by the business to operate
- *Information systems*—the IT holdings of the business, which comprise deployed software (bought to perform a task, such as accounting or design), product software, product data (via Cloud or other), and internet presence (website, social media platforms)
- *Information system management plan*
- *Operational plan*—describes how the business will be operated and manned
- *Social media strategy*

First Sale

The third group deals with the commercial model of the asset. It defines how the asset will generate revenue, how the business will sustain itself financially, and how the product will be supported once it is in the hands of the buyer. The work in this case is prescriptive in the following areas:

- Revenue model
- Financing requirements

- Warranty and insurance strategy, for example, standard terms and conditions, reliability management, client feedback tracking (associated with product data)
- Sales plan, including sales methods, channels, staffing, compensation models, staff training, pitch development, points of sale locations, after-sale support
- Diffusion, or in other words, the release of information into the public domain, including types of articles to be written, magazine selection, white papers, conference presentations, seminars, and trade shows
- Marketing plan, which consists of strategies, website, materials and brochures, social media platforms, advertisement platforms, public relation messages, and message development
- Sale of the product to the first customer
- Rollout of the product data mechanics (see *Production Readiness*) to gather user data

It is important to remark that the various plans developed in TRL 9 have not yet been implemented into the day-to-day running of the business. The implementation should wait until the experience of the first customer has confirmed the commercial viability of the product. If customer issues arise during this critical stage, they must be addressed by the innovator (who has now taken on the role of business manager) without delay. No product rollout to the wider market should be undertaken while unresolved issues fester with the first customer. Otherwise, the innovator will end up dealing with monumental pressures to simultaneously fix the internal workings of the business and help the sales efforts to the outside world. This is akin to the proverbial war being waged on two fronts, a surefire recipe for rapid collapse.

THE SCHEMA PRODUCT CLIENT

The Many-Headed Client

The *schema product* differs, once again, from the other types in the first client category. The latter is more *Hydra* than single client on account of the underlying unit transformation process (in Greek mythology, the Hydra was a serpent with several heads). A given *schema product* invariably involves several parties (individuals, functional groups, or departments) with an interest in the outcome of the process (outputs, characteristics, metrics), if not as well with the inputs, attributes, and targets (refer to Figure 4.5). Each one of these parties has a say and, consequently, acts as a buyer. The challenge to the innovator in this instance is to align the interests of these parties with the necessities of the UTP. Take, for example, the *schema product* associated with ordering a batch of fasteners to replenish production inventory levels. The fastener specifications will be supplied by one party (presumably the engineering group or perhaps production control), but the quantity will be dictated by the consumption rate of the inventory (warehouse line manager), the minimum order quantity (vendor via the procurement specialist), and the delivery date (planner). The process will yield a purchase order, which may in turn trigger the requirement for follow-up action by the accounting, logistics, transportation, job controller, and third-party inspection groups. The interplay of these various groups will be characterized by the nature of the information exchanged, the timing of the exchange, and the input requirements of each party. The very simple action of placing a single purchase order is accompanied by an explosion in transactional complexity driven by the many clients involved.

W5H to the Rescue!

Clearly, the success of this schema product hinges on the aggregate successes of all client interactions implicated in it. Nevertheless, the more meaningful harbinger of that success lies in the rationalization of these interactions—in other words, who must really be involved in the process, in what capacity (accountable, responsible, or probate), and at what moment in time. Figuring out who's who in the essential zoo is readily achieved by applying the W5H approach described in Chapter 4:

- First, ask why an action is required in order to define the purpose of this action. In our example, the purpose is to replenish the inventory level (notice that we did not say *to procure new fasteners*).
- Immediately, the formulation of that answer opens up the possible answers to the second question of *what must be done to realize the purpose?* Buying new fasteners is, of course, one approach, but so is borrowing them from another bin in the warehouse if production planning allows. Yet another possibility would be to reuse fasteners that were previously removed from an inactive piece of equipment. A fourth option could be to utilize a new type of fastener.
- Once the *what* is settled, the matter of *how* is addressed. In the example, this could be a new purchase order to an existing vendor, a new purchase order to a new vendor, a material transfer form to borrow from an existing bin, a work order to remove fasteners from one piece of equipment and put them in the new one, or the issuance of an engineering change request to obtain the correct replacement/substitute fastening solution.
- With the *how* determined, the next two questions are *where* and *when*, which determine the mechanics of implementing the *how* and the timing for doing so.

- Finally, the question of *who* is answered for each one of the elements of the UTP in Figure 4.7. That is, who provides the attributes and the targets, who specifies the inputs and the outputs, who needs to see the characteristics and the metrics, who approves the output-input and the output-input junctions, who approves the characteristics and metrics, who imposes the constraints, and who provides the enablers to get all of this done in time.

Uncovering the Efficiencies

The application of the W5H method to the analysis of the UTP results in the clear and concise identification of the first *clients* for the activity under consideration. The next step by the innovator is to carry out a second round of rationalization for the input, output, and probate requirements of each client, again with the help of the W5H method. It is in this second coming of the W5H analysis that the *status quo* of doing business will be challenged and either justified or abandoned in favor of genuine improvements. For example, a particular client may be accustomed to receiving the information on a signed form, whereas the efficiency of the process will be improved by transacting the information electronically without any need of an ink signature. Predictably, these rationalization mechanics are bound to encounter resistance, objections, and belligerence, even from people shackled by chains of habitualness. The needs and requirements of some clients may differ or even counter those of other clients. The resulting conflicts must be resolved harmoniously among the clients for the activity to succeed.

PAMPERING THE GOLDEN CHILD

Dress Rehearsal

The importance of the success with the first customer should be glaringly obvious to the reader by now. This first customer offers the innovator a golden opportunity to conduct a full dress rehearsal of the product before unleashing it upon the market. The rehearsal is the one instance when imperfections and irritants will be tolerated (as long as they get fixed quickly) without derailing the commercial venture. The innovator will never get that leeway from any other client in the future.

Conversely, the innovator can offer the same benefits to the first client by conducting a full dress rehearsal of his own ahead of the first sale. Someone outside of the development team takes on the role of fictitious client and goes through the motion of ordering, receiving, installing, and using the product, and creates fictitious feedback data to test the asset's business infrastructure. It's amazing what can be discovered by this simple artifice, especially in the integration of the business processes, or lack thereof. Finding out the pain points now, rather than in full view of the first client, is a blessing.

The Client Is King

One cannot emphasize enough the importance of achieving success with the first client. Once the precious first sale is secured, this client becomes your golden child. You must do everything in your power to help the child succeed. You must be prepared to hold the client's hand throughout the process, step in as soon as a difficulty arises, and even set up shop in the client's facility to better monitor the product and assist the client at the drop of a hat. Whatever the issue, the blame is on you, not the client. If the client breaks the product because an operating instruction was not followed, it is your fault for not emphasizing the importance of that instruction in text and in words. If the product is used beyond its design envelope, it is your fault for failing to caution the client adequately.

> *Always remember that the prime objective is to have your first client declare the product a success—not only for its use, but also for the business framework supporting it. There can be no blame game if things don't work out. The blame is yours and yours alone—but so is success when it comes.*

6

TRANSFORMERS

Venture or vanish.

THE BUYER'S PERSPECTIVE

Reality Always Trumps Avoidance

Given the preponderance of the *buyer's perspective* throughout the text of this book, it is only logical that Part 1—The Innovation Journey—should conclude along that particular viewpoint. The term *buyer* is representative of the party making the buying decision; be it a person, a group of people, a business division, or a company. This representation continues herein. Chapters 2 and 3 went to great lengths to reveal the motivations of the buyer, both internal and external. We saw how a fear of change formed an undercurrent of reluctance on the part of the buyer to embrace anything new. The pull of the *status quo* is a strong and dark force. It acts as a bulwark—protecting the buyer against disruptive threats yonder. It conceals the buyer's common, everyday experience and dresses it in a familiar garb of anticipated predictability. Even when reality is plagued with hiccups, obstacles, and frustrations, the *status quo* offers the buyer the pretense of mastery over his own domain. "Better the devil you know . . ." as the saying goes. Whereas bad ideas have their own museum (see Chapter 1), the alumni of missed good ideas form a distinguished luminary set of their own:

- *Albert Einstein*—"There is not the slightest indication that nuclear energy will ever be obtainable. It would mean that the atom would have to be shattered at will."
- *The president of Michigan Savings Bank* urging Henry Ford not to invest in The Ford Motor Company—"The horse is here to stay but the automobile is only a novelty—a fad."

- *Ken Olsen* (president of Digital Equipment and MIT graduate)—"There is no reason for any individual to have a computer in their home."
- *Tom Watson*, IBM chairman (1943)—"I think there is a world market for maybe five computers."
- *Robert Metcalfe* (inventor of ethernet)—"I predict the Internet will soon go spectacularly supernova and in 1996 catastrophically collapse."
- *Darryl F. Zanuck* (founder of 20th Century Fox studio)—"People will soon get tired of staring at a plywood box (a.k.a. the television set) every night."
- *Clifford Stoll* (astronomer and author of Silicon Snake Oil (1995)—"Nicholas Negroponte, director of the MIT Media Lab, predicts that we'll soon use books and newspapers straight over the Internet. Uh, sure!"
- *Steve Ballmer*, former Microsoft CEO (2007)—"There's no chance that the iPhone is going to get any significant market share. No chance."
- *Padmasree Warrior*, Motorola CTO, about the original release of the iPhone—"There is nothing revolutionary or disruptive about this technology."
- *Jon Rubinstein*, Palm CEO, also about the new iPhone—"Is there a toaster that also knows how to brew coffee? [No], because it would not make anything better than an individual toaster or coffee machine."
- *Olli-Pekka Kallasvuo*, Nokia CEO, still on the iPhone—"I don't think that what we have seen [from Apple] is something that would necessitate us changing our thinking."
- *TechCrunch*, unimpressed with the iPhone—"That virtual keyboard will be about as useful for text messages as a rotary phone. I can't see the buttons for the screen."
- *Steve Jobs* (2008) in discussing Amazon Kindle—"The whole conception is flawed at the top because people don't read any more."
- *New York Times* (1936)—"A rocket will never be able to leave the earth's atmosphere."
- *Henry Morton*, president of Stevens Institute of Technology on Thomas Edison's lightbulb (1880)—"Everyone acquainted with the subject will recognize it as a conspicuous failure."
- *Variety*, an entertainment magazine, passing judgment on rock 'n roll (1955)—"It will be gone by June."
- *Book publishing executive* writing to J. K. Rowling (1996)—"Children just aren't interested in witches and wizards anymore."

Such quaint attitudes are the rule rather the exception, which is why the innovation game is so difficult to play *for the buyer*. The buyer's proclivity will lean toward the preservation of the *status quo* over the intangible promise of better-by-newer. The belief in one's control over one's environment is the cornerstone of self-preservation. People will actively seek out ways of eliminating any risk, any threat, any act of aggression to their perceived sense of security. This sense of security is an illusion, but that matters not—it can still overwhelm a person's rationale. The matter always seems to devolve down to the question of what's in it for me? A buyer will ask: why waste time tinkering with the new, when the old is good enough? Why fix what isn't broken? Why put a stop to inertia when it seems to work regardless?

The question is misleading because it starts from the wrong premise. The *old* is assumed to exist and persist because of its merits. It is accepted as entrenched on the strength of its *value* to its adherents. It is presumed to be insulated from external threats because of its track record. In other words, it is taken for granted, hence the delusion of control. In reality, the *old* never exists impervious to the outside world. How could it? Everything around it exists in a state of perpetual flux through the relentless advance of technology—what the economist Schumpeter called creative destruction. On the flip side, this forward motion actually accelerates technology's own propensity for deterioration. New advances bring forth inevitable changes in processes, procedures, techniques, and management schemas. Business operations and regulatory regimes are forced to follow suit. Supply chains have no choice but to get on board and abandon offerings that are becoming rapidly irrelevant or incompatible with the state of the art. Last, but not least, the competition may have already embraced it. The march of innovation is ruthless and unforgiving. Its pace sets the rhythm of reality with the utter and complete indifference to the objections of its victims. Innovations are like the Borg from Star Trek TNG: *resistance is futile*. The iconoclast may cling stubbornly to his typewriter but he will never stop the digitization of the alphabet.

Innovation Is Self-Preservation

There is a silver lining to all this doom and gloom. The inevitability of change coalesces into a fantastic opportunity for the buyer to *enhance his or her own self-preservation and job security*. The crux of the argument is simple:

> The futility of resisting innovations presents a binary choice to the buyer—resist and go extinct or control your faith by anticipating them.

A caveat is needed. This choice for the buyer does not imply a wholesale embrace of anything new, any time it comes out, at whatever the price. It implies qualifying one's reality first, then gauging the merit of a potential innovation in terms of its economics. If your competition has already adopted an innovation, you're already behind the eight ball with the commercial edge to them. You have no choice but to play catch up. Hoping that this turns out to be a fad is a dangerous stance; wishful thinking and faith are no way to run a business. Absent an innovation, it behooves the buyer to ask the question: what is the actual cost of one's *status quo*? How does the economic performance of this *status quo* compare with that of the competition? Is your technology so old as to be orphaned or too onerous to maintain profitably? Where are the shortcomings, the deficiencies, and the frustrations caused by this *status quo*? Regardless of your level of comfort with it, you, the buyer, owe it to yourself to assess these cost drivers with facts, not whims. Then, look outward, beyond the firm's horizon, to see what solutions exist to assuage or eliminate the cost drivers. *You cannot afford to not consider them.* Do not let the transition costs (changeover, implementation, process disruptions) be the final arbiters of the buying decision. Cash flow alone should not be the sheriff, as the opportunity cost may be greater. Long-term shareholder returns on investments are the rightful arbiters of the decision.

Even if your *status quo* is competitive now, the real question is whether it will continue to be so *in the future*. Your firm may be severely allergic to any spending that is not absolutely essential, but it will be of little solace to wake up one day lagging behind the times and losing money or market share or both to the competition. What are the technological trends that are carving out new troughs unto the market landscape? What are the innovations that are clearly offering benefits over your current assets? How will these assets fare in a future collision with an enhanced landscape? What will be the costs then to make the inevitable changeover? Can you afford to wait without taking a hit to your market share or your profitability? And will you be able to retain your people inside an archaic infrastructure that has no hope of a future?

These mundane issues illustrate what happens when the question, "What's in it for me?" is turned into "How threatened am I now, and later?" It is utter folly to assume that your job is permanently secure because you are good at it. The productivity and expertise of an individual will make little difference to a business that sees greater valunomy in some new innovation (think automation and robots, for example). The prudent employee (or contractor, for that matter) will be much better served by facing his current reality as it truly is. Often, this will mean accepting the ugliness of what lies ahead in terms of threats to oneself. It may require a degree of honesty and courage that cannot be stripped of uncertainty, lack of control, or frightening consequences. One of the hardest things to do is to stand up to these fears, rather than recoil with horror at their implications and hide behind a veil of denial.

Innovation Is Control

Facing reality head-on grants the buyer the power of control. Starting with the premise that all things must pass, since all things must change, the buyer can take immediate control of his destiny by being proactive in gauging his *now* against possible *then*. First, quantify the *status quo* within which the buyer operates. Second, quantify the costs of this *status quo* and, more critically, the opportunity costs of changing nothing. Third, survey the outside landscape to discover what is done differently, using what innovative means, with what skill sets, and at what costs. Together, these three actions empower the buyer to conduct a fact-based analysis of the pros and cons of his circumstances. This knowledge puts the buyer in the driver's seat and positions him to broach the subject intelligently with the firm's management.

> *The status quo is often justified but rarely justifiable.*

The truly beautiful thing for the buyer is that these efforts can be pursued as an integral part of one's job. There is no need to spend excessive hours on the topic at the detriment of the daily routine. Indeed, the bulk of these observations will come naturally to the competent worker. For management, this proactive attitude yields priceless operational insights *at no additional costs to the business* since the true operational effectiveness of a firm is best surmised from the knowledge of those closest to the issues. It is a rare instance of a win-win-win situation (the third win belonging to the shareholders). For the buyer, the benefits are greater control, greater visibility, greater valunomy, and enhanced employment prospects.

Clearly, the proactive buyer cannot expect across-the-board acceptance of all innovation opportunities at first glance; but the mere act of pursuing this agenda will foster goodwill between the buyer and management. Conversely, if management refuses to acknowledge the issues and lends a deaf ear to innovative prospects, the message conveyed to the buyer will be one of employment caution. The buyer in this case may heed the warning signs and look for a back-up plan elsewhere. This is another form of control available to the buyer. He may not want to leave the business, but the decision to stay will at least be made from an informed basis rather than emotional fear.

YOU ARE A CHAMPION, MY FRIEND

The Beginning of a Beautiful Friendship

The next logical step for the buyer who is interested in self-preservation is to become a champion of an innovator's vision. The role offers a double whammy of professional growth. When the innovation springs from within the firm, the champion operates with a higher level of visibility to management (who must, of course, endorse the initiative). The champion gets to articulate a vision, sell it to management, and perhaps even get a budget. He sets the aims, the objectives, and the all-important functional requirements of the innovation contemplated. This level of control is at least one order of magnitude greater than the self-preservation case.

If the opportunity is beyond the firm's purview, the involvement of the champion is lighter. But the benefits of controlling the message remain with the champion. There is, obviously, always a risk of condemnation from failure in keeping with our principle of *perform or justify* (explored in Chapter 7). The would-be champion would be well advised to keep his management informed and interested before committing to the role. The mandate, once approved by management, cannot be taken lightly as it will literally make or break the outcome of the innovation journey. In both cases, the upside of the mandate is greater than the downside. It is for this reason that the risk to one's career is worth taking. The flip side has zero downside to the more reluctant convert unless, that is, someone else in the organization is willing to walk the plank. Any glory will accrue to that person, leaving the hesitant unscathed but unseen.

How does one discover where the champion opportunity lies outside of the firm? One should always start with a completed *status quo analysis*. Then, identify a pertinent vendor with a commercial history with the firm and let them know that you are open to championing innovations. The would-be champion can go so far as to share the analysis of his *status quo* with the vendor and outline what success would look like. In a different scenario, the would-be champion determines that no vendor can tap the opportunity presented in the *status quo* analysis. In this case, the champion can query the competition or seek the counsel of government agencies operating in the innovation sphere (free of charge!). In a third instance, it is the vendor who will approach his client with the hope of enlisting him as a champion. A derivative of this third scenario is the participation of the would-be champion in trade associations that provide a platform to express the innovation's need.

But First, Own the Problem

A cautionary warning is in order at this juncture. When the champion decides to take the lead in finding a solution to a problem, it is essential that the problem definition be owned by the champion. For example, it is not enough to declare the premise from a need to cut costs or improve reliability; it is not adequate to declare the need to modernize an old system nor is it sufficient to chase after the latest and greatest because the competition is already doing it. To go to the marketplace with such a vaguely defined objective is a surefire recipe for inviting the riffraff in the house and wasting precious time, effort, and money. The champion must, first of all, understand the underlying structure of his *status quo* (discussed earlier). He must possess a comprehensive understanding of the answers to the 8Q set (refer to Chapter 2). And he must quantify the problem from the outset, whether the anticipated solution is unclear or certain. In short, the champion must own the problem and formalize it in a *problem statement* (see the upcoming section, Problem Statement).

Ownership stems from understanding what works well, not so well, and not at all; and have a clue as to the reasons beneath it all. Such an understanding is derived from a systemic analysis of the situation through problem analysis. The analysis of a problem can be broken down into three types: Type A—Modernization; Type B—Performance; and Type C—Ownership. The choice is a function of the competitive pressures pressing against the champion. When we superimpose the pressures on Figure 3.1, we obtain Figure 6.1, which gives us a clue as to the motivations of the champion.

The pressures associated with Type A motivate the champion to finally get on with the outside world and either play catch-up with the rest of the competition or make a quantum leap and circle back to the next wave of innovation. Going from horse-drawn buggies to automobiles is a classic example. The key insight for Type A problems is the fact that the solution, while new and novel to the champion, is wholly ironed out and understood on the outside.

Type B problems deal with the revenue-generation aspect of the circumstances under review. The problem may be at the plant, installation, system, or even component level. The problem's consequence is either a reduction or a loss of generated revenues that are relative to the actual potential of the existing

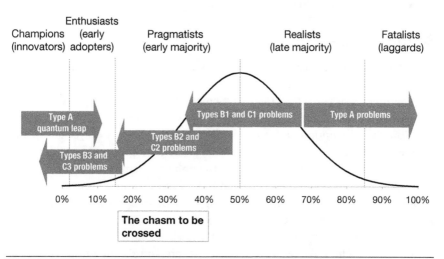

Figure 6.1 The range of solution sources available to the champion: the choice of a solution is a function of the problem's type (A, B, or C) and the motivations driving the champion to seek a change to the existing status quo

solution. A machine may have become undersized or oversized or it may be incompatible with other elements of the installation. The process may not be able to meet higher throughput requirements. The overall reliability may be trending downward and provoking more frequent shutdowns and production losses. The instrumentation and controls may be out-of-date and unable to communicate with the newest digital signature architecture. Type B problems can be solved by bringing in new kinds of commercially available solutions already embraced by the competition (B1 in Figure 6.1), or solutions that are exploited in different industries foreign to the champion (B2 in Figure 6.1), or new solution approaches that offer the promise of quantum gains but require innovation development (B3 in Figure 6.1). In all three cases, the solution chosen by the champion will represent an innovation within the organization (in every sense of the term).

The final Type C problems are characterized by their ownership costs (borne by the champion's organization) and reflected in a decrease or loss of profits (the other side of the revenue ledger). Type C problems are found at the operational level where labor, material, and production cycles are negatively impacted. A machine may require a larger number of operators than required by newer solutions (think automation replacing people or two pilots and a navigator versus two pilots and an advanced cockpit). It may be fuel inefficient and emission fraught. A process could be costly in terms of consumables and utility streams (water, chemicals, electricity), and prone to frequent maintenance requirements. The solutions available to the champion piggyback on the three B categories as C1, C2, and C3 in Figure 6.1.

Solution Risks

Each type of problem carries its own sets of risks. Type A solutions may be no-brainers to the competition who have already implemented them, but to the champion's organization their implementation may be harbingers of profound structural and operational needs for reform. The biggest risk of Type A solutions is a disruption and possible dismantling of a trusted-yet-antiquated business process. The overarching concern of the champion will be to devise an implementation strategy that addresses the upheaval ramifications of the solution upon the *people and processes* that bind them together. Process modeling (engineered as product schemas), training, information technology (IT) infrastructure, and rollout dry runs will be required.

Types B and C carry essentially the same risks along a progressively greater severity scale, where B1 risks are the least severe and B3 the most severe. For B1, B2, C1, and C2 solutions, the champion will benefit from the experiences and learnings of past implementations by others. It behooves the champion to research these learnings painstakingly as they will vastly lower the possible risks in his or her own implementation program. B3 and C3 solutions do not carry this benefit and, as a result, present the highest risk profile to the champion. Nevertheless, this risk intensity is compensated by the potential to devise a thoroughly potent and novel solution that is capable of leapfrogging both the competition and the marketplace.

Problem Statement

The final controlling act of the champion is to formally state the problem to be solved. The champion is aided in this endeavor by the mechanics and mechanisms developed in Chapter 4. The *problem statement* must be written concisely. The measure of its effectiveness is found in the clarity of the case made, rather than in the number of pages printed. First and foremost, it must be tailored to the needs of the organization. Except in rare circumstances (namely Type A cases where a single solution is mandated), the *problem statement* does not specify what the solution is but rather what the *outcomes* of the eventual solution must be. In other words, the *problem statement* declares what the solution must deliver and the criteria against which the success of this delivery will be measured. In this respect, the *problem statement* abides by the philosophy underscoring the *landscape basis*, the purpose, and the *function prioritization* that was developed in Steps 1 through 5 in Chapter 4. An example of a *problem statement*, pertinent to a B3 and C3 problem type, can be downloaded from the publisher's website at www.jrosspub.com/wav.

It is imperative that the champion refrain from limiting the options at this time by specifying particular technologies or approaches (pursuant to the section *The Pitfalls of Preconceived Notions* in Chapter 4). As a matter of fact, the exercise presents the champion with an opportunity to question the underlying reasons as to why the existing status quo is the way it is. For example, an industrial process may require gas compression that has traditionally been provided by a screw compressor. The champion should, at the very least, question why compression is required in the first place; can it be replaced, reduced, improved, or eliminated; and what drives the equipment selection. These questions are best asked and answered by abstracting the investigation beyond machines into the conceptual realm of functions (see, in this case, the W5H section of Chapter 4). Abstracting the discussion in this way, in the case of problem Types B3 and C3 in particular, is the surest path to uncovering genuinely novel solutions that lie beyond the champion's current horizon.

The Execution Plan

The follow up to the *problem statement* is the creation of an *execution plan* for the selection of an eventual solution and its implementation within the organization. For problem Types A, B1, and C1, the selection process is adequately served by technology readiness levels (TRL) 8 and 9. For Types B2 and C2, TRL 7, a *selection plan* based on a lean *technology development plan* is advised. By lean, we mean culling the original contents of the technology development plan (say, through the deletion of Section 3, for example) and focus principally on the scope of work. An example of a *selection plan* can be downloaded from the publisher's website at www.jrosspub.com/wav. For Types B3 and C3, the assessment requires a proper technology development plan and is initiated with a comparative analysis pursuant to Article 1.1 of the *selection plan*.

Next comes the implementation phase. The nature of the work, the timelines, and the costs are a function of the operational readiness of the existing organization. In essence, the perspective is akin to bringing online an *integrated product* into the organization. If the implementation will disrupt the old ways of doing things, the champion is genuinely facing a sales job in the same vein as what the innovator faced with the challenges of the first sale in Chapter 5. There is essentially no difference between the implementation program and the innovator being involved with ramping up his organization to get to the first sale. Except for the activities associated with the sales team, all other activities and tasks discussed in Chapter 5 under the heading of *Getting to First Sale* will be necessary, especially the need for a dry run or dress rehearsal.

FINAL CONSIDERATIONS

A Question of Selfishness

The altruistic appeal to the role of champion is undeniable, especially when a vendor leads the charge. The champion provides guidance and mentoring and watches his contribution move the project along on a path of success. The role is a very effective way for seasoned professionals to give back without undue burdens upon their daily travails. It can be a little bit like the grandparent who enjoys playing with the grandkids—but leave the diapering to the parents. Altruism notwithstanding, the greatest reward to the champion remains a selfish one: it helps one's career to help another's career. One can, of course, get into the game purely on laudable grounds to help, to guide, and to nurture. But the emotional stance may prove lacking in stamina when the project goes on for months on end, or shows signs of going off the rails. The selfish gene is still better adapted to staying the course—no matter what. It comes equipped with a built-in sense of purpose and urgency to keep the innovator on track when the execution starts to fray. Goodwill and patience will rapidly evaporate if the innovator insists on his or her own way. At which point, the champion will want to terminate the relationship.

Whether for self-preservation or for altruism, the pursuit of innovation by a buyer boils down to the imperative for continued employment. The imperative, incidentally, increases with age; older workers are historically more threatened by innovations than younger ones. Let us once again emphasize that experience, expertise, and know-how may not win a battle with innovations. The best defense will always be offense—to head off constructively the unfettered advances of innovations' promises. It may well be that the buyer may be able to prove an innovation wrong in some cases, which is equally valuable knowledge to management. The call to arms is to remain always vigilant about the balance between one's *status quo* and the world's thirst for the new.

The Manager's Take

The buyer, in our context, is independent of his position in the corporate structure. This was done on purpose to extend the franchise to whomever it may apply. We now make a distinction between the buyer and the manager (according to the usual hierarchical meaning). The manager has a role to play in the consideration of innovations beyond acceptance and implementation. The role is closely related to the product evolution strategy that will be discussed in Chapter 7. The aim is to quantify the strengths, weaknesses, opportunities, and threats of the manager's environment. The objective is to devise an *evolution strategy environment*. Naturally, a significant portion of the environment will involve information systems, IT infrastructure, and software assets. The digital realm is, by its very nature, subject to a never-ending innovation cycle and must therefore be managed proactively to control the ever-changing state of its configuration. The innovation cycle, however, extends beyond the digital divide. Business processes, transaction flows, execution procedures, supply chain interactions, and production systems also fall under the yoke of innovations—*even when technology is not involved*. Take, for example, the issue of customer relations, which at an elemental level is about human interactions (with software playing a secondary role). Over time, the art of customer relations has progressed dramatically in keeping up with evolving attitudes and mores. In short, that evolution is innovation manifested. The state of the manager's environment provides the inputs to the *evolution strategy environment*, which in turn, is designed as a framework to decide upon the adoption of innovations. The effort is an exercise in synthesis to extract order from the complexity of the environment's coupled interactions. The guiding principle is to *do no harm*: do not implement an innovation that can disrupt the smooth and efficient running of interwoven processes. That is the job of the manager—to figure out what's needed, how to bring it in, and how to integrate it without busting things up.

The tools and techniques pertinent to the *evolution strategy environment* are those associated with the *schema product*. The schema product perfectly describes the innovation impetus of the manager's role. Managers are, by nature, implicated in the transactional features of a firm. Information is transacted across a network of paths joined together by nodes where managers sit. Managers are ultimately positioned to peer across the transaction's landscape and see where bottlenecks fester. Bottlenecks are markers of inefficiencies and authors of delays. Bottlenecks metastasize into malignant procedural tumors that tend to spread and infect the rest of the organization like cancerous cells. Treatment is possible through the pursuit of schema product innovations—led by at least one manager who is ready to take up the champion mantle.

> *Firms grow and thrive in accordance with the strength of their inside champions. Too few of them spell corporate failure. Too much plodding hierarchy kills their effectiveness. Too much risk aversion destroys their motivation. But institutionalized freedom of curiosity will foster their blossoming until their collective volition leads to a fattening of the bottom line.*

Part 2

The Business Journey

From first sale to wealth: in this second part of the book, the emphasis changes from succeeding at the innovation process to starting the innovation-driven business and getting it to survive and thrive as a steady commercial concern.

7

MANAGING THE JOURNEY

Cajole, convince, coerce, repeat: the art of management.

MANAGEMENT VERSUS DEVELOPMENT

The Odd Couple

The innovation business is unlike any other with its never-ending parade of surprises, wrong turns, dead ends, black swans, and funding droughts. Predictability is counteractive to the environment. Success hinges in part on alertness and suppleness of mind to handle the almost daily quirks of the development journey. The innovator has no choice but to embrace a state of perpetual flux. The expression *managed chaos* is appropriate.

Nevertheless, chaos management is no way to manage a business, innovation, or anything else. Allaying the contrast between development fickleness and steadfastness of operations represents the greatest challenge to the innovator who is running the whole show. On the one hand, we have development which dwells at the boundary between known and unknown and requires boldness and a free-wheeling imagination. It thrives on the unexpected and the rush of discovery. On the other hand, running the business calls for an approach that is anchored to predictable reality. The very act of managing should banish randomness in all its forms. Surprises of any kind are the bane of any manager. The tools of the trade shun imagination and embrace stoic control to achieve repeatability of predictability. If development is an artist, management is the impresario. They need each other to succeed, but either can make both fail.

A note to the reader: in this chapter, references to the innovator will always imply that this person is the ultimate decision maker, unless the context states otherwise.

A Collection of Hats

This symbiotic reality is the reason why management must be structured throughout the development journey and across commercial operations. Formalism acts as a bulwark against the random effects of development. Balance, however, is critical to success. Too much structure threatens to choke development while too little unleashes the rampaging hordes of *what-if* innovation warriors. Furthermore, the appearance of management changes over time. In the early stages, the innovator wears the idea hat: he is the prime advocate, the supreme cheerleader, the converted believer. His focus is twofold: define what needs to be developed (technology readiness level (TRL) 1, TRL 2) and find the means to pay for it. At TRL 3, he puts on the team-leader hat. His job is to assemble the team, assign the work, and get things started. He remains mindful of the funding pressures and, if need be, puts on his idea hat to drum up more investors and funding sources. By the time TRL 6 rolls in, the hat changes once again to that of project manager—with a dual mandate: lead the development and lead the externalities (everything else that is not development-specific). If the product is sufficiently simple, the innovator can wear the two hats—team leader and project manager—simultaneously. If not, two separate heads are necessary. This split is usually necessary for an *integrated product*. The hat separation is inevitable at TRL 7 for the integrated product. Indeed, if it is a full-blown industrial installation, the methodology advocated in *Investment-Centric Project Management* is advised. At TRL 8, yet another hat change takes place: the innovator becomes business manager. His focus shifts from technology development to commercialization. The mandate is clear: put in place the pieces of the business foundation that will enable the firm to succeed in selling the product. The final hat swap takes place at TRL 9. Here, the innovation assumes the executive mantle (CEO, COO, VP, etc.). The priority is the same regardless of the title: get to breakeven as fast as possible and start generating return on investment (ROI) for shareholders. This particular role will be explored further in Chapter 10.

Of course, this hat sequence is but one among many. For example, if the innovator is an employee of an existing, well-established firm, he may remain limited to the roles of team leader and project manager over time. The other functions will naturally be assumed by other individuals within the organization. If the innovator is the CEO of a small enterprise, he may elect to retain the funding mandate but delegate the other roles to other people within the organization. If the company is a start-up, one person often ends up assuming all roles simultaneously. There are no hard-and-fast rules. Circumstances will dictate what must be done by whom and at what time.

The important thing to remember is that the daily management activities of everyone involved will vary over time. Money, ultimately, will govern the role assignments.

The Funding Threshold

The act of reconciliation between development and management is made more difficult when funding forces the innovator to take on all roles as is often the case for small start-up companies. Then, necessity trumps all other consider-ations even when the innovator becomes mired in areas that are clearly beyond his expertise. This is, sadly, a reality that is all too common at the smallest of company scales. No easy remedy is at hand to ease the innovator's burden. In the absence of adequate funding, the innovator's journey will be a slow, arduous, subsistence affair. Friends and family may be willing to lend a financial hand, but that money could only prolong the ordeal rather than propitiate the endeavor.

To put it bluntly: there is no point in undertaking a development initia-tive if the funding does not exceed whatever threshold has been estimated to achieve commercial success.

To proceed otherwise by canvassing family members, friends, and acquain-tances will only increase the stress of the innovator tenfold without *any* increase in the likelihood of success of the innovation—which begs the question of how to determine this funding threshold? The process sends the question back to Chapter 4 and is comprised of four pieces:

1. Execute TRL 1 diligently with an emphasis on Step 1
2. Carry out Steps 2 through 5 with the help of people who understand the product's functions
3. Compile the functional requirements (Step 6) with the help of peo-ple knowledgeable in the design/engineering/programming of these functions
4. Scope out the work and the allocations required to do this work

Obviously, these four steps will need to be funded as well. In all but the rarest cases, the innovator will not possess the know-how to carry out these steps sat-isfactorily and outside help will be necessary. The good news here is the invalu-able help that is offered by all manners of governments. The value of this initial cash outlay when scoping out the project cannot be overstated. The idea that the innovator would skip the expense at this early stage in order not to *waste precious development money* is not only fallacious but nefarious. *This initial expense is the most important spending in the life of a product.* Only with it can the innovator obtain the information necessary to put a dollar figure and duration to the expected work from which a budget is compiled.

> *This early spending includes intellectual property (IP) surveys and prior art searches, but not application filings.*

The scope of work compiled by the end of TRL 1 and 2 is quantified *without regard to the funding requirements.* In other words, figure out first what work needs to be done over what time frame; then—and only then—figure out how much money will be needed. Funding applications, grants, and angel investments should be pursued. Once the funding is completed, the scope of work is adjusted to fit the money on hand. If there is not enough money, the scope must be scaled back, or a new round of funding is needed.

> *The reverse order does not work. That is, if you start with funding rounds without previous knowledge of the anticipated scope of work, it can only result in an exercise in spending the money and creating the illusion of progress.*

The Exclusion Principle

One critical element of the funding threshold assessment is the identification of the skills required by the anticipated work. It is a straightforward matter to figure out what expertise will be required for a given technical feature of the work. The more delicate task is the self-assessment of the innovator's strengths and limitations. In all cases, the following compound exclusion principle applies:

> *Work to your strengths; train to your weaknesses; hire to your shortcomings; and outsource to your ignorance.*

This principle is derived from the obvious fact that one cannot be an expert at everything. The greatest labor valunomy ensues from working in one's area of expertise. The next level of valunomy is the upgrading of skills *as long as the process is expedient.* If the training requires months of dedicated effort, it is better to revert to the third priority—hire someone who can hit the ground running. Finally, everyone is plagued with vast tracts of ignorance across innumerable fields. If a skill set will be required permanently, hire the expertise; otherwise, retain a consultant who will get the answers quickly (see *Speed to Market Demands Real Expertise* in Chapter 3).

The exclusion principle suffices to quantify the head count and effort levels that are necessary to get the work done. The cost of that labor is readily derived. Be sure to heed this advice: you cannot do everything, nor should you; therefore, work to your strengths. If you are a technology wizard, the project will be best served with you in the development lead while the management of the overall project is left to someone else. If you are the owner, you are likely better at managing work and money than dwelling in the physics weeds. If you are a product-line manager, your deal is front-line management, not computational fluid dynamics. Whatever the case is, it is imperative that you, as the innovator, limit yourself to one specific lead role at the exclusion of all others. Do not try to be technology lead, COO, marketing head, and investor relation expert all at once: you will not succeed. There are not enough hours in a week to cover all of these bases *competently*.

The Curse of Riches

The reverse scenario of a funding famine is a cash bonanza, whereby the innovation project has successfully attracted more investor money than it can spend on the development works. It is the ideal position to start with. At the same time, it can rapidly devolve into a more precarious development than its disadvantaged brethren when it is allowed to lull the organization into a sense of budgetary comfort. Riches tend to dilapidate urgency for comfort has an insidious way of relaxing one's hunger for speed. It also gives greater reign to unbridled imagination to frolic far and wide across the *what-if* landscape. From there, it is but one step to getting off the primary function path that is so critical to the development process. Riches can also imbue the organization with an entitlement mindset that is stubbornly opposed to compromise. Easy money emboldens the need for ease. Why work around a shortcoming when you can buy a fix outright? Why make do with what one has rather than splurge on what one wants? Why not go all-in rather than what's essential? Why not hire more bodies rather than push for greater efficiencies? Why not paint over problems with expensive solutions rather than go through the pain of solving arduous problems? Why be frugal in the midst of affluence?

It only takes a couple of months following the successful funding round for an organization to get comfortable. It begins to go about its business under a false sense of financial stability. In these two months, people settle into their routines without giving a passing thought to the cash burn rate. The absence of immediate, tangible cash pressures rapidly crushes the imperative for speed. The preservation of capital (always precious, regardless of the pile height) loses its primacy on managers' minds. The environment undergoes a subtle, nearly imperceptible transformation from developmental (transience, urgency, focus) to operational (permanence, routine, periphery). Once the transformation takes hold (usually unbeknown to everyone), the innovation process reaches its highest risk of failure. Why? Simply because the entire operation is no longer motivated by the urgency of getting to Version 1.

The fact of the matter is that a cash-rich environment requires more, not less, discipline than a cash-starved one. Having money removes the immediate problem of having to worry about money—which is infinitely better than not having enough money as a starting premise; but that lack of worry cannot be allowed to spread throughout the organization, to taint the need for speed, and to relax the fiduciary duty of the innovator to protect investors' money. The innovator has no claim on this money unless it was his to start with. Nothing should ever change in control, cost discipline, execution oversight, processes and procedures, and the urgency to get to Version 1. At best, this money enables the innovator to *accelerate* the development process, but not to expand it just because there's money to do so. The development process must always be based on the scope of work that was developed at the end of TRL 2.

Investor Interactions

There are two, and only two, types of funding sources within a management context: the innovator's own cash and outside cash. That is it. The outside cash can come from a variety of sources (friends, family, private investors, venture capitalists, government programs, initial public offering (IPO)); nevertheless, all outside cash must be considered by the innovator as investment capital. In the case of the innovator's own money, he is free to spend it whichever way he wants. The better way will always be under the protection of an investment mindset, of course. But if it is your money, it's yours and you can spend it any way you want. If it is not your money, you don't get to call the shots.

The case of the public company funded through an IPO is beyond the scope of this text and will not be discussed. This discussion is limited to funding sources from individual investors and government programs. In certain cases, the innovator is bound by a fiduciary duty in the management of the funds that are supplied by external sources. This is no light matter and the innovator would do well to seek legal counsel to understand the implications. Fundamentally, the fiduciary duty is the highest standard of care that can be expected of a person. Breaching a fiduciary duty can land a person in prison.

With or without a fiduciary duty, the innovator will be expected to manage the work in such a way that it protects the invested capital. Never forget that the external money is *never, ever* allocated to enable the innovator to believe in the power of his dream. External money *always* comes with an expectation of *significant* ROI. Even family and friends will expect to make money from their generosity. Private investors will usually expect to earn $10 for each dollar invested within three to five years of the first sale. If the innovator cannot demonstrate a realistic path to this revenue threshold, he will stir no investor interest. Venture capitalists are risk adverse and of a mind to get into the game no earlier than TRL 8 or 9 as a general rule. They will want to get in and get out within five years and expect a 10 to 1 return on the valuation of the business. Governments will usually expect job creation, opportunities for minorities, and tax revenues down the road. The common thread uniting these examples of shareholders is the expectation of maximized investment returns.

> *The supreme duty of the innovator is to manage the innovation journey in order to maximize ROI for all shareholders once commercialization starts.*

The consequence of this duty has profound ramifications on the relationship between the innovator and his investors. He may run the show on a daily basis, but he is ultimately subservient to the will of the investors. The innovator does not have the freedom to take the development process wherever he or she wishes. The innovator is beholden to the expectations of the shareholders by ultimately acting as their agent, not as first among equals. As agent, the innovator's duty is to keep them informed at all times on the actual, fact-based state of the journey. The truth is all the more essential when things are dire. Shareholders can smell a snake-oil sales pitch from the other side of the conference room door. The innovator who tries to pull a fast one over shareholders by painting a positive picture for a dismal state of affairs will be sniffed out in a minute and lose all credibility. If he or she flat out lies to hide an ugly reality, the ugliness could soon morph into a lawsuit, at which point the entire innovation journey will be sacrificed in the pursuit of attorney justice.

DECISION MANAGEMENT

The Prime Directives

By now, the reader may be feeling unsettled, unpleasant even, in the face of so many directives imposed on the innovator. They can certainly put a damper on things and take the joy out of the journey. But fear no longer—solace is at hand. The innovator does not have to operate under the guise of a drone that is remote-controlled by shareholders. Furthermore, the latter are neither in a position to arbitrarily dictate their whims upon the innovator. They are too far removed from the reality in the shop to understand the intricacies of the development process. They are at best casual observers on the outside looking in. That knowledge sits with the innovator, who is best positioned to know what's going on and why. By virtue of this knowledge, the innovator is able to restore the balance of power with the shareholders, especially in the realm of decision making.

The innovator must be vested with this power by default—and checked by exception. If any one of the shareholders does not trust the innovator with this power, one or the other will have to go. Shareholders are motivated to distrust any discretionary power over the fate of their investment; it is human nature. But, mistrust is unhealthy—trust is possible but requires that a formal framework within the power of decision making can be exercised transparently. The framework can be readily established upon seven prime directives that are meant to circumscribe all project decisions. This Group of Seven comprises:[1]

- *Prime purpose*—To realize *the commercially successful business* anchored to the innovation; all decisions must be made by doing what's right for the purpose
- *Prime priority*—The buyer's *purpose* governs
- *Prime execution*—Feel the need for speed in development, in Version 1, and in breakeven
- *Prime mindset*—The budget is the investment vehicle to realize the successful business
- *Prime control*—The TRL sequence structured upon the *function* taxonomy
- *Prime tool*—The twelve steps of the development mechanics (Chapter 4)
- *Prime governance*—Direct accountability (see ensuing text)

This framework will succeed when everyone involved in the journey agrees to abide by the seven principles, including shareholders. Then, it will provide a transparent environment to discuss whatever issue might come up and define who gets to say what in each case.

Ego versus Project

Decision making forms the essence of management. Decisions by consensus are the easiest to implement—although not necessarily the best for the situation. Consensus is a fickle thing and decision making is not just an exercise in getting there. Decision making is the embodiment of the prime purpose. All decisions must be ultimately to do right by the innovation business. In the majority of cases, the decision will pit two or more options against each other. In other words, one option will win out over the rest, leaving the noble aim of consensus emaciated.

The decision maker is paid to make these choices. The ego invariably influences the individual's internal dialogue that is always going on while options are stewing. Blind spots compound the effect of that ego. All too often, sadly, the need to see blinds the decision maker's sight. Taken together, these self-serving actors make it difficult to gain clarity through the fog of competing interests. Indeed, the greatest challenge to the decision maker is to make his or her ego subservient to the greater good of the business; a choice between *being right* and *doing right by the project*. Most people would agree that, when framed in this manner, the latter is unequivocally the better outcome. Alas, it is far easier said than done. In the heat of an argument and in the intensity of a debate, the ego springs forth in an unconscious attempt to get its way. It is supremely difficult for someone in the thick of things to observe the scenario as it unfolds within one's mind and then willfully pull one's ego back. The consequence might very well be to end up on the losing side of the argument. Yet, that is exactly what the decision maker must do in such circumstances. The mark of a great manager is the ability to corral one's ego and marshal it unto the path that will benefit the project's outcome. Conversely, the sign of an incompetent or adverse manager is to always fight to be right regardless of the impact to the prime purpose. Fortunately, the Group of Seven equips the decision maker with the means to avoid this zero-sum game. The prime purpose eliminates the confrontational clash of egos altogether. It assigns zero value to the *source* of an option. It cares not one bit who came up with the right option; it cares only for the right outcome. There are no winners or losers in the pursuit of doing right by the project. There is only a winner: the project.

Output Acceptance

The acceptance mechanics for the outcome of a task is another aspect of decision making. The value of the mechanics increases with the number of people involved and becomes significant when a piece of work is carried out by an external party. If an outside expert does the work, who within the development team is competent enough to approve the outcome? When the scope of work involves several disciplines—say chemical, civil, electrical, mechanical, and environmental engineering—it is not entirely evident who should approve the aggregate outcome.

The concept of outcome acceptance is a management issue. The nature of the acceptance mechanics is directly linked to the staffing level required to execute it.[2] There are essentially two basic approaches: to *review and approve* or to *trust but check*. The *review and approve* philosophy dictates that every outcome of every task must be reviewed by two or more members of the development team. The expertise and/or motives of the people chosen to do the work is doubted implicitly. The aim of the mechanics is an in-depth examination of the contents of the output/outcome in order to uncover errors and mistakes. The *trust but check* mechanic, on the other hand, suggests that the people who have been chosen to perform the work are competent and trustworthy. The acceptance process assumes that the contents are inherently correct without the need for a deep-dive analysis with every revision of the work.[3] The seminal difference between the two approaches lies with head count, which affects funding. The level of effort entailed by the *review and approve* mechanic can be five to ten times higher than for the *trust but check* mechanic. The former is also slower, more cumbersome, and prone to a greater number of iterations—*without greater quality to the work's outcome.* The bottom line: *trust but check* aligns with the prime objective of protecting the investment capital.

Perform or Justify

Decisions can be viewed in terms of management performance. Great performance and great decisions go hand in hand. The opposite is also true: poor decisions reflect poor performance. At its heart, performance is but expectation materialized, which is tied to a measurable outcome. But how can one reconcile this notion of expectation with a decision that may not be drawn from consensus? After all, the decision maker is expected to carry out his duty without creating animosity within the group. The group will be expected to carry out the decision, which brings us back to the issue of egos. The project side of a decision is clear cut: do right by the project. The human side of a decision is far more nuanced and therefore of greater import to the management of the project.

Once again, we are dealing with an issue that can be boiled down to a choice between two outcomes: to *perform* or to *justify*. Managing by performance requires knowing beforehand the decision framework, the individual expectations, the lines of authority, the objectives, and the metrics by which any measured outcome will be gauged. The onus is on the manager to put these definitions in place *and enforce them.* It entails much more work than *management by justification,* but with a clear and unassailable benefit in the end—expectations will be judged by homogenous norms, impervious to whims and personalities. The approach simplifies decision making and accelerates a decision's implementation. The drawback is to put the human aspect in second place in the hierarchy of priorities. The challenge for the decision maker will therefore be primarily driven by the need to manage the human aspect.

The alternative, *management by justification,* switches the priorities around. The decision maker places greater emphasis on group harmony than on wringing out performance. The quest for harmony can reach, in the extreme, the quicksand of conflict avoidance, especially with outsourced work. For example, the decision maker may elect to retain the services of a contractor who continually fails to meet expectations rather than go through the stressful cancellation of the contract. A similar scenario occurs when an employee consistently turns in a subpar performance. The decision maker may be reluctant to deal with the intensity of the personal confrontation that could ensue if the employee were called to account. In these and other similar instances, the decision maker will find ways to justify *not* making the decisions required to fix the problem. He may invoke external circumstances, bad luck, inexperience, personal issues, health, and whatever else could present a credible explanation. Regardless of the explanation, the outcome is always the same: the project will suffer in favor of harmony. The challenge for the decision maker is to overcome his conflict aversion, which would be a tall order for most people so disposed.

Managing by performance is the better choice. It is the only philosophy that can be relied upon to execute the work in accordance with the budget and the schedule. But the reader is cautioned against concluding that the dictator-type, top-down style of management is ideal for this role. Over the long run, the dictator will do more harm than good. Staff turnover could explode and continuity of development could become nonexistent. The firm's bad reputation will find its way into social media. Clearly, the dictator is not the best type for the job; the ideal candidate is the polar opposite. He or she must be, first and foremost, comfortable with the dynamics of human relations. At the same time, the person must be willing to embrace the expectations of the project and formulate an execution framework that is understood by all—with expectations baked into the cornerstone and outcomes measured transparently.

MANAGEMENT FRAMEWORK

One Ring to Rule Them All

A management framework is a set of principles, rules, and structures corralling the work that is done under its guidance. It is a virtual ring inside which action takes place. An effective framework is transparent, consistent, predictable, and logically orchestrated. It defines who is who in the zoo and who decides what and when. It prescribes the minimum number of processes and procedures that are mandatory for the organization. It also prescribes the hierarchy of authority and the remedies to be applied when contraventions are observed. It should also set out the consequences for success and for failure.

Ultimately, the framework exists to manage risk. It has no business meddling into the daily travails of the organization's people and groups. It operates at an arm's length from everyday operations and hovers above them with an eye on what might be going off the rails. The true measure of a framework is its ability (or lack thereof) to anticipate problems, trends, and dangers, and mitigate them *proactively*. When a framework only gets involved *postmortem*, it is a sign that it views its role as journalism rather than management. The effective framework manages for performance, never for justification.

The organizing principle of a framework is the separation of risks into endogenous (internal) and exogenous (external) sources. The person mandated to execute the work across the TRL phases (presumably the innovator or his delegate) assumes the mantle of endogenous risk manager. This person must manage the work always and foremost in relation to the internal risks at play. Conversely, the person vested with management oversight of the business (presumably a hired manager or the innovator, again in compliance with the exclusion principle) takes ownership of the risks external to the business. In both instances, the act of managing must be anticipatory and proactive, before an emerging issue is allowed to manifest itself. Too many project managers spring into action *after the issue has done its deed.* Reporting after the fact, when costs and schedule delays have already been incurred, isn't project management—it is journalism.

The Meaning of Accountability

The reader may recoil with fright from the impression that the framework is an organizational burden on overhead. The scale of the framework is a function of the project's scope. Large capital projects will require a dedicated framework team, for example. Remember that the framework is first a management concept that can function well with the smallest of resources. For a small development team, the framework mandate can be vested in the overall project manager—a one-man show. The framework is justified because it is arises as a logical consequence of the exclusion principle. It is not an extra layer of oversight bolted to a business' management structure. The framework sets the boundaries between who's who in the zoo to manifest, in practice, the exclusion principle in theory.

The framework serves to assign accountability across the organization.

Accountability is one of those terms that, like the word leadership, everybody's heard of but nobody can correctly define. Its meaning is taken to be understood implicitly; its usage is routinely swapped indiscriminately with *responsibility.* When accountability is distributed or absent, an organization will tend to compensate with larger head counts, which appease an environment in which dabbling and dabblers abound. Dabbling is a grave concern to the manager who is wanting to manage for performance. It should be eradicated the instant it is uncovered. No good can come from it, at any time, on any subject. Fortunately, dabbling cannot exist where accountability rules.

In investment-centric project management (ICPM), an individual is accountable when he can be hailed for success or nailed for failure. Accountability is always an individual mandate that is never applied to a group or shared; we then speak of *direct accountability*. Direct accountability is achieved when three conditions are met: (1) the decision of the individual determines the success or failure of an outcome; (2) the individual can be singled out for reward or punishment for the outcome flowing from the decision; and (3) the individual must live with the consequences of the decision. *Note that all three conditions are necessary to guarantee that deciders will have skin in the game.*

The *accountability* mandate is limited to the planning, execution, and delivery of a specified scope of work. To be *accountable* is not the same as being *responsible* in ICPM. The latter is the mandate given to an individual for putting in place the environment and the resources required by the individual who is accountable to do the work. Hence, we see that accountability and responsibility are distinct from each other. The former gets the works done, while the latter enables the work to be done. This distinction is crucial to the delineation of the boundaries between the various management functions of the business. The distinction is also relational: *accountability* and *responsibility* exist symbiotically relative to their place in the organizational hierarchy. For example, at the executive level, the management framework operates as a triad comprised of the owner, the business manager, and the development manager. In the relationship between the owner (single or multiple shareholders) and the business manager, the former is responsible and the latter is accountable for the innovation journey. The business manager is, in turn, responsible for the development manager's work mandate, himself being accountable for it. This dual construct is repeated at all organizational levels. For instance, within the development team, two or more team leaders will report to the manager, each with a specified accountability mandate, leaving the manager responsible for enabling their simultaneous work. The duality is directly linked to the structure of the reporting hierarchy and organizational chart. To each accountable party there corresponds at least one responsible party (note however that the reverse does not always apply).

The final piece of the puzzle concerns *authority*, which is equally distinct from *accountability* and *responsibility*. *Authority* designates the person (again, never a group) vested with the mandate to approve what the accountable person produces (the output). The two roles are mutually exclusive: one either executes the work or approves it, but never both simultaneously.

The accountable person cannot grant the final approval of an outcome.

The two roles must always be assigned to different people *with respect to a given output*. It is perfectly acceptable for two people to have, relative to each other, one mandate for one output and a different mandate for another output. In the organizational chart of a project, all boxes represent an accountability mandate. The responsibility and authority mandates are task specific and will normally not appear in the chart. They are carried out as discrete assignments.[4]

To summarize—accountability, responsibility, and authority are defined as follows:

- Accountability is the mandate to execute a specified scope of work
- Responsibility is the mandate to marshal the resources required by the accountable work
- Authority is the mandate to approve the outputs of the accountable work

The formulation of the accountability, responsibility, and authority mandates is derived from the need to eliminate overlaps between organizational functions and to concentrate their holders' focus on the specifics of their mandates.

Always Go Domestic

The prospect of executing a project with global resources can be a potent aphrodisiac. It creates the illusion of being in the big leagues. It flatters the innovator's ego and the investors' acumen. It is also an exceedingly dangerous game for going global entails a host of complex problems and difficulties in communications, cultural alignment, priorities, and productivity. It also carries a constant risk of breaches to budget and schedule. Worse yet, information technology lulls the innovator into believing, erroneously, that once communication has taken place, it implies that the message was received and understood. More often than not, the opposite occurs.

The most reliable communication path between two parties is through direct, in-person contact (with both parties fluent in the language in play). Moving one step away through e-mail or text immediately causes a loss of information in the message conveyed (owing to the absence of body language). Move another step away, across different locations, and the loss of immediacy introduces the necessity of implicit trust, which is a form of risk. Move yet again across time zones and you lose the convergence of chronological priorities. Going international introduces cultural, linguistic, and priority choke points.

Staying local should always be the starting position; going global, the last resort.

Decision No-Nos

The plethora of collaboration tools available at the office makes business communication frictionless and instantaneous. They are unavoidable in the context of teams distributed widely in space and time. Naturally, managers have evolved the reflex of utilizing these tools (e-mail and others) by default when reaching out to team members on virtually all manners of issues, including decision making. Immediacy of action comes at the high price of damaged human relations. The latter should always have right of way over immediacy by default if one aspires to maintain a healthy employee culture. Accordingly, the following rules of engagement should be embraced in day-to-day exchanges:

- Never have people listed as carbon copy (CC) in a distribution list. Either a person must be included in the exchange or not at all. CC and blind CC recipients only invite dabbling and meddling, which is never desirable under any circumstance.
- Use the collaboration tool to communicate information and decisions uniformly.
- *Do not* use the tool as a platform to engage people in decision making. When a decision requires input from two or more people, the venue should be either in a live group setting or by teleconference. Such discussions must never be carried out by e-mail or Snapchat or any other collaboration platforms. Proper decisions require sound, sights, and body language.
- *Do not* use these tools to handle personnel issues. Whether the concern is with one person or an entire department, that concern *must* be dealt with in person. If a manager cannot handle this aspect of the job, he has no business being in that job in the first place.
- *Never* rant or rage or blow steam or vent in written or recorded form.

TALENT MANAGEMENT

The People Conundrum

The issue of talent management is a perennial challenge to businesses everywhere. The topic is far too vast to address in this book so our discussion will be limited to three aspects that affect innovators during the development journey: staffing, information leakage, and messaging. Staffing is front and center at all times. The hiring process is tedious, time consuming, costly, and inherently risky. The process of firing is stressful, disruptive, and possibly costly as well. Funding constraints exacerbate things even more. The issue is of prime importance to the innovator. At the end of the day, people are the single most important variable in the nature of the journey's outcome. Success or failure rides on their abilities and limitations.

- *Hire the skill sets that are deemed strategically key to the future business—* These are the core skill sets that will constitute the knowledge assets of the business, the intimate knowledge of the innovation, and the production acumen of the product. Choose carefully what qualifies as key, then move heaven and earth to keep these people happy. In particular, assign them their mandates, then get completely out of the way.

- *Acquire key knowledge through your key people*—The way to get the most bang for your buck, in this instance, is to train your people to recognize whatever core competency is deficient or missing.
- *Outsource the rest*—No organization can ever hope to acquire all the knowledge, expertise, and know-how that go into the innovation. Stick to your knitting (through your core people) and bring in the expertise piecemeal from outside sources—or send the work out to outside contractors and consultants. In so doing, always ensure that the terms of engagement repatriate all outcomes, outputs, deliverables, and knowledge yielded by the contractor's work.

Leaking Secrets

Another universal challenge is the protection of corporate knowledge. Employees and contractors alike must be bound by confidentiality and nondisclosure agreements that establish a primary legal bulwark against information leakage to the outside world. But legal agreements are no panacea; they are, at best, akin to a padlock that keeps honest people honest. The innovator must envision the worst and plan for it. Outside threats from hackers, fraudsters, and industrial spies may be realistic, in which case expert consultants should be brought in to customize the protection barriers. Inside threats are far more difficult to counter, owing to the need for trust in the people doing the work. Here again, expert consultants can be rapidly deployed to design robust document management processes and systems. Proprietary calculation schemes should be created in math-specific applications rather than Excel spreadsheets. Engineering design and data need to sit behind sturdy firewalls that are unreachable by outside internet connections. Simulation results and test data must be physically protected even more as they contain the essence of the innovation's limits and secrets.

Bottling the Message

The third challenge is linked to communication and public messages. The need for information protection is self-evident. Even when an information bulwark is erected and working, there is still one source of leakage that can wreak havoc with the firm's secrecy plans: messaging. Think of all the communications that go on every day within and outside the firm as a matter of course. Some employees will attend seminars, conferences, and trade shows. Some will publish papers; others will be invited speakers at public events. The scale of those communications cannot be gauged nor can it be fully controlled for content. The solution in this case is message management. The innovator should devise a plan whereby all external communications are vetted against an approved, predefined message. All written publications that are intended for public release must be vetted internally for compliance to the message and verification of confidentiality. People called to deal with the public should be counseled first on the need for information preservation and knowledge protection. The bottom line is simple enough: to control the message effectively, you must effectively define that message, constrain its language, and indoctrinate those meant to convey it in the public domain (discussed in Chapter 9 under the heading *Diffusion Strategy*).

VENDOR MANAGEMENT

Greed Is Good

Dealing with the supply chain is inevitable in any business. Despite its routine nature, the management of vendors can be intimidating to very small start-up firms who are learning the ropes at the same time that they are pulling on them. The vendor relation is fundamentally transactional in nature for the most part. That is, the vendor supplies you with a product or service, you pay for it, and each party moves on. Some vendors will be more important than others and may even become a strategic element of the innovator's success strategy. In that case, the relationship may go beyond transactional and become akin to a partnership. Never ever forget, however, the golden rule of supply chain management:

> *Each party in the relationship is in it to make money and will never sacrifice its self-interest to preserve yours.*

Even when the parties agree to form a joint venture or partnership, they remain ultimately driven by their own success within the venture. Hence, any relationship involving money must be based on a contract. A solid contract will set out unambiguously the accountability, responsibility, and authority limits of each party, the execution requirements, conflict resolution, and ownership assignments. The reader is warned against assuming that the contract provides each party with the proper leverage to enforce the successful outcome of the contract.

> *All contracts start from a position of mistrust. In effect, they declare that the parties cannot be trusted to fulfill their obligations. Their existence serves to replace trust and honesty with explicit obligations and duties*

defined for each party to be enforced by the threat of legal proceedings. The contract, in other words, is offensive to a relationship resting on a handshake.

The implied absence of ethics, trust, or honesty makes it exceedingly difficult to genuinely align the contracted parties along a common axis of interest (i.e., the success of the project). When acrimony sets in, the first thing that gets sacrificed is the success of the project in the pursuit of each party's commercial interests. The innovator will derive little solace from winning a legal argument, should it come to that, if the price is a project completely derailed. Nobody can afford that kind of Pyrrhic victory.

Safe Proceedings

There is no doubt that the insights of a competent lawyer offer the innovator the strongest guarantee of protection in a contract. This is one area where the novice party should never improvise in the name of cost savings. The expense is well warranted and will cost less in the long run than avoiding it at the outset. The innovator can still do many things to help reduce the magnitude of this expense, but must not fool himself into thinking that he can figure it all out without legal help. All contracts being written, it stands to reason that the first action of the innovator should be to pay attention to content writing. Lawyers get paid to do this. The innovator is better positioned, however, to write things like scope of work, statements of work, procedures, plans, reports, and proposals. In all of these instances, clarity, concision, and prescriptive style are *required*. The upside of prescription writing is the willful absence of artistic creativity. One does not need to be an accomplished writer at all. As a matter of fact, people who struggle with writing well will do well to avoid creative styles entirely. Prescribe in all cases; describe in none. The smallest number of words, properly chosen, is always best. What must be done must be quantifiable. What is assessed or approved must be measurable against specific criteria. Wishy-washy fluff must be avoided like the plague. Consider the following examples:

> *"The manager will ensure that the work has been done in accordance with the requirements of the quality assurance plan."*

> *"The engineer shall diligently carry out the work."*

Exactly how, pray tell, would someone go about verifying this? Words like *ensure, in accordance with, quality, plan,* and *diligently* are devoid of prescriptive intent. They are tacitly immeasurable, unquantifiable, and therefore unreliable means of contract enforcement. So, how does one go about writing in a prescriptive style?

- The first step is to avoid general statements in the first place.
- The second step is never to write in the passive voice. The sentence, *it has been observed that the results were incorrect* is useless. This one isn't: *Tests showed that the results were wrong.* Neither is this one: *the results were wrong.*
- The third step is to limit prescriptions to outputs and deliverables. Don't describe the nature of the work underlying the output; prescribe the acceptance criteria for the output.
- The fourth step is to never explain or provide reasons for why an output is required. For instance, if a pump system is required in a plant, do not write, *the pump selection must comply with API 610 in order to satisfy the regulatory requirements of the plant's operating license*; simply write, *the pump selection shall comply to articles X, Y, and Z for API 610, 7th edition.*
- The fifth step complements the fourth. When referencing a governing document, always spell out every pertaining article. For example, do not write, *the wall thickness of the pressure vessel shall be in accordance with ASME B31.3*; write, *the wall thickness of the pipe shall be calculated by Articles 304.1.1 and 304.1.2(a) in ASME B31-3-2014.*
- The sixth step calls for never repeating a text that was previously introduced. Instead, refer the reader to the appropriate article or paragraph number that introduced the text.

We conclude these tips with a recall of the W5H approach that was introduced in Chapter 4. A complete prescription will be comprised of the answers to the why, what, where, when, who, and how questions. The text need not be explained; often, a bulleted list will be more than adequate to cover the W5H.

The Statement of Work

The statement of work (SOW) is the workhorse of the vendor relationship. Its purpose is self-explanatory: to state what is to be done by the vendor, over what time frame, and against what acceptance criteria. When the work is done by the innovator's people, it goes by the name: *scope of work.* Since every job is unique, so will the SOW. Writing an SOW can be intimidating to newcomers so our discussion henceforth will focus on good practices for developing a competent document.

The value of an SOW lies in its prescriptions, not in the number of pages.

The writing tips offered in the previous article apply equally to the writing effort. The SOW is never:

- A summary of the work to be done
- A set of profuse descriptions of the roles and responsibilities of the people doing the work

- A justification of functions and processes
- An invitation to *ensure* and *assure*; don't ensure that a procedure is followed—prescribe it
- A list of purposeless actions (which do yield a reviewable output)
- A regurgitation of published contents—this prohibition extends to processes, procedures, and plans; these documents are either references or appendices to the SOW
- The list of terms and conditions (these belong in the contract or purchase order)

The SOW can be a one-line request for a deliverable or a more comprehensive document. In the latter case, the following sections should be included as a minimum:

- *Section 1—Presentation*: includes project title, SOW number and date, and contact information
- *Section 2—Introduction*: purpose, results sought, list of supplied information, list of applicable codes and standards, and list of standard processes and procedures
- *Section 3—Prescriptions*: deliverables required, compliance criteria (codes and standards), acceptance criteria, list of assumptions, list of work exclusion, list of applicable exceptions, and authentication requirements (stamping, certification, validation); also, when testing is required, the testing protocols must be included in this section
- *Section 4—Management*: milestone schedule, accountability matrix, meetings (types, frequency, recurrence, minutes), review mechanics and attendance matrix, change management mechanics, and reporting requirements
- *Section 5—Document management*: naming and numbering conventions, file format prescriptions, file exchange process, comments and markups conservation, abbreviations and acronyms, standard templates (contents and presentation), software and Cloud transaction, and version control (note that this last section is required only when the standard procedures specified in Section 2 are silent on the matter)

Terms and Conditions

Regardless of the type of contractual mechanism that is adopted (contract, purchase order, invitation to tender, work authorization, etc.), the document will be accompanied by a set of terms and conditions that are specified by the innovator. The vendor will also present his own set of terms and conditions, appended to his proposal. Clearly, both parties will need to come to an agreement for what is kept in and out. Complex agreements will benefit from a competent lawyer. Consider the following lessons that were learned from the trenches of innovation management:

- IP ownership: whoever pays for the work owns the sole rights to *everything* that is designed, discovered, understood, modeled, created, and otherwise documented as a result of the work performed under the contract. In other words, when the innovator issues a contract, the vendor has no claim to any IP, period.

- Always include a nondisclosure agreement to bind the vendor to the innovator's confidentiality requirements. The issuer of the contract dictates the terms—always.

- All outputs and deliverables that are produced in the course of the work belong to the issuer of the contract and must be so supplied in their native formats—in a form that is editable by the issuer. This means no password-protected files and no pdf. The issuer can also prescribe the program and file format if he so desires.

- In the case of software codes and algorithms, each instance must be accompanied by an editable text file to explain their construction, data structure, variable lexicon, and logic diagrams.

- At the end of the project, *everything* received or created by the vendor must be returned to the issuer of the contract in their native format. The vendor should be allowed to keep copies of the documentation and codes created.

- The issuer should consider imposing a naming and numbering convention scheme for all documents, drawings, 3-D models, and algorithms. The scheme should include, among other things, a mechanism for managing version releases over time.

- The issuer should always prescribe a minimum number of review meetings with the vendors, and specify the topics, frequency, and mandatory attendance for each type of meeting. Meeting minutes should be mandatory for every meeting, and published within two business days after they ended.

- The issuer must specify his requirements for technical reviews and deliverable approval.

- The issuer should prescribe the process for final acceptance of the complete works by the vendor. The prescription must include the pass-fail criteria, the required documentation, and the quality documentation to be supplied by the vendor.

- Invoicing and payment terms need to be specified clearly, along with the submission, review, and contestation processes. When a final acceptance condition is included, the issuer should insist on a hold-back provision, upon final payment, that is tied to a successful completion.
- Finally, the terms and conditions should prescribe the project close-out mechanics as imposed by the issuer.

When the Vendor Is from Academia

More controls are needed when the innovator contemplates soliciting expertise from academia. The realm is obsessed with two objectives: employ students on research projects and publish scientific papers. Cited publications are the yardstick by which researchers are graded. As a result, to hire an academic researcher is to invite, unwillingly, a work ethic that is driven by the ritual of paper writing and the pursuit of complexity for complexity's sake. Simplicity and speed to completion are detrimental to execution. This character will often conflict with the innovator's need for prompt results and simplicity of implementation. If academia cannot be avoided, the innovator would be well advised to take heed of the following tips in addition to aforementioned lessons:

- *Shop locally*—That is, seek out the expertise in your immediate vicinity. The further afield you go, the greater the management risks. Beyond your local borders, language and culture may become exceedingly challenging.
- *Dictate the timelines*—Academics tend to work at a pace that is incompatible with the exigencies of business. Urgency is defined in relation to publication deadlines and end-of-term exams. If the researcher cannot or will not abide by your timeline, seek someone else.
- *Research student capabilities*—Allow the participation of a student *only* when you know that your timeline will be respected.
- *Impose a publication ban from the outset*—If the researcher wants to publish anything, insist on participating as coauthor and on reviewing the final paper prior to submission. This paper is an output of the work you paid for; in other words, you own this IP.
- *Impose a gag order on all public disclosures*—This includes the very existence of the effort.
- *Assure complete understanding*—Make sure the researcher(s) recognizes precisely the answers you seek and the deliverables you require.
- *Specify decision gates to control the incremental progress of the work over time*—Do not allow the work to progress beyond a missing answer.

- *Verify key information*—If the answers are critical to the success of the innovation, have the results independently verified and validated.
- *Stay in control*—Manage the work for performance forcefully.

The Fourth Shift

The *fourth shift* is a term employed in globalization circles to describe the practice by foreign manufacturers to complete their contract orders, then continue producing the outputs for their own benefits in their markets without permission. The concept extends to IP (patents, trademarks, copyrights, etc.). The fourth shift is typically tolerated or downright encouraged in jurisdictions that give domestic industry priority over international laws—in other words, orchestrated thievery. The point should be obvious by now: outsourcing anything to jurisdictions that flaunt the rule of law as understood in the West is the riskiest cost decision that an innovator can make. Never mind that the cheapest cost *now* will always cost the most *later* (to seller and buyer alike); the risk of IP loss, market share destruction, and brand valuation should never be put in play for the putative benefit of lower manufacturing costs. The golden rule of staying domestic, enunciated previously, applies equally to the manufacturing function, particularly before TRL 7. Never outsource on the sole basis of cost savings: the price will always catch up with you later.

FUNDING MANAGEMENT

The Importance of Being Earnest

Financing is an essential component of the innovation journey—right from inception and all the way to growth and exit strategy. An inventor can conceivably get away with doing things on the cheap but at the price of over-extended development timelines. The innovator does not have this luxury as he is running a marathon that can only be won by being first to the finish line. Getting financing for the endeavor *before the need for cash arises* must be a recurring priority of the innovator. The source of this financing will vary over time as a function of the risk to the investor. Furthermore, and this is absolutely critical to the discussion, the innovator must understand that financing is fundamentally about getting money in exchange for something else. Many investors fail to appreciate this fact and go into the sales pitch thinking exclusively about extracting a money commitment from the other party. In this context, the other party is the would-be *buyer* in exactly the same sense of selling a product to a would-be customer. Investors will only offer their money if their own motiva-tions for doing so are satisfied. Families, friends, and fools may be swayed at an emotional level; however, any other person or organization with money to spare will buy into your vision if and only if it matches their internal compass. Hence, one must understand the motivations of the investor before making the pitch. The latter must be tailored to address them explicitly.

These motivations form a continuum that reflects the segmentation of the *investor market*. At one end of the spectrum are motivations that are driven by social gains (erase poverty, increase literacy, raise standards of living, create jobs). These motivations are typical of programs that enact government pol-icy, non-government organizations (NGOs), and charitable foundations. At the other end of the spectrum we find motivations driven by financial gains. This is the realm of the professional venture capitalists, the banks, and private equity. At this end, money trumps all. The goal is to multiply the initial investment by a factor of 3 to 10 over five years, then move on to the next deal. The continuum is shown in Figure 7.1. Observe the dilution over time of an innovator's ownership as a function of the sources of funding. Dilution is inevitable when non-govern-mental sources are involved. It is part of the exchange in return for the money.

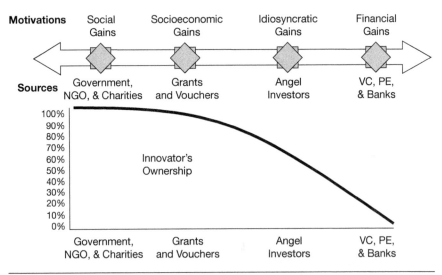

Figure 7.1   Continuum of the investor market: the market is segmented along motivation sources that range from altruism to pure greed

Order of Solicitation

The other part of the exchange is determined by the motivations of the funding sources. They form a hierarchy as illustrated in Figure 7.2. The hierarchy sets out the order of solicitation. The bottom layer is the first source that should be tapped by the innovator and is, incidentally, the ideal scenario. A customer who is willing to put money up front to develop the innovation is the strongest statement of viability possible. The customer will, of course, negotiate an exchange that will benefit him in the long run, such as preferential pricing, priority of supply, or exclusivity of access. He may also ask for a minority stake in the innovator's company, which should be regarded as an excellent potential exit strategy in the future.

Predictably, getting the customer to participate in this financial risk is difficult. The fall back position is to seek out help from friends and family. This is always a very risky path, mind you, because of the unique emotional component. As the logic goes, if you cannot convince this group of people to put money into your venture, why would strangers have any faith in doing so? The downside should be weighed very carefully by the innovator against the possibility of failure. Would an outcome of this sort wreck relationships? Money

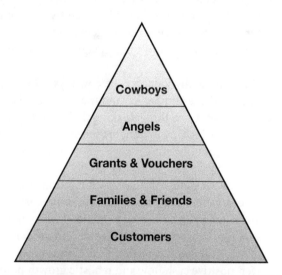

Figure 7.2 The solicitation pyramid: the order of priority in seeking external funding is erected as a pyramid that typically frowns upon jumping levels out of sequence

matters, especially when they include losses, have a way of destroying human relationships. The upside, however, is a source of funding with lesser constraints than with angels and cowboys. And, with money in hand, making the case for additional funding from the latter becomes slightly easier (at the very least, it becomes possible, as opposed to impossible).

The third layer in the hierarchy comprises the funding programs offered by governments, nonprofit and profit foundations, and NGOs. This source of funding offers the great benefit of being nondilutive—that is, the innovator does not give up ownership in the company. These programs are often geared toward the front-end, high-risk developmental stages of an innovation where few angels and cowboys dare tread. The motivations of this level are tilted heavily toward societal benefits rather than pure profits. Governments always want to see job creation and increased tax revenues; NGOs and charities are motivated by the human element first.

The fourth layer represents angel investors. They will usually become involved once the high-risk development is completed (TRL 3 or higher), although some will have no qualms about getting in on the action right from the get-go. Angel investors are motivated by personal curiosity and passion, first. Money—as in making more of it—comes second, or third, and sometimes not at all. The angel investor is a highly prized contributor to any innovation journey. By virtue of the person's career, wealth, and network, the innovator stands to gain infinitely more than mere funding from such a relationship. On the other hand, angel investors move in packs usually out of the limelight. For that reason, they are the hardest people to find.

The last layer of the hierarchy includes the cowboys. These are the venture capitalists, private equity firms and banks, and merchant banks. These sources are motivated by one and only one thing; making their money back, many times over. Venture capitalists are looking to double their money over a three- to five-year period with a minimum investment between $2 and $20M and a majority stake in the company. Private equity firms like to run the business they take over and look to prep them up for a huge payday by selling to an established competitor. Banks want to preserve their capital and earn their interest. Merchant banks seek to maximize the share price as long as possible, then leverage that increase with further investments. Cowboys are risk averse and are rarely interested in getting involved before TRL 8 at the earliest. The business must already be established with proven positive cash flow and realistic growth potential. The Silicon Valley story tends to create the impression in the public's eye that they are always at the ready to jump on the next potential big thing. In reality, they are not. Out of 100 projects, venture capitalists typically invest in only two (hence, they face a 98% chance of picking the wrong bet). In a portfolio of 10 projects, one project will hit the jackpot and pay for all the rest; two will make one half to three times the initial investment; the remaining seven will be smoking holes. This is the reason why cowboys are so risk averse and why they *are not a realistic source of funding for innovators in general.*

PRODUCT EVOLUTION STRATEGY

Stay One Step Ahead of the Competition

We close this chapter with the subject of evolution, or more precisely, how to keep competitors at bay. They make up the highest risk to the innovator; as a group, they transcend the mortal threat to the commercial sustainability of the innovator's business. Your product could be the greatest thing since sliced bread, yet it makes no difference; whereas it is your profit generator, the competition is your revenue killer. The product rollout, to paraphrase Churchill, is not the end of development, nor is it even the beginning of its end; but it is the end of the business' beginning. Indeed, with commercialization in full bloom, the innovator cannot risk resting on his or her laurels. The priority is on making the operation profitable. But the competition will not sit idly by while your product gains traction in the marketplace. As a matter of fact, there is ample probability that at least one of the competitors has already noticed the opportunity that led to your product—and that he has been hard at work to seize it. The arrival of your product will only intensify the sense of urgency felt by him. The rest of the competition will watch your success closely and wish for your failure. Your success will only exacerbate their state of mind. The competitive onslaught is about to unfold. Are you prepared for it?

The best defense is, of course, offense and the same goes for the innovator. It is far more important to understand why the product is succeeding than why it is failing—in which case, you may be done anyway for the factors underlying the success will be equally visible to the competition. The sense of urgency takes on a new mantle for the innovator who must now figure out how to follow up the initial success with new versions of the product. That is what *going on the offensive* means. The advantage is with you, the market incumbent. The competition is playing catch up. Your objective is to stay ahead of the pack, embodied in the *product evolution strategy.*

The first step calls for circling all the way back to the initial definition of the primary functions. Which ones are well received by buyers? Which ones are irrelevant or even detrimental? Which ones are missing? What are buyers asking for, above and beyond what the product gives them? More important, what is the competition offering in response to your product that is desired by buyers? These questions are at the heart of the evolution strategy. There are no hard and fast rules for setting a timeline for the next development cycle. That timeline will be dictated by buyers' feedback. If it comes in quickly, the next development cycle also needs to get started quickly. If the feedback is slow in coming, the sales team must be dispatched to scour the countryside to bring it into the light.

Design to Destroy

The pace of the evolution is tightly woven into the fabric of the technology beneath the product. Consumer products are notoriously fickle. Software surfs an incessant wave of releases every few months or so. Big industrial products are far less prone to changes; as a matter of fact, once they are known to work, they become stubbornly resistant to change! But changes can never be avoided. If not at the product level, it will be with the internal components. Electronic components are in a constant state of design flux. Mechanical components that are prone to wear and tear will always change with emerging materials. Legal and regulatory regimes will inject their own kind of randomness by changing the rules of the game over time. Inflation itself might price out age-old components and age-old components eventually come to a timeworn end. The question of technological aging is fundamental to the design process. It is also one of the hardest design variables to manage. In the ideal world, the design of a product will anticipate future changes suffered by its components and integrate the corresponding constraints into the product such that new bits and pieces can be quickly installed without any ancillary design changes to the rest of the product. This is easier said than done. It is harder still with physical components whose interfaces are controlled in part by their geometric envelopes. Mating standardization goes a long way toward minimizing collateral design changes. Physical placement also helps manage the space in which installation and handling takes place. The list of possibilities is immeasurable, obviously. Given that prediction is usually not possible, anticipation is the antidote to extensive design modifications.

> *Design should take into account the eventual death of a feature and account for it in the layout to increase the flexibility of future modifications in place.*

Version Management

Evolution implies *configuration management*, which can be defined as:[5]

> *The surveillance of the functional, physical, and modification characteristics of a product.*

Configuration management tracks all information associated with an element of a product. This information extends to the sources of supplies, the backward and forward design compatibilities, the associated manuals, the quality records, the part numbers, the technical documents (drawings, datasheets, etc.), and any other piece of information that defines the element in part or in total. The reader can readily see that the configuration management flows through everything that makes up the product—from the bottom-up and the top-down.

Configuration management and product usage data go hand in hand; the former for tracking what exists and the latter for what performs how. Usage data are required to derive reliability statistics, which are essential to the profitability of the business—warranty, inventory, and after-sale costs are all driven by them. It is therefore imperative that the business be equipped with a stalwart configuration management system that is capable of being linked to the document management system and the product data usage infrastructure.

Documentation Management

Evolution also implies aggregate knowledge if lessons are meant to be learned with each new generation of the product. The subject was discussed in previous chapters, except for two new items: technical writing and translation. The finer points of good writing are not limited to SOWs and proposals. Good writing is also essential at the technical level where highly specialized information must be captured and documented. Take, for example, a troubleshooting manual; despite being utterly devoid of stylistic prose, such a document is beyond the writing abilities of most people, including technical professionals like engineers, designers, and scientists. The same goes for all other forms of technical documentation (engineering reports, technical analyses, operating manuals, parts list, etc.). The value, and therefore usefulness of these documents, can only be realized by employing writers who are trained in the esoteric art of technical writing. The work is ideally suited for outsourcing since most products will not require a full-time writer once the document set has been published. The cost of this work isn't an expense against the development budget, it is an investment into the profitability of the business.

The corollary to the writer requirement is translation. The instant that the product finds its way into a market where the language differs from the innovator's business, the need for translation will manifest itself. The world of translation is even more arcane than technical writing. It would be folly for anyone to take on the task in name of expediency or cost savings. There is *nothing worse than a bad translation* for the reputation of the business. A bad translation comes across as sloppy work or an amateurish business attitude or even disrespect to the culture of the buyer. It is better to do nothing rather than release a bad translation. This is another instance of an expense that isn't actually an expense: it is an investment into the business' commercial success.

MIGRATION COMPLETED

This chapter transitioned the perspective of the text from the innovation journey to the onset of the commercial operation of the innovation-driven business. The management angle, or rather angles, helped make the segue natural without explicitly pointing out the fact that the development program was done. The various management functions brought to bear the fact that the innovator has reached the stage where the innovation journey is subsiding, to be replaced by the emerging business that has derived from it. From this point forward, the prime directive of the innovator is to get this business to make money. Things like vision, mission, and strategy have been put in motion and will continue to carry the innovator's dream forward. It is an exciting time for everyone and especially for those who have lived, breathed, sweated, and paid for what has gone before. Nevertheless, the vision to change the world or whatever, cannot—at least not yet—be permitted to roam free across the commercial landscape. From the business standpoint, *nothing has happened until sales thrive*. This is a harsh fact of life. It matters not whether you spent a month or a decade on development. Nor does it matter whether that development consumed a thousand dollars or a million. Until there is money being made in sufficient quantities, nothing that came before amounts to a hill of beans.

The imperative to make money and to do so profitably and continuously will underscore the remaining three chapters of Part 2. The *revenue attitude* (explored in Chapter 8) will blossom, or not, from the volitions of those who are entrusted to lead the business and mold its *culture*. The *profit attitude* (exposed in Chapter 11) will reveal the gravity of the bottom line and the importance of the mechanics involved in nurturing it.

NOTES

1. These directives are inspired by the original version of the seven primes introduced in *Investment-Centric Project Management*.
2. Ibid, Chapter 6.
3. Ibid. The trust-but-check mechanic relies on the acceptance maturity model.
4. The three mandates (accountable, responsible, and authority) form what is called the *directrix*. The directrix is the orchestrating principle underlying the unit transformation process and is the guiding principle behind the hierarchical relations between team members. See *Investment-Centric Project Management*, Chapter 13.
5. See Mil-Std-973. Military Standard: Configuration Management (http://everyspec.com/MIL-STD/MIL-STD-0900-1099/MIL_STD_973_1146/).

8

CULTURE

Dreams float; visions anchor.

THE REVENUE MINDSET

One for All and All for One

We need a new analogy. Throughout the first seven chapters, the development endeavor was described as a journey of discovery and exploration. When we fold the development works into the bigger picture, we see that the end of development occurs *prior* to the launch of the commercial operations. These operations are in turn intended to conquer the market with the roll out of the innovative product. The appropriate analogy is that of a pirate ship's mission. Everything that has gone on and culminated in technology readiness level (TRL) 9 consisted of equipping the ship with the crew, provisions, charts, ammunition, weapons, and orders to engage the enemy. The second part of the mission is the voyage proper, whose purpose is the hunt for treasure. Despite the preparations, it would be folly to launch the ship without first indoctrinating the crew, who would otherwise be nothing more than obtuse pieces of driftwood in waiting.

The voyage commences with the unification of the crew's power of will.

This indoctrination—for that is the precise term—goes beyond job descriptions, organizational charts, accountability matrices, and functional training. These things are necessary, it goes without saying, but do not suffice to align people along a shared mindset. What is needed from the very get-go is a *culture* that is unique to the ship's journey. There will be one to sprout in time, out of nothing more than the amalgamation of the hopes and fears of the individual crew members if nothing else is done. Culture is an emergent feature of organizations in the same vein as complexity. The firm is, and always remains, a living organism driven to survive, striving to multiply, and prone to diseases, conflicts, and emotions. What this culture will look like, nobody can predict: it's the greater whole of the sum of its individual parts. It will reflect the composite personalities of those who partake in it. A single personnel change could permanently alter this culture or have no effect whatsoever. In the former case, it is said to be fragile; in the latter case, antifragile. The recipe for one or the other was brilliantly explored in *Built to Last* and *Good to Great* by Jim Collins, et al. The culture of an organization is foundational to its longevity and one of the key factors that will determine how a firm will survive an extreme success or an existential threat.

Cultural Insemination

The emergent quality of a group's culture does not preclude the ability to influence what it will become. Since it emerges from the symbiosis of the volitions of each person in the group, it stands to reason that the selection of these persons will play a seminal role in shaping the culture of a place over time. Collins, in *Built to Last*, emphasized the importance of corporate values pervading an organization (as opposed to the declarations of management) *whether or not they were introduced by the firm's leaders*. Collins concluded that these values will traverse the passage of time unscathed when they are completely suffused within the organization to the point where they are taken for granted and transparent to everyday dealings. Clearly, the long-term success of our innovator's commercial enterprise must recognize the role that culture will play. Three mechanics of cultural cultivation will occupy a central role: the vision, the reflection, and the clash. The vision originates with the innovator and flows downward throughout the troops. It serves as impetus of the entire affair, from Chapter 1 through Chapter 11. It is the equivalent of the pirate captain setting his sights on the domination of the seas.[1] It also guides the firm's leadership team in matters of hiring, firing, strategic decisions, and daily operational management.

The second mechanic, reflection, is the interpretation of the vision by the people within the organization, who in turn manifest these values through their daily travails. It is now that the emergence of the corporate culture takes place. When the vision is articulated, the culture does not exist; at best, it will be hoped to take a certain shape. Through the reflection mechanic, the staff internalizes the vision of the leadership team, gains inspiration from it, and buys into it lock, stock, and barrel. Or, they could pick and choose what suits them—or straight out decide to reject it. Emergence reaches reality through the interactions of the people from within and without. These interactions unfold along the recesses of the internalized vision or in contradiction to them. If they agree, the culture is on its way to sowing deep, stalwart roots. Otherwise, they plant the seeds of dissent that could eventually prove the firm's downfall.

The clash mechanic serves as final arbiter of the firm's vaulted aspirations. There will always come a time in the life of a business when circumstances (internal or external) will force a stark choice upon the firm's leadership between loyalty to the vision or sacrifice of it on the altar of opportunity. Take the simple example of a senior manager running an astonishingly successful sales department but who is known to be willing to ignore the firm's vision if it can secure a sale. By the same token, this behavior encourages the sales staff to adopt a similar judgment basis when chasing the next deal. In a similar scenario (experienced by myself), a vice president repeatedly breached the firm's commitment to respect in the workplace and zero tolerance for bullying employees, but continued to be held in high esteem by his superior because of a positive cash flow that had been achieved from his activities. In both cases the question is: should the manager be fired for failing to live up to the vision, thereby foregoing precious revenues? This is the essence of the clash. The firm must decide if the vision, along with the ramifications that it entails, must prevail or not. In a purely speculative scenario, it is easy to take the high ground and pretend to make the right decision in favor of the vision. However, more often than not, the opposite occurs in the actual heat of the moment. Adjudicating between moral integrity and riches is one of the most difficult decisions for a firm's leadership to make. When money is on the line, so is allegiance to an ethical or moral standard.

The Substance of Culture

The reader should observe that the culture of an organization is not the same as its vision or its mission (which will be explored shortly). Nor is it an abstract concept that is intended to satisfy the individual aspirations, motivations, and needs of the staff. Such a thing is impossible to achieve. Some people are motivated by money, others are obsessed with positional power, and still others seek social standing and reputational recognition. For some, job security and health benefits are the primary drivers. Many people value work-life balance the most. Some people will gladly be on call 24/7 if it advances their career objectives. Some will seek a purely inspirational reason to get up in the morning and save the world (or a small corner of it). The more potent approach to cultural design is one that leads people to find their own motivations within a finite accentuated frame. This notion of finding one's impetus from without lies at the heart of the importance of *cultural fit* of prospective employees. *Fitting in* is by the far the most important quality to such corporate giants as Google, Apple, and Ferrari. No amount of extreme functional expertise can overcome a perceived divergence between interviewee and culture for these firms. This is why firms who value culture above technical prowess will spend enormous time and effort to select new employees. They will be brutally honest about what they care about, what they value, how they prioritize values within their decision-making processes, and why they will fire those who don't fit. Where culture genuinely matters, hiring is slow and firing swift.

The definition of success is an integral component of any culture. By juxtaposition, the definition of failure and how to react to it also partakes in this definition. The latter can be explicit and inscribed in the founding tenets of a firm. Or, it can be more generic, even unclear as long as the outcome is deemed worthy. In some cases, the definition is absent, which itself says something about what the organization stands for.

A Culture Is What a Culture Does

When the culture of a firm is strong, its people have clarity—clarity of purpose, clarity of expectations, clarity of decisions, and clarity of compliance. One can readily gauge the strength of this culture in the language of its people. Clarity permeates the organization with a form of language whose subtleties are understood by everyone. The language rides an undercurrent of values both tacit and stated that color the message. A shared culture is one in which *people express themselves with the same words*. Once again, we can detect the importance of *fitting in* to the strength of a culture. The clarity of the culture itself percolates to the surface by itself. Newcomers to an organization are able to determine how they can belong to it. They will rapidly learn what success means, what it looks like, and how to achieve it. They will, by the same token, know what to expect in the event of a failure. Employees old and new will know how accountability, responsibility, and authority are parsed across the hierarchy. They will also understand the latter and grasp the limits of the feedback mechanics.

We can look upon the culture of a firm in terms of a flowing undercurrent that carries its business activities across a mercantile ocean. The waves undulating at the surface portray the subset culture of the leadership team. Hence, we can discern two distinct movements over time in both the undercurrent and the visible waves. Calm waters point to a homogeneous culture. Raging waves at the surface indicate troublesome turbulence dominated by a clash of divergent values between management and the rest of the staff. Storm fronts may come and go over time without causing too many disruptions to the undercurrent patterns. However, continual tempests could reach down to the depths of the currents and change them in the process. In that instance, we have a company that is in turmoil and unlikely to survive unscathed.

Clearly, the influence of management is enormous to the firm's emergent culture. It is readily observed in management's approach to promotions and rewards.

The true values of management's culture are revealed by who gets promoted and how the C-suite gets paid.

The promotion track is the clearest outward sign of a management team's tacit values, which in turn, sets the tone for how the firm's culture will evolve over time. These intrinsic values are reinforced by who gets fired or demoted. Eloquent inspirational declarations of inclusion, diversity, and ethical practices amount to precious little if the organization rewards behaviors that, at best, harbor tenuous connections to them. A firm that proclaims loudly its belief that its people are its greatest asset, but lays them off in droves in hard times while simultaneously doling out fat bonuses to its executives will be found wanting in its cultural foundation. A pirate ship that views its crew as assets will be able to carry out its mission successfully more frequently than one whose crew is viewed as a collection of hired, undifferentiated bodies. That latter will abandon ship much sooner than the former when troubles lie ahead.

When layoffs are a firm's first option to protect the bottom line, its culture regards people as disposable commodities, not as assets.

The Top Matters

One simply cannot ignore the outsized influence of a firm's leadership values upon the shape of the emergent culture. Even in established companies with decades of successful history behind them, those values must continue to reflect their deeply rooted firm culture. When those values diverge, the resulting contrast can wreck the entire operation in rapid order. The abysmal track record of large corporate mergers over the decades is living proof of this predictable outcome. Examples also abound where the firm's emergent culture was strong enough to resist and ultimately defeat brutal bosses who were brought in from the outside to shake things up for the sake of the immediate health of the bottom line.

Culture starts and ends at the top.

It should be clear by now that the tone set by the firm's leadership is key to the emergence of the culture born by future employees. The values of the innovator, now running the company, form the cornerstone of this tone. Her dream, her vision, must be articulated in a way that will inspire others to sign up for the journey. Her actions—especially his decisions when a clash between values and money arises—will demonstrate to the rest of the people in the company the depth of her allegiance to those articulated values. Convergence of values and decisions will tell the story that this innovator walks her talk, regardless if adversity exists. Her crew will, in turn, understand the value of the currency offered by the innovator in exchange for their service. What is nonnegotiable to the innovator becomes decision bulwarks for the managers who are then hired. The firm's leadership team will be the first promoters of the budding culture. Their actions and decisions will, in turn, disseminate the seeds of that culture throughout the staff. Cementing the shape of that culture will take place organically from the bottom up, by the people carrying out the day-to-day activities of the business. The culture that emerges will be characterized by a tangible homogeneity of values embraced across the hierarchy, as well as a uniformity of the words spoken by everyone to express the shared values.

The Flip Side of Aspirational Precepts

There is a certain poetry to the idea of a shared culture that is highly satisfying to a motivated person. There is no denying the allure, the pull, the attraction of a great culture to an outsider looking in. It was a potent motivator behind eighteenth century pirate adventures despite the gore and dangers that awaited their recruits. Our modern-day pirates are not immune to its appeal as millennials everywhere illustrate. A strong, inspiring culture is not just a cure-all, but carries deep within its bowels a cornucopia of expectations that, if broken, can lead to mutiny. The stronger the culture, the greater the expectations of its adherents upon those called to manage by it. Woe betides the line manager who makes a decision that betrays the firm's culture! The severity of the impact of a broken expectation increases in lockstep with the firm's hierarchy. At the very top, the innovator will be afforded no wiggle room by the crew and could lose in the blink of an eye the trust of his peers and subordinates by a decision contravening the tacit directives of the firm's culture. A strong culture guided from the top and embraced at the bottom can act as a prickly straitjacket in decision making. Hard economic times may leave management with no good choice to sustain its survival without singeing the culture. Such circumstances call for genuine leadership (not management) to prevent divisive feelings from permeating the organization. Great success may also challenge management to allocate its future capital investments if the firm's culture upheld a mantra of employees first with the implicit grant of financial rewards to people who stuck with them through thick and thin.

Expectations can morph into dogmatic rules of governance that are incapable of adapting to changing market circumstances and threatening external innovations (Nokia, the original cell phone giant, is a case in point). A culture once fully emerged and immersed into the very fabric of a firm's activity can become a bulwark against progress, a defender of the status quo, or a bottomless pit of inertia that cannot be overcome by necessary forces (unionized workplaces are a good example). The firm's leadership team is also prone to the same propensity toward dogmatic strictures. Blind spots and confirmation bias may take hold unbeknown to decision makers. Past successes and current cash flow performance create a sense of self-validation for management's past strategic choices. Such self-validation is inherently cultural in execution, and hence, hard to question or doubt.

Business expansion is another potential source of friction between expectations and conformity. Every business management book out there warns its readers about the dangers of losing one's culture when expansion is too rapid. Rapid expansions imply the hiring of more people more often and under less controlled conditions. Such an influx of new blood carries with it the very real risk of cultural infection, or worse, obliteration. It is a simple thing to indoctrinate a handful of people and monitor their cultural fit in the first few weeks. It is radically more difficult to achieve uniformity of cultural indoctrination when dealing with dozens or hundreds of new people across many locations.

There is no magic formula to stop these conflicts from flaring up. The prudent leader will, as a matter of course, pay close attention to the vibes of the place and keep his finger on the pulse of the organization. When hard decisions must be made with attending cultural clashes, the leaders are advised to discuss the matter with staff well ahead of their rollout. Communications, proactive and bidirectional, are always encouraged as a principal tool of reaction control. By contrast, unilateral impositions of decisions will always cause rumbles within the firm. They may lead to general discontent, stagnation, or rage, whose intensity will act as an amplifier of people's frustrations. The end result can be ugly: loss of productivity, higher staff turnovers, sabotage, or even mutiny.

THE VISION

Turning Aspiration into Inspiration

One cannot speak of culture without first addressing the vision, which implies, among other things, the innovator's role in it. Vision is one of those formless, ethereal concepts that are familiar to everyone yet grasped by few. It is often confounded with other fleeting words like dream, mission, strategy, or value proposition. In fact, vision is an element of the organizing concept as illustrated in Figure 8.1.

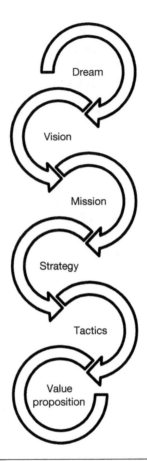

Figure 8.1   The vision: one of six components of an organizing principle

All of these terms have a place in our discussion as we will see shortly. However, it is essential to clarify what they each mean in our context. The dream is the source of all aspirations. It is a beacon, a brilliant light that points the way to a mind searching for a destination out of a barren landscape. The dream floats above the mundane, the trivial, and the pragmatic; unshackled from the bounds of reality, it thrives on its own existential plane oblivious to negativity and aspersions alike. The dream, in other words, gives form to the aspiration germinating in the heart of the innovator.

A dream is useless without a connection back to reality. This connection is the vision, which turns aspiration into inspiration. The vision is anchored to the real world. The vision is aware of the world's boundaries yet sees a path to pushing them or obliterating them outright. The vision outlines what the innovator's world will be when it has become reality. It is, in a sense, the legacy that will remain once the innovator has gone. It is the vision that impels a person to persevere against all odds that may be encountered on the innovation journey. It is the *thymos*[2] that sustains the firm in times of upheaval. The vision is the imprint of the innovator upon the firm. It is the message that calls forth a new reality, expressed in words that will resonate unapologetically with certain people who buy into this vision. This vision sets the end point of the business journey—the destination of the pirate ship's voyage. It illuminates what success will look like when you finally get there. It is the rallying cry of the crew desiring to manifest through actions what they aspire to achieve in will.

The vision also helps the innovator articulate what the values will be that will power the ship. The vision and the values exist independently of each other; yet, as they come together in mutually reinforcing symbiosis, they blossom into the genesis of the culture of the firm. The vision becomes the great unifier of the people toward the same goals, the same objectives, and the same destination. It is the common thread that unifies the people's individual needs into a beautiful tapestry. But it will invariably sow the seeds of expectations in the fertile minds of people on board this ship; with the darker side to appear when they are broken, ignored, dismissed, or betrayed. Indeed, nothing is more damaging to the survivability of a firm whose leadership acts in contradiction with the founding vision.

While the vision acts as a bulwark against the quirks of time or the assaults of competition, it should be sufficiently malleable to admit tweaks and adjustments when circumstances dictate. The seascape may change dramatically as the ship sails across new horizons. The ship itself may need repairs, improvements, or even replacement in order to continue on. The crew's skills may need adjusting in many ways. Whatever the causes, it behooves the innovator to remain attentive to the appearance of dichotomy between vision and opportunity. At times, a wholesale recasting of the vision may be needed (the history of the giant 3M is a sublime example of the evolution of a firm's vision across time).

The Poisoned Chalice

A stalwart vision is profoundly empowering for the innovator, the leadership team, the crew, and even the firm. It possesses a harmonizing quality that is wondrous to managers and leaders alike. It is easy to get wrapped up in the romance of its ideals to the point where people giddily drink the proverbial corporate Kool-Aid. At that point, the vision stops being a helping factor and transforms instead into a roadblock. The changing seascape could signify seminal changes to reality, but receive a cold reception in defense of the vision's assumed invincibility. The vision cannot be allowed to reign supreme, impervious to the evolving character of the outside world. It is one thing to believe in one's vision; it is an altogether stupid and deadly thing to staunchly cling to it against the throes of a new reality. The very passage of time, the ultimate arbiter of all things novel and obsolete, may suffice to erode the essence of your vision to the point of nothingness.

Do not fall prey to romanticizing the nobility of your vision.

The onus is on the innovator, surrounded by the firm's leadership team, to remain vigilant at all times lest reality suddenly turns around to bite. Once again, the call for facing reality head on without fear and with full awareness of one's confirmation biases is the best policy. Foster a discussion framework that encourages frank opinions, divergent views, and doubting mindsets. If you know that your vision is right for a set of conflicting externalities, do not fear confrontation, but stand upon the shoulders of that vision to make your case. But if the opposite occurs and you realize that the vision is antiquated, orphaned, or crippled, have the courage to allow reality to prevail and your vision to evolve.

There are a number of antidotes available in the management marketplace to neutralize the poisonous effects of a persistent Kool-Aid. The first one is to foster an environment that encourages frank exchanges and respect of differing opinions. In the clash between reality and vision, faith is not enough. The flattery that accompanies a rigid ideological structure is detrimental to an idea ecology that rejects arbitrary rejections. Dissent that is rooted in observed facts must be permitted to flourish—if only to flush out the arguments defending the *status quo*. What does it say of a vision whose belief system cannot withstand questions regarding its legitimacy lest it falls apart. Dissent will spring from within when this is clearly detectable to the crew. It will also flow from without, through the agency of new hires, which constitutes another antidote. This is where diversity can make a seminal impact. But not just any kind of diversity dictated by arbitrary edicts to conform to the law; the kind that transpires through a multiplicity of skill sets (technical and relational) that have been gained in other industries. It is of a kind that emanates from a wide spectrum of ages, talents, motivations, and life experiences. The kind, in other words, that shuns uniforms, uniform job descriptions, and uniformity of emotional dispositions. There remains, of course, an essential expectation that new hires will fit the culture of the place. But those expectations should not lead to a proclivity for clones of the crew, nor drones to authority.

In the arena where ideas are admitted, it is imperative that the judgment of their respective merits be made strictly from the message they convey without regard to the messengers. A brilliant manager can come up with a stupid idea just as easily as a dumb-as-a-post worker can stumble across an inspiring thought. People must be respected and their contributions to a debate encouraged and rewarded. In the end, the best idea is the one that is best *for the firm*. There should be no winner or loser from such a debate for it is their very input that helps sort out the diamonds from the dirt.

The True Master of Your Vision

One may wax lyrical about a poignant vision, but the fact remains that the vision is not truly mastered by its originator. As long as the firm has not passed the break-even point *and* proven itself sustainably profitable in the eyes of its shareholders, the vision is subservient to the cash flow giant. Let us repeat this plainly:

> *Your vision can drive when it is driving profits. Until then, cash flow rules.*

The reader may take offense to this suggestion that cash should take precedence over vision. On the face of it, this order of priorities would seem contrary to the usefulness of a guiding vision. The vision is an *essential* ingredient of a successful business venture. It is what will sustain the firm in tough times and keep it honest with itself in good times. The preeminence of money cannot, on the other hand, be relegated to a supporting role. All else being equal, no firm can survive—let alone thrive—in the long run without making money. Money is what nourishes and nurtures a vision. Without it, no amount of persuading, cheering, or grandiose pronouncement can expect to see the light of day. This reality, harsh though it may be, is encapsulated in Figure 8.2.

In the early days of a business, there is no choice between vision integrity and revenue generation. Unless a deal threatens the very purpose of a business, it is best to compromise on the vision to secure the precious revenues. This mortal choice is rare; in most instances, the compromise will not nullify the purity of the vision. It will merely set it aside temporarily to obtain its survival to fight

Financial state	Survival	Subsistence	Affluence	Freedom
Cash flow	Negative	Break-even	Profitable	Abundance
Decisions by	Necessity	Buyer	Shareholders	Vision

Figure 8.2   Calling the shots: the ability of a vision to dictate to the business is directly proportional to the business's cash pile—no money, no say by the vision, save perhaps a few words to convince the few braves to fund it until it grows up into a real force

another day. If the vision cannot withstand a compromise, chances are it is better suited to a nonprofit than a corporate experiment.

> *Remember that the prime objective of the innovation journey is to achieve a sustainably profitable business from the innovation. You are not getting paid to believe in the power of your dreams; you are getting funded to create a commercial asset that will generate future returns on investment.*

Inspiration into Motivation

A business cannot thrive on inspiration alone. It must find the motivation to board the ship and set sail with determination. In other words, it needs a *mission* to turn inspiration into that motivation. Whereas the vision anchors the dream, the mission is the cord that tethers it to a grounded reality. The mission qualifies and quantifies the vision's end game. It determines how the vision's success will be gauged. It instructs the firm on how to make the vision a reality. For instance, say the dream is to rid the world of hydrocarbons (go big or go home, eh!). The vision is to create a company that will power the world from the sun. The mission is to develop the technologies to harness the sun's power and deploy it far and wide across the planet. The mission is necessarily grounded in what's tangible to make the vision a reality. It addresses the nature of the journey that is about to be undertaken; the means of carrying out the journey; the kinds of targets that will be attacked; and hints at the types of equipment, provisions, and crew skills that will be required to get things going. In business terms, the mission tells a firm what markets will be attacked with what solutions (at the exclusion of all other markets and solutions), what scales will be called for, what competitors will be engaged (and which will not), and finally, what will be the lay of the land at the final destination.

Motivation into Actions

Next on the agenda is the *strategy*, which is the plan devised to put the mission in motion. The strategy goes one step deeper into the execution weeds. The key word is *plan*. The strategy is, in effect, a detailed plan to orchestrate the resources, budgets, schedules, and major paths across which the mission will take form. The strategy breaks the work down into *discrete work units* and then sets out the targets and the metrics to achieve them. The strategy defines up front what is to be included and excluded from the endeavor. The strategy defines the overall hierarchy, the decision-making principles, the conflict-resolution mechanics, and the accountability assignments for crews and for the work. The major paths will often include the components: technology development, production planning, supply chain, commercialization, financing, and management. In effect, the strategy translates into actionable pieces the various TRL elements developed in Part 1 of this book.

The heart of a potent and *realistic* strategy exploits the strengths of the organization while simultaneously neutering the organization's weaknesses. Most readers will be familiar with SWOT analysis, which is a common analytical tool of the management consulting set for gauging a firm's prowess. The tool enumerates and quantifies the strengths, weaknesses, opportunities, and threats (hence the acronym SWOT) that exist today and possibly tomorrow within an organization.[3] The strengths are bankable assets that can be deployed right now to benefit the strategy. The weaknesses must be avoided through judicious tactical choices, mitigated through immediate hiring/consulting, or planned for future corrective actions. The strategy itself may become a liability or a weakness to the organization if it is not realistically achievable either because it makes too many assumptions that are unlikely to be correct or timely or because it sets goals and objectives that are simply impossible to achieve within the known SWOT profile of the firm. This last point is frequently overlooked by sales and/ or marketing groups who set out aggressive quotas to instill an extra oomph into the spirit of competition between the sales staff—only to end up creating an environment where success means gaming the system through cheats and deception if need be.[4]

> *No strategy can succeed if it is disconnected from the constraints of the reality in which it is meant to unfold.*

Tied to the strategy are the *tactics*, which are the mechanics and mechanisms required to carry out the tasks and activities being called out by the discrete work units. Processes, procedures, methods, tools, templates, and personnel assignments are part and parcel of the tactics. A simple way to distinguish between strategy (why, what) and tactics (who, when, how) is to look at strategy as the *head* and tactics as the *hands*. Effectively, a *tactic* is a unit transformation process pursuant to Figure 4.7.

Actions into Results

Finally, we come to the concept of *value proposition* sitting at the bottom of the organizing concept from Figure 8.1. The proposition differs from the other five in one particular way: it is the only one that is oriented externally, toward potential buyers. The other five components are turned inward and are explicitly geared toward the firm and its employees. One can go a step further by restricting the public domain to the value proposition. Indeed, given the motivational and strategic importance of the dream, vision, mission, strategy, and tactics to the overall success of the business, it may be best for the innovator to keep them close to the vest away from the public.

The value proposition is a statement, concise and succinct, of the reasons why a buyer should buy your product at the exclusion of others. It is not a sales pitch, mind you, meant to extoll the virtues of a product. The value proposition extolls the benefits to the buyer. It speaks directly to the needs and pains of the buyer. The measure of the value, and indeed, its meaning, is entirely controlled by the buyer. It may be a lower cost, but it could just as well be a higher operating reliability. What is critical is to articulate this value in terms that resonate with the buyer. And whatever that value turns out to be, your value proposition should be able to deliver at least a 20% increase in that value *as perceived by the buyer*. At this juncture, a warning is timely to the reader who promotes the *newness* of his product as the primary measure of value. As we mentioned in Chapters 1 and 2, being new is usually *not* seen as a viable benefit by existing buyers. The buyer's experience will instead push him to view anything new as too risky. His immediate reflex will be to wait until someone else tries it out first. Only when the product is proven will he then reconsider his initial hesitation.

LAST WORDS FROM OUR SPONSOR

The Ruler Returns

There are four lessons that the reader should take away from this chapter:

- *Lesson 1*—The firm will always evolve a culture from within given enough time
- *Lesson 2*—The values of the innovator will flow through the organization via the culture that he instills in it from his actions
- *Lesson 3*—When the culture from within aligns with the culture from the top, the firm will be able to face whatever comes its way
- *Lesson 4*—When alignment fails, the firm could fail under the slightest of outside provocations

To these lessons we add an alternate interpretation to the organizing principle of Figure 8.1. As long as a firm has not reached sustainable profitability (milestone 3 in Figure 8.2), Figure 8.1 reads like Figure 8.3. The vision is nothing more than being able to stay in business while the mission is to generate revenues to keep the doors opened. When the vision conflicts with revenue generation, ask yourself if staying faithful to it is worth losing the business or if

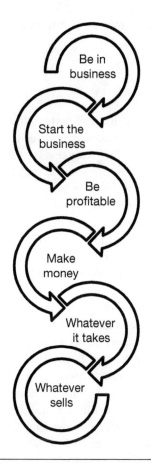

Figure 8.3   A start-up's vision reality: the flip side of having no money is the ascendency of the profit motive over the philosophical presumptions of the vision

you'd be better off taking the money now to have another day to fight to make the vision a reality.

To Be or Not to Be

As long as the firm is not profitable, that is the true nature of the vision. Once it turns the corner, the vision can commence its ascendancy over the future of the firm. If the vision is right, the market will send you the signals to that effect. If it is not right, the market will tell you via the silence of the order lines. Ultimately, it is the world that will sit in judgment over the rightfulness of your vision. The world will not change to fit your vision of it; it is you who must change the vision to adapt to the world.

NOTES

1. The reader may learn with surprise that pirates were the most advanced form of democratic organizations during the golden era (the 16–18th centuries). Crews chose their captains by a vote, wrote out the engagement contract (bounty divisions, work conditions, punishments, limits of the captain's power), and freely followed their captain *as long as he lived up to the expectations of the crew*. The crew could replace a captain at will by voting in a new one. Compare these conditions to the reality of the Royal British Navy of the time where officers had absolute powers over the life and death of their crews, who were treated as nothing more than slaves. See *Pirates: The Complete History from 1300 BC to the Present Day* by Angus Konstam.

2. Plato described *thymos* as the part of the soul comprising pride, indignation, shame, and the need for recognition. *Thymotic* impulses are among the most powerful to power a need to act.

3. The literature on the subject is profuse. Virtually all business books dealing with corporate structures, marketing and sales strategies, business plan development, or corporate strategy will include a section on strengths, weaknesses, opportunities, and threats (SWOT).

4. This scenario played out exactly as described in late 2016 when the American bank Wells Fargo was discovered with millions of bogus accounts created by an army of employees who were laboring under a top-down imposed hard-driving sales culture mandating a 10 to 1 product sale per customer when the industry average was 2.7. These quotas were realistically impossible, as everyone knew. So, employees were left with a choice between cheating and gaming the system illegally, or facing management scorn and possible firing.

9

THE SECOND CUSTOMER

Show me the money.

YOU ARE IN BUSINESS NOW

Finish What You Started

We have addressed the matter of management and explored the ramifications of the innovator's cultural tendencies, which laid the foundation of the business. It is time to put them both to work and start making some real money. We concluded Chapter 5 with a purchase order in hand from the all-important first customer—now we need more. The transition from first to second customer marks a seminal moment in the innovation's journey. Up till now, what has been an obsessive product focus for the innovator must be switched to an asset perspective. The transition time also marks the end of the technology development process. Critically, this transition can only start when the product was proven successful *in the eyes of the first customer*; otherwise, something is not right and must be fixed *immediately*. The urgency of the corrective action cannot be overstated since it would be folly to launch the product rollout while simultaneously working to fix what must be fixed. The product rollout is a stressful time for the innovator, the team, and the business. The last thing they need is to have to deal with the additional stress of problem remediation.

The asset perspective comes into full force in preparation for the product rollout. The immediate objective of the product rollout is to get to the breakeven point as soon as possible (recall Figure 3.2). Getting to that point depends entirely on the success of the product rollout, which depends on a flawless implementation of the plans that were addressed in Chapter 5 (see *Production Readiness* and *Asset Readiness*). These plans will be incarnated into business functions and integrated into a finely tuned framework simultaneously. For instance, the physical and information technology infrastructures are erected; the departments are staffed and activated; supply chain contracts are signed; marketing and sales materials are completed, printed, and uploaded to the website; staff training is carried out; satellite offices are opened; system tests of the machinery, computer systems, digital networks, and Cloud location are completed. Quality assurance (QA) processes are put in place at this time while minimum inventory levels are acquired and stacked. Mundane processes such as packaging and preservation are put at the ready. Financing is secured for the ramp-up period. Intellectual property (IP) applications are monitored (patents, trademarks, copyrights, etc.). The business is made ready to ensure that the second sale is an immediate success.

Nucleation

The other asset activity that requires completion prior to product rollout is nucleation (discussed in Chapter 4). Recall that this process numerically models the theoretical state of the asset. The datum set obtained from nucleation is essential to the innovator for the pursuit of continual improvements and to the buyer for his pursuit of long-term returns on investment. The scope of a nucleation is, obviously, a function of the complexity of the product. When the product is a component, the triple nucleation could, for example, be limited to a spreadsheet file. A complex installation (say a wind turbine) will yield a massive amount of data that can only be managed effectively within a comprehensive digital framework.

The importance of nucleation manifests itself when user data are gathered in real time by the business (see *Product Data* in Chapter 5) to quantify the product's operational performance. The *product data* convey the real-time behavior of the product in the form of a performance envelope, failure modes and rates, reliability predictors, maintenance requirements, function deficiencies, software problems, and *cost of ownership* metrics. The data tie right back to the *nucleation information* from which corrective actions, component improvements, configuration changes, documentation changes, and future version objectives are inferred by the innovator.

DIFFUSION STRATEGY

The Art of Putting Out the Word

The product rollout marks a seminal moment in the life of the innovator; all the hopes, dreams, expectations, visions of riches, and sense of vindication are at their peak. The work is done, the stage is set, the curtain will soon rise, and the rubber is about to meet the road. There is nothing left to do but await the acclaim (or condemnation) of the audience—or is there?

As a matter of fact, product rollout is but the end of an information campaign that will have started weeks before. The campaign is meant to *diffuse* information far and wide about the new product. This diffusion lets the world know about the innovator's new offering, educates the intended buyers on its merits, and creates the buzz to stimulate these buyers to await the actual rollout with excitement. Marketing campaigns are unique to each product; there is no magic bullet or universal recipe (and is thus beyond the scope of this book).[1] Our focus will instead be placed on ways of maximizing diffusion without breaking the bank, which should commence during technology readiness level (TRL) 7 and be implemented within the organization by the end of TRL 9.

The Message

The first and quintessential element of the diffusion endeavor is the message initiated in TRL 7. It must be scripted before anything else is put out in the public domain. *The message precedes everything else.* It must be succinct, yet meaningful. Whatever the intent, it must carry. Intent must permeate *everything* within the marketing and sales strategies. The message is the foundation for all content development, including the scientific articles. It will be the *elevator pitch* for every sales rep from this moment forward.

The Presentation

The second cornerstone of a diffusion strategy concerns the presentation, which is initiated in TRL 8. The sum of the brochures, literature, articles, publications, postings, and website contents must be aligned uniformly and homogeneously. *Whatever claim is made in one place, it must be written in the same exact way everywhere else.* Other prescriptions include:

- *Never* make claims that cannot be substantiated. State the truth or say nothing at all.
- *Never* make claims that are wishy-washy, misleading, or unverifiable. For example: *this gadget will make your life easier compared to our competitor's product.* Pray tell, how can you possibly quantify this?
- Be consistent. Use the same expressions, the same terminology, the same abbreviations, and the same message across the board. Do not introduce terms and notions in one place that are never to be used again elsewhere.
- Consistency also applies to colors, fonts, and presentation schema. The presentation template must be the same across all media formats and

recognizable at once. Keep the color scheme simple (three colors max, except in technical charts).

- *Be direct.* Fluff, bland words, and digital filler material add no value to the contents and only corrode the message. Use words concisely without complex sentence structures or esoteric meanings. Maximize your use of terms and expressions that are standard in the target industry. Spell out all acronyms and abbreviations without exception and provide a link to your terminology dictionary for proprietary expressions and sector-specific language.
- Do not state the obvious or overemphasize what is widely known in the target industry. Avoid boring expressions like *best in class, world class, category killer, cost effective,* and *one-stop shop* to name but a few; these and other like expressions have lost all measure of textual validity from an excess of exposure.
- Do not address the competition by name or product brand. Do not say anything negative about competing solutions. Focus instead on the tangible benefits of your product.
- Keep the presentation clear (visually and textually). Be brief with words and generous with images, graphics, charts, and pictures.
- Make all printed material freely available from the website. But require that downloaders provide their contact information first.
- Copyright everything all the time.
- Include on all materials (printed and online) a single contact name for questions and enquiries. This contact should be a person rather than a department (johndoe@firm.com instead of sales@firm.com).
- Emphasize digital downloads over printed materials. The former is free; the latter, costly.
- Make the business cards conform to the color and presentation scheme found in the published materials.
- *Translate professionally.* Saving money on translation will cost you credibility if the results are nonsensical. It is better to stick to English rather than come up with comical, embarrassing, or humiliating *Engrish*.

The Wonders of Free Speech

Large companies have the luxury of throwing money at a marketing campaign. That blessing can turn into a curse (*New Coke,* for example) since money is no guarantor of success in generating sales. A successful marketing campaign is achievable on a tight budget and should begin in the early days of TRL 9. Thanks to social media, the innovator has access to a multitude of platforms on which to release information freely in order to reach a wide audience. The trick is in knowing which one to use, what tone to strike, and what not to say or do.

Diffusion can start small by targeting trade magazines, technical journals, and industry association newsletters/newspapers. These types of publications are always looking for novel contents and will be willing partners to do write-ups on what's new and exciting. Such coverage is free to the innovator and has the advantage of reaching a prescreened audience. Throw in a paid quarter-, half-, or full-page advertisement and the editor will doubly embrace the article. In a similar vein, trade publications also like to feature success stories on people and businesses. Offer your own story without reserve! This is one instance when tooting one's own horn is entirely acceptable. When the product has a meaningful technological or scientific aspect, it could be beneficial to expand its exposure through academic and scientific publications, too. Keep in mind, however, that these publications are usually peer reviewed, which implies much longer review cycles (weeks or months, compared to days for the previous kinds of publications). The white paper approach is quite efficient as it lends itself to putting up the article on the innovator's website and other venues like conferences and trade shows.

Trade shows are the natural segue to the budgeted marketing strategy. Conferences, trade shows, and industry powwows can be valunomic diffusion channels. The best option is always to be a presenter or speaker—either about the product or on the issue solved by it. In both cases, keep the presentation technical and abstain from turning it into a sales pitch (you will lose the audience's interest in three blinks of an eye). By emphasizing the technical aspects, you allow the audience to come to its own conclusions on the viability and desirability of the product. It is better to be the engaging engineer extolling the mechanics of the machine than the predictable slick salesman whose words fall on deaf ears. Just make sure that the engineer is not socially challenged and is well practiced in the art of public speaking.

What about exhibitor booths? These can add considerable costs to the escapade. If you do not have a fully functional, sales-ready product, don't go that route, lest you are forced to make unsubstantiated claims; in which case, the whole thing will come across as vapid sales pitching. If the product is on hand, make sure that the literature you give out is the final version. Make sure that the website is up, fully aligned with the conference handouts, and has a live tie-in with what's going on during the conference. Finally, when you cannot avoid the exhibitor booth, make sure that you stand out. Wear unapologetically noticeable uniforms and find a socially acceptable way to create a line up to your booth.

The website is essential to the diffusion process *and access is free*. It is, by default, the entry portal for the world into yours. Presentation is everything. The visuals must be clean and pleasing to the eye. Navigation must be intuitive, logical, and bug free. Minimize text and maximize images; never describe in text what you can animate and narrate. The effective website presents the product with a scarcity of words buttressed by a plethora of images and a few animations. Use recorded video files *only* when professionally produced. Otherwise, it will come across as an amateurish, cheap, and done-in-the-basement improvisation. 3-D animations can be created at a fraction of the cost and presented in realistic rendering that adds flair to the viewing experience.

PRODUCT ROLLOUT

The Sales Team

Product rollout must be carried out by the sales team. The marketing team will, of course, be intimately involved in the creation of the development of the message, the marketing campaign, and the orchestration of the product rollout event; nevertheless, the onus for its public unveiling rests solely with the sales team. The sales team will make or break the rollout (more than all the glitz, cocktails, video streams, and social media blitzes).

The ramifications of this awesome responsibility lay at the feet of the innovator (acting as business manager by now). In practical terms, this means getting the sales group ramped up during TRL 8 as follows:

- *Training*—Sales personnel must be thoroughly educated on the design, operations, usage, and limits of the product. Salespeople must understand the product inside out at the functional level. They must be able to explain its intricacies to a novice buyer along with the resulting justifications for its preference over the competition.
- *Indoctrination*—Sales personnel must believe in the product unconditionally.[2] The dubious, the doubtful, and the merely interested must be weeded out from the outset. The business cannot afford the risk of unleashing such a person upon a virgin market audience.
- *Awareness*—Whereas training speaks to the product itself, the education of sales personnel speaks to the diffusion materials discussed previously. They must be fully cognizant of the publications that are available (printed and posted), their contents, and their location.
- *Relations*—Each member of the sales team must understand the organizational structure of the business, who's who in the zoo, and what mechanics and mechanisms exist to connect an outside person to the pertinent departments within. This knowledge is especially critical in the realm of product data where user-generated data are captured by

the business. The critical departments and points of contacts will always include the sales department, the customer help desk, the commercial group (payments, invoices, and warranties), the product documentation group, the spare parts group, the training group, and the after-sales group.

- *Advocacy*—Sales personnel are the bridge between customers and the business. They represent the first line of defense *for customers* when an issue arises. In such instances, the pertinent salesperson should become the sole point of contact for the buyer in his dealings with the business. Recall from Chapter 5 the importance of doing everything to ensure the product's success *in the buyer's eyes*. The best way to solve a customer's problem is to empower sales personnel to drill down the organization to get to the answer.

Before the Premiere

The very last step leading to the actual product rollout is the full dress rehearsal for the marketing and sales teams, which will happen at the end of TRL 9. This rehearsal should take place in the days prior to opening night. The aim is to run both teams through various event scenarios such as: questions and queries from would-be buyers, first contacts between sales and buyer, on-the-spot sale and customer registration, requests for later demonstration, connecting the customer to the business (see advocacy), user problem with a defective product (see advocacy), quick retrieval of publications, guiding a customer on the website, etc. The objective of these hypothetical scenarios is to uncover problems (with the processes, the systems, or the personnel) and fix them. Suffice it to say, no rollout should ever proceed if problems remain.

Opening Night

Time to raise the curtain! The rollout event will take whatever form is deemed best by the marketing group. It could be a big media event, an open house with selected guests, or a simple visit of one potential customer by one salesperson. Whatever the form, the following pieces of advice may come in handy to everyone involved in the momentous event:

- *You will not sell anything that day*—This will usually be the case when the product is the *integrated* type and destined to non-retail clients. What matters to the team is to drum up interest from would-be customers and schedule follow-up meetings with these customers to close the sale.
- *Be prepared*—If you sell, then you must be prepared to make the sale successful *immediately*. That means having enough stock on hand to meet

demand, training the customer on the spot if required, carrying out the registration process on the spot, and doing all the other things that flow from the sale.

- *Always get contact information*—When the rollout is a public event (a place or online), the sales team must focus on generating interest and getting contact information from potential customers. Letting people roam the floor without at least getting their business cards is a waste of time and money.
- *Always follow up*—In the days following the event, each business card must be followed up with a call by the sales team. The sooner the better—no later than five business days after the show ended.
- *Always follow through*—If a salesperson happens to make a promise or a commitment to someone during the rollout event, it is imperative that the individual delivers on that promise or commitment, and soon—this means no later than five business days after the event.

SUPPLY CHAINS

Vital Plumbing

The criticality of being able to complete the sale in the early days of the rollout is *essential*. Following through on the sale implies that all departments and business functions of the firm are in place, operational, and ready to spring into action. One of these functions is supply chain management, whose inner workings are performed during TRL 8 and 9. It is the opposite of sexy and is often overlooked by eager innovators. Supply chain management is a study into the minutia of sub-minutia—a grinder of details, decisions, and prescriptions that make up the vital sausage that feeds your production. A supply chain embodies everything that is empirical, prosaic, and realistic. It thrives on a voluminous library of specifications covering the entire gamut of existence of the bit or piece that you buy. Logistics is always in the background, ready to spring to the fore when it was neglected by the procurement process. Simple things like custom forms, factory inspection reports, minimum shipping quantities, raw material sourcing, metal composition, preservation requirements of a wet part, lifting and handling, and calibration records are but a sample of the multitude of information pieces that will be transacted between the innovator's firm and a vendor; not to mention price, payment terms, holdback terms, warranty clauses, shipping and handling, and conflict resolutions. So, what is the point of all this? Supply chains require diligent attention by all parties involved. Improvisation is a death wish. The scale of the task is often misread by beginners who would rather deal with everything that is visionary, glamorous, and inspirational to the business. Your innovation may one day change the world, but to get there, you need to look after your plumbing first. It's messy, but it's inevitable.

The Rule of the Written Word

One may wax eloquently about the vision, the mission, or the objectives of the innovation. Vendors and suppliers may buy into your inspiring business model and even volunteer to help you along the way. However, when all is said and done, your suppliers and vendors are in it to make money first (just like you). No vendor will ever willingly sacrifice its financial wellbeing to serve your greater purpose. If the vendor can't make money or anticipates losing money in the long run, he will have zero motivation to do right by you. Even when the terms of a contract are entirely in your favor, they offer little solace if the vendor decides to cut his losses and see you in court rather than continue to lose money. You may yet prevail in the eyes of the law, but at the cost of endangering your own financial position.

A happy vendor will move heaven and earth to help you get out of a bind. A forlorn vendor will shun you like the plague.

Key Processes

The best policy to adopt by the innovator is one that will create a win-win situation for all parties involved. The onus is on the innovator to create a business framework that promotes the success of the vendors. If your sole driver is to buy the cheapest there is, you will get exactly what you bought: the lowest value on offer (with zero margin for error). If you are genuinely interested in nurturing a strong commercial relationship with a vendor, you end up cementing a foundation that will resist tremors in the marketplace when they shake the industry. Getting there calls forth these key elements:

- *You get what you negotiate, not what you deserve*[3]—The reader may have seen this statement in airplane brochures; it is true, pure and simple. Parties to a commercial transaction, whether it be a one-time deal or a long-term standing order, seek to extract as much value from the relationship as possible (which usually implies profit maximization in one form or another). It is not about fairness or righteousness or even sharing in your vision; it is about maximizing each side's benefits (which could be motivated, for example, by the need to keep the shop open in lean times).
- *The written word rules, governs, and adjudicates (judge, jury, and executioner, if you prefer)*—What is written is what gets done. If it is not

written, for whatever reason, it does not exist. If you missed it the first time around, try to get an amendment in. For contracts as well as standard terms and conditions, consult a lawyer if they are new to you; do not skimp on this cost, as the savings will be obliterated in the future should something go wrong and find you on the hook.

- *Technical prescriptions are critical*—These could be fabrication drawings, datasheets, scope of supply, inspection requirements, etc. If you do not know what is needed, ask the vendor for an example; he or she will be most happy to help you put in an order. If you create a template from the vendor's example, make sure to eliminate their logo and change the document's properties in the property pop-up menu with your information.

- *You get what you inspect, not what you expect*—Vendor relationships take time to nurture and trust. Until such time when you can fully trust the quality and consistency of the vendor's deliverables, you will need to put in place an inspection, verification, and validation (IV&V) program to vet what you buy from vendors. Things like shop inspections, final acceptance testing, incoming inspections, dimensional checks, performance runs, and calibration measurements may be required—likewise for the paperwork, documents, and datasets that accompany the deliverables. The scale of the IV&V program is a function of the complexity of the part counts in your product. Do not improvise yourself into this role in the name of cost savings. A single screwup can cost you many times the salary of a production specialist. The best policy is simple: hire a competent production professional from the get-go and give him or her the mandate to set this IV&V program as his or her first priority.

- *Document management*—The accumulation of datum sets never ends. These sets include the engineering documents, the procurement specifications, the purchase orders, the inspection reports, bills of lading, certification records, shipping manifests, custom clearances, operating manuals, troubleshooting software, calibration charts, etc. The list can go on *indefinitely*. Many companies in the start-up stage fail to anticipate the magnitude of the task and imagine that they can muddle through with spreadsheet lists. That is a big mistake. Document management must be planned and implemented before the first product is ever sold. It will require industrial-strength software to handle the inevitable scaling up that will ensue. The system must be engineered through and through as a *functional procedure* that is internal to the firm's operations.

- *Identification system*—In tandem with document management, the innovator must also engineer a system for naming and numbering every piece of information that will be transacted over time (including parts, documents, software, and audio/video files, to name a few). The part numbering system must be able to handle future revisions, backward and forward effectivity, and obsolete and outdated parts. And, it must be able to expand over time to capture new products and new configurations. Finally, the naming system (or convention) should be accompanied by a master lexicon of acronyms, abbreviations, and custom definitions, along with correct translations when applicable. Once again, the innovator will be best served by hiring the right expertise rather than improvising himself into this role. The subject can be surprisingly complex and obscure.

The Right Way to Getting Things Done Right

Next on the list of setup priorities is the matter of quality. Quality is as much a mindset as it is a process. It is an emergent feature of any unit transformation process (UTP), constructed upon the overarching goal of doing things right the first time within acceptable limits. That is the very essence of *quality* and the interpretation that avoids defining it as a *noumenon*. But quality does not follow merely from publishing a quality management plan or putting out mounds of paper to describe the countless elements of a QA program after the other plans discussed in Chapter 5 are developed. There is no such thing as achieving quality through inspections and checklists. *You cannot inspect quality into a product.* After-the-fact inspections and verifications only confirm what is there and what is absent.

Quality must be engineered into every function of the business as an input variable *from the outset*. A *valunomic* QA program need not be a ponderous document that by its very development could overwhelm the budding business. It only needs to be pursuant to the UTP described in Chapter 4. If the company is a small start-up with no prior experience in this field, there is every possibility to end up with a bulky, ponderous quality management system that looks good on paper but fails to meet the actual needs of the business. One may aspire to master the finer art of GE's Six Sigma methodology, Toyota's production system, or the more prosaic ISO 9001 quality philosophy. One may believe in the potency of just-in-time manufacturing, just-in-time inventory, lean manufacturing, and Kanban scheduling, to name but a few. However, these complex management systems, while fine in theory, demand a level of organizational sophistication that will rarely be available to emerging firms.

The prudent implementation of a quality-delivery environment is best carried out in baby steps, taking care to master each step involved in a set of interconnected UTPs. Advanced methodologies require more time, effort, and funding—beyond what the innovator can deploy effectively.

Going Global

International supply chains are possible even for the smallest of start-ups, especially in the procurement of commodities. But going global is no panacea. The price discrepancies that occur with foreign suppliers contain hidden transaction costs that can easily wipe out any initial cost benefit. The previous caution that you *get what you inspect, not what you expect* is especially poignant when one is forced to have faith in the internal QA processes of a vendor on the other side of the planet. If the supply agreement requires the innovator to travel regularly to the foreign country, the cost of those trips can rapidly blow your budget (traveling from North America to China, for instance, will take at least three days when you consider acclimation and cost several thousand dollars per person, notwithstanding the opportunity costs of being away from the office). As with engineering and manufacturing, supply chains are easier to manage the closer they are to the innovator. The cost difference may be disadvantageous on a unit basis but still be cheaper in the overall transactional process. By all means, go global if you must, but do so knowing all of the cost drivers up front, not just the unit price list. Remember that the cheapest *now* always costs the most *later*. Before you go global, give some thoughts to the following common problem areas.

Import/Export

Going beyond your country's borders means dealing with import and export requirements that are dictated by government policies, international trade agreements, shipping limitations, weather, dishonesty and corruption, paperwork, and fees. This is a realm that is self-serving, complex, peculiar, and obtuse to outsiders. It behooves the innovator to enlist the help of a logistics professional to form an understanding of what will be involved once a deal with the foreign vendor is struck. *Do not wait until the deal is done to figure things out.* Indeed, the best time to do so is *before* any negotiations are undertaken with the would-be vendor.

Taxes and Duties

The logistics expert is to import/export issues as the accountant expert is to international taxes and duties. This realm is also a world unto itself, one that is impossible to navigate at first sail. The assistance of a professional who is well versed in the matter is essential to the global sourcing strategy espoused by the innovator. And, just like its logistic counterpart, it is best to iron out this aspect of the strategy *before* any deal is struck with a foreign vendor.

Currencies

The question of currency denomination is often overlooked by the novice supply chain player, who will assume that U.S. dollars will suffice to settle outstanding accounts. They may in some cases, but not always (European suppliers will be paid in euros, for example). Dealing with non-domestic currencies introduces a significant financial risk in the buyer-vendor relationship. Currencies are forever prone to fluctuations, which means that the innovator cannot make the mistake of assuming that his purchase costs will remain constant. Procurement deals that span months or even years will need to be buttressed against money market fluctuations. In other words, the innovator must now plan for financial hedging, which calls for yet another kind of expertise—this time in financial management.

IP Protection

This topic has already been covered in Chapter 3. The decision to buy from a foreign buyer must be made in full cognizance of the real IP protection afforded the innovator *in that jurisdiction*. Do not take this matter lightly and allow yourself to be blinded by the promise of rock-bottom pricing. If the trade-off is a high risk of intellectual pilferage or piracy, the deal should be avoided.

Regulatory Compliance

Knowing one's domestic regulatory requirements is straightforward and easily controlled. The mistake is to assume that the foreign vendor is equally cognizant of the implications of those requirements; an error that is compounded when the requirements call for independent inspections and testing by third parties accredited by those regulatory bodies. The situation is aggravated further when the foreign regulatory framework is completely different than the innovator's situation. In that instance, the qualifications of the vendor may simply be incongruous with those expected by the innovator. Whatever the case may be, the issue must be quantified and validated by the innovator before going too far down the negotiation road. Above all, the innovator must get the complete picture of the expectations, requirements, and obligations mandated by his regulatory bodies.

Cultural Sensitivity Training

Never assume that people and businesses from different parts of the world share your business values. Even within one's own country, regional differences may taint the business relationship in ways that could work against the innovator's aims. If a commercial relationship is to be built for the long term, the innovator will be expected to meet frequently with his prospective supply chain partner.

The best policy, and indeed the best commercial strategy, is to contact one's foreign affairs department and seek out help and training to educate oneself on the dominant characteristics of a given country's culture. Such training can be obtained in just a few hours often for free or minimal costs. Upon visiting the vendor for the first time, try to enlist the help of your government's diplomatic presence or hire a local handler who will be able to enlighten you on the finer points of cultural no-no's.

Lingua Franca

Obviously, language is an inevitable barrier to foreign exchanges. Once again, never assume your foreign associate speaks English or understands its nuances. When in doubt, hire a translator. When dealing with written communications: first develop a precise lexicon of acronyms, abbreviations, and custom definitions that will underscore the exchanges, then hire a professional translator to develop the corresponding glossary in the vendor's native language. At the same time, develop a set of templates to define the expected contents of the technical documentation that will be transacted between the two parties. This is especially important when the vendor's scope of work includes the creation of technical documents (say, a drawing or a functional specification for example).

Queue Priority

The balance of power between the innovator and an established foreign vendor tilts in favor of the latter. The effect is readily felt in each party's scheduling priorities. The innovator will want his orders fulfilled without delay. The vendor, on the otherhand, will look upon this new buyer merely as another order to be slotted into his existing production schedule. The two schedules may not accord, especially if the vendor prioritizes his clients as a function of volumes. Naturally, bigger orders will tend to accord precedence by the vendor over the smaller quantities of the innovator. Hence, the innovator is cautioned against putting undue faith in a contract with a vendor whose size dwarfs the innovator's.

Meetings

Distance inevitably makes in-person meetings, reviews, and paper exchanges more costly. Business trips from North America to Asia or Europe are week-long affairs (at the very least) and cost upward of $5,000 per person. Clearly, online venues will be the norm. The internet is awash with potent virtual meeting applications that are affordable, convenient, and easy to use—maximize your use of them. Alternatively, one could up the ante with virtual reality rooms that, although more costly than online meetings, remain significantly cheaper than business travel when you realize the elimination of lost productivity from travel, jet lag, fatigue, and workload disruptions. In fact, business travel should be the exception, not the rule.

Do not underestimate the adverse effects of time zones. The ideal supply chain will be comprised exclusively of vendors situated in the same time zone as the innovator. The effects are minimal within two time zones on either side of the innovator's meridian. Beyond this band, disruptive effects will start to appear in the form of scheduling difficulties. Four time zones will cut in half the meeting window inside normal working hours. Eight time zones effectively forces the innovator's organization to operate in overtime, which is tiring to personnel and can be unproductive. Once you get to the point where night and day have been switched, both the innovator and the vendor teams will begin to operate in a virtual 24-hour cycle that will kill productivity, quality, motivation, and profitability.

Paperless Transactions

Another bane of the distant vendor relationship arises when documentation is transacted on paper. The problem appears instantly when ink signatures are required. It is increasingly compounded when annotations by hand are offered—say a technical drawing containing several changes made by a review team. Dealing with paper is cumbersome in the best of times; it is downright counterproductive and profit-killing in the worst of times. The solution is simple: insist on paper transactions when the handwritten text is required by law or regulation. Otherwise, adopt a paperless framework, complete with markup software (for example, www.bluebeam.com) and digital signature systems.

Regulator Whims

The matter of regulatory expectations is quite often overlooked by the innovator and his distant vendor. Never assume that the vendor understands the idiosyncrasies of your ecosystem, nor assume that you understand the one underlying the vendor's business environment. As much as possible, both parties should spend some time together to explore the regulatory reality of each one to gain an understanding of what is expected, acceptable, and rejected.

THINGS ARE ROLLING. NOW WHAT?

The Future Starts Now

The business is now up and running, doing deals, selling, and generating long-awaited cash flow. The development journey is complete. The numerous milestones illustrated in Table 9.1 have been reached and the first sale is shown by

Table 9.1 Milestones of the innovation journey: the development program comprises a number of milestones (each one discussed in the chapter indicated by the number in parentheses). The first sale marks the end of TRL 9; it is shown as a star at the bottom right of the table

	TRL								
	1	2	3	4	5	6	7	8	9
IP search (3)				IP licensing (3)		Patent application (3)		Other IP application (3,6)	IP grants
Landscape basis	Product objectives and purpose (4)	Wish list (4)		Pick a winner (5)	Buyer and recovery criteria (5)	Pilot champion feedback (5)		Buyer success factors (5)	
TDP v1.0 (4)	TDP v2.0	TDP v3.0	TDP v4.0	TDP v5.0	TDP v6.0	TDP v7.0	TDP v8.0		
Burden of proof (1)	Champion search	Champion sign-up		Permit plan (3)	Permit applications (3)	Permit applications (3)	Permits and licenses (5)	Operating permits and licenses (6)	
8Q (2)			Specification document (4) v1	Specification document v2	Specification document v3	Specification document v4	Pilot test plan (5) and Specification document v5	Final Specification document v6	

Initial funding	New funding	New funding	Completion funding	Product completion plan (5)	Product
			Code certifications (3)	Certificates granted (3)	
				Nucleation begins (4)	Nucleation ends (4)
				Product version 0 (5)	Product version 1 (5)
				Production and asset readiness (5)	Production and asset readiness (5)
				Supply chain plan (6)	Supply chain activation (6)
			Diffusion message (6)	Diffusion materials (6)	Marketing campaign (6)
				Sales training (6)	Dress rehearsal (6)

the star. The innovator's mind is fully occupied by the commercial operations of the business. For the time being at least, talks of innovation and future product development take a backseat to the profit imperative.

The next milestone on the road to financial success is the breakeven point. The third prime directive (see Chapter 4) governs everything from this point forward: protect the investment. The business is now in a race to generate enough profits to recover the development investment (see *Recovery Criterion* in Chapter 5). Profitability is the name of the game (unless market share is the objective, in which case the investment stream must continue unabated in greater intensity).

Nevertheless, the innovation cycle is not quite done yet, especially when the product is the innovator's first entry into the marketplace. The performance of the product, while in the hands of the buyer, must be tightly monitored for any trend pointing to problems or issues. This is the reason behind the insistence on the *product data* plan (see *Production Readiness* in Chapter 5). The sales team plays the pivotal role in this act: the onus is on the team to encourage buyers to provide their feedback or make use of the online feedback system if it exists. The worst possible outcome is to cease contact with buyers once the sale is made. The effect will be to leave the business in utter darkness as to the acceptance of the product. Crossing the chasm, shown in Figure 3.1, is not a milestone that occurs organically; the innovator must shepherd the product all along and lead the market to get beyond the *pragmatic* threshold.

Plotting the Next Move

Keeping in touch with customers promotes the success of the business in three ways. First, it enables the sales team to control the narrative, which can lead to additional orders from those customers. Second, it helps uncover marketable insights from the same customers as to new potential customers. And third, the customer feedback helps define the baseline for the next round of product improvements. This third benefit is crucial to the long-term growth of the business. It is the mechanism by which the innovator circles back to Step 3 (see *The Wish List* in Chapter 4), when the primary functions were divided into *essential, desirable,* and *discarded* functions. The *essential* functions exist in Version 1 of the product. The *desirable* functions come back to the fore via the customer feedback mechanics. Some of them will percolate to the top of the feedback stack, thus confirming their merit. Other functions will show up unexpectedly. Finally, some of the functions from the original list will appear in the feedback stack. For those, the next step is to mandate the sales team to suggest them to the customers and see what sticks; what doesn't will get reassigned to the list of *discarded functions*. Note also that items from the discarded list may also show up in the feedback stack in which case they are transferred back to the desirable list.

The innovator's development, marketing, and sales teams begin a compilation of the *desirable functions* that are deemed by the teams to expand the value proposition of the product. The first version of the list is assessed by the parsing sequence (see *From Purpose to Functions* in Chapter 4). Alternatively, the innovator could invite selected customers to participate in a group discussion about which function should be considered for the next version release (other feedback venues are, of course, possible). The final version of the list belongs to the business manager, whose job it will be to put together the financing and technology development plan for the next iteration of the product.

Dealing with Mr. Murphy

Murphy's Law is certain to strike, especially in the early days following the rollout. Something that can go wrong will assuredly do so—with potentially devastating impacts—prior to the chasm-crossing milestone. The key to mitigating the impact to the bottom line and, more important, to the market's impression of the product, is to act fast. Once again, the reader is reminded of the truism that the innovator really gets only one shot at this. Whatever circumstance arises to threaten success, it must be nipped in the bud *without ever blaming the buyer for it—even when he or she is the root cause*. It is a simple choice between being right or doing right by the business. The former is driven by ego; the latter by success. Always remember the damage that can be wreaked by words flowing from the mouth of a disgruntled customer. When properly handled, a problem is a great opportunity to prove your worth in the eyes of a customer. The more severe the problem, the greater will be the appreciation.

It is, of course, impossible to plan for all manners of *Murphy's Law* manifestations. But it is possible to lay out a resolution strategy before pandemonium ensues.

Product Failure

This is the best problem to have. Once the failure has become known (hopefully as a direct communication from the customer to you), the idea is to rapidly assemble a resolution team and dispatch it to the customer's site. Once there, pull out all the stops to fix the problem or simply replace the failed unit with a brand new one. As long as you are on the left side of the chasm (see Figure 3.1), you want to assume all costs and go the extra mile to get the customer back on track as soon as possible—worry about the paperwork later.

If a second failure occurs soon after, you have a design problem on your hands and the simple dump-and-replace will not suffice. Dispatch an engineering team to the site with the mandate of figuring out why things are failing and to get the customer back on track without delay. Stick around if you must, but take ownership of the situation.

Customer Failure

In this instance, the product may be working perfectly well, yet leave the customer unhappy—perhaps ready to pull the plug. You have basically two choices: (1) send the sales team to meet with the customer to determine why he is unhappy or (2) make an offer to the client to take the system out and reimburse the purchase price. In most instances, the problem will either be a lack of training, a lack of operational understanding, or frustration with his dealings with the business. Here, you want to empower the sales team to fix the problem on the spot, no questions asked. If the customer's dissatisfaction stems from another emotional source, the matter becomes one of beliefs and values, which means logical arguments will not work. If you cannot turn things around, opt for choice number two, and then walk away without anger. At least this way you will have minimized the risk of the customer venting his disapproval publicly.

System Failure

This is the case of the business failing at one or more internal processes. If the issue is procedural, get the right people in the room, including the sales team; figure out what is not working and come up with a fix. If the issue is software related (as in a server crash, a denial of service, a corrupted database, etc.), mobilize the IT and software team to 1) take things offline, 2) let customers know that you are doing this, and 3) work on it until things are fixed. If the issue is with the supply chain, get the executive team involved immediately. Regardless of the nature of the failure, the prime objective is the same: fix it immediately. Do not linger or wait in the hope that the problem will go away on its own; *it never does.*

IP Failure

IP failure is a more sinister problem. It concerns the infringement or downright theft of the business' IP. It also concerns the discovery of disparaging messages promoted by your competition. Your solution must involve a legal team, which will not be cheap. But the cost of doing nothing is likely going to exceed whatever you may spend on lawyers. You must protect your IP unflinchingly.

Made Elsewhere

If your product achieves rapid success and acceptance, it will for sure attract unwanted attention from competitors. If it is really good, someone will buy it and reverse engineer it. Never assume that your IP strategy is sufficient to win this battle; it is not. Savvy companies will find ways to go around your patents. Your best defense is offense, meaning that you must expect the competition to do all of these things and counter their plans with an aggressive product evolution strategy (discussed earlier in this chapter and also in Chapter 7). Alternatively, you may discover that a foreign country is already selling copycats, with complete disregard to your legal claims (see *The Fourth Shift* in Chapter 7). Sadly, there is little you can do in that instance, except to learn the painful lesson and avoid repeating it in the future.

Let us reiterate the importance of reacting quickly to the news of any problem, either perceived or confirmed. Ultimately, the executive team owns the accountability for maintaining constant vigilance and for marshalling the required resources to fix things without delay. The head of sales is the logical accountable party for issues that are external to the business. The head of operations should in turn own the accountability for internal issues. And the head of the business (presumably the innovator) owns the accountability for holding these two people's feet to the fire.

NOTES

1. The interested reader is invited to consult *Crossing the Chasm: Marketing and Selling Technology Project* by Geoffrey Moore; *Diffusion of Innovations* by Everett Rogers; *The Lean Startup: How Today's Entrepreneurs Use Continuous Innovation to Create Radically Successful Businesses* by Eric Ries; *Blue Ocean Strategy, Expanded Edition: How to Create Uncontested Market Space and Make the Competition Irrelevant* by Chan Kim and Renée Mauborgne; and *Growth Hacker Marketing: A Primer on the Future of PR, Marketing, and Advertising* by Ryan Holiday.

2. The importance of this fact was set in stone by Geoffrey Moore in his classic book *Crossing the Chasm*.

3. See *Getting to Yes* by R. Fisher, W. Ury, and B. Patton and the seminars offered by https://www.karrass.com/.

10

THE PURSUIT

To rake in the money, one must thrive. To thrive, one must first strive.

THE BUSINESS OF BUSINESS

Leading the Way

The innovation journey reached its destination at the end of Chapter 5. The transformation of the voyage from exploration into exploitation began at Chapter 7 and finished with Chapter 9. At this point, the innovator is entirely immersed in the business and making it work. Sale revenues may have started to flow in—or may still be sputtering. The end game is actually not an end, but a process of continuous strengthening of the commercial viability of the whole operation. The immediate milestone objective is to break even or it may be to achieve rapid market penetration to attract potential suitors. In either case, the means to get there will be the same: a steadfast leadership team, a stalwart growth strategy, and a proactive obsession with metrics. Neither the innovator nor the firm can afford to sit back on their laurels and watch from the sidelines as the business moves beyond the adolescent age into commercial adulthood where the promise of riches lies. Growing up requires dedication, attention to details, and unwavering vigilance. This is no time for autopilot; on the contrary, the circumstances call for a healthy dose of directed paranoia. The pirate ship may have reached Treasure Island, but by virtue of the discovery it is bound to attract the attention of bigger, more numerous pirates circling about ready to pounce by stealth or shock.

Keeping the ship on course, away from predators, requires seasoned leaders who will know how to navigate treacherous waters. For no ship, no matter its size or armament, can remain master of its own domain without strong leadership at the helm. Such leadership is inherently different than the one needed for the innovation journey. The business literature is replete with examples of great start-up companies that were built on stupendous innovations that could not make the transition from innovation to start-up or from start-up to growth. The visionary innovator may strive in the murky waters of uncertainty, but fail miserably to keep the ship afloat amidst a flurry of routine tasks. The bottom line is simple: managing the innovation process is entirely different than managing a business day after day. The challenges are different, the unknowns are unique, and the risks are spawned of a distinct species.

The Top Line

It can be a soul-wrenching exercise for the innovator to face this managerial reality and make the right choice *for the good of the business.* The business is his baby, after all; stepping aside to promote its path to adulthood can be emotionally impossible to do. The same conflict afflicts revolutionary political leaders who are extraordinary in upsetting the establishment, but pathetic at governing the new world order that they ushered in. Fortunately, the choice does not have to be so stark. The innovator can still play an essential role that is suited to his strengths. The choice lies in recognizing one's weaknesses and abdicating the attendant duties in favor of someone who is better suited to carry them out. No single person is a leadership team. The innovator can lead this team—or be part of it. That is the necessary choice that he must make.

We will call this leadership team the *top line.* It is made up of five individuals: the visionary/leader, the technology champion, the revenue chief, the head of operations, and the finance champion. The lineup finds a pleasant analogy in hockey where the offense line is made up of the center (leader), the right winger (technology champion), and left winger (revenue chief) and where the defense includes the right and left defensemen (finance and operations, respectively).[1]

- *The visionary/leader*—is the CEO who embodies the culture and values of the organization and was hired to steer the ship in the right direction at all times
- *The technology champion*—is vested with the know-how of the innovation products, oversees design and research and development activities, and owns the product evolution strategy (discussed in Chapter 7)
- *The revenue chief*—looks after sales and marketing; pursues the activities that will generate revenue for the firm
- *The finance champion*—is the CFO. This is the money man, the person accountable for monitoring the profitability of the firm.
- *The head of operations*—is the COO. Production, supply chains, logistics, and after-sale support falls under their purview. The COO is the primary driver of profits for the firm.

Top of the Line

It goes without saying that these five individuals must be chosen judiciously. Each one must be a seasoned veteran in his/her realm of expertise—this is no place to improvise, especially on defense. The top line must fit together like a glove and share the vision, values, and cultural objectives of the visionary leader. They cannot—let me emphasize—be cut from the same cloth or be animated by flattery. Nepotism here is a double-edged sword; loyalty and shared values may come at the expense of truth. As a group, the top line owns the accountability for developing the business strategy and aligns the sales strategy with it. The top line is also vested with the accountability of overseeing the execution of this overall strategy.

BUSINESS STRATEGY

Strategy Options

The shape and priorities of a business strategy will vary according to the objectives of the firm. These objectives divide into three separate paths: profitability, growth, and exit. The profitability path implies a desire to stay in business in the medium term at which time its future plans may be reassessed. It strives to reach the breakeven point (BEP) as soon as possible. It will do so by achieving rapid market acceptance, by securing enough customers to go beyond the *enthusiast class* (see Figure 3.1). Sales volumes are secondary to unit profits; the point is to make the most money from whatever sales are generated. Once the BEP is achieved, the business strategy comes to a crossroad where the leadership team must decide whether the next phase of the evolution of the firm is to grow the business or set it up for an exit strategy.

The growth path reflects the intention of the shareholders to grow the business in the long run and stick with it. The growth strategy strives to realize three goals: achieve market acceptance at a slower pace (relative to the first path); increase the firm's market share; and reach the BEP under controlled conditions. Everything the firm does, says, or avoids must be geared toward the realization of these three goals. Profits, on a unit basis, may be sacrificed in the short term to drive sales numbers in the medium term. Breakeven will take longer to achieve, but will enable the acceleration of growth of the firm's market share.

The exit path, as the name suggests, aims at selling the business to the highest bidder usually in 3 to 5 years after product roll-out. In this case, the innovation must be shown to be genuinely disruptive in its chosen marketplace. Sales must generate superior profits quickly or achieve very rapid market share in a highly visible manner. Either scenario is intended to prop up the product's perception by competitors that it is threatening to their business to the point that it must be stopped. The whole point of the exit strategy is to make the firm highly attractive to a takeover, a merger, or a buyout. The leadership of the firm, along with the shareholders, are interested primarily in maximizing their returns now and moving on to something else. Let someone else worry about long-term growth.

Of course, it may not be clear at the outset which long-term strategy should be selected. Either one has its benefits and trade-offs. When there is no clarity provided by the shareholders, the prudent policy would be to adopt the profitability path as a starting point. This selection focuses everyone's mind on the need to run an efficient operation that shuns wasteful pursuits and mercantile nonchalance. Getting to the BEP quickly means that the firm will have money in the bank soon after, which is the strongest position to be in when entertaining different strategies in the future.

The Effects on Intellectual Property (IP)

The choice of a strategy path has an impact on the IP objectives of the firm. This IP can take several forms as we saw in Chapter 3 (patents, trademarks, copyrights, industrial designs, and trade secrets). The patent is by far the more onerous to pursue and the most ruinous to defend. One may ask whether a patent is worth the investment for all three strategic paths. The answer is an unequivocal, *it depends*. For example, if the innovation belongs to a class of products that are characterized by short commercial life cycles, this new product may become obsolete in a manner of months. Such a short life makes it extraordinarily difficult to reverse engineer by a competitor. The patent protection in this case could be superfluous—unless it covers a fundamental element of the product that will itself survive the cycle. If the product itself is not radically novel, a patent may not be able to protect it against legal variations on a theme pursued by others. Conversely, if the internal workings of the patentable features are known to be very difficult to design (and, by extension, very difficult to reverse engineer), the innovator may skip the patent entirely and rely instead on the potency of the embedded trade secrets to proceed with commercialization (the recipe for Coca-Cola is the classic example).

In other cases, the invention may include enough secretive insights that it may be better protected by confidentiality or nondisclosure agreements (especially if the small inventor is dealing with a prominent firm). These agreements are at least one order of magnitude cheaper than patents and carry within them a stronger legal bulwark for the inventor. The innovator should seriously consider this option in technology readiness level (TRL) 3 if the larger partner can be signed up before TRL 6 or the innovator is confident in his ability to maintain the secrecy during commercialization. The upside is that the trade secret will outlast the 20-year term of a patent. Ultimately, the strength of the alternate trade secret is supplied by the strength of the agreement.

The scope of protection conferred by a patent is another consideration that should be a factor in the filing decision. In this instance, the insights of the patent attorney are essential. If the protection is sufficiently expansive, the innovator may be able to gain dominance over the market with minimal infringement threats from competitors. On the other hand, if the protection is very specific and therefore limited, a savvy competitor may be able to find legal workarounds that could greatly weaken the value of your IP in commercial terms. In that case, not pursuing the patent may be the best approach.

The strategic path itself influences the decision. The exit path dictates the possession of a patent. The investment value of a product (or the firm for that matter) is amplified by a patent, but lessened without it. Very few companies will consider the purchase of a product devoid of patent protection. The growth path tends to be enhanced by the existence of a patent, although the trade secret option discussed previously bears equal importance to the IP decision. The profitability path is the least obvious one to decide. For short lifespan products, not getting a patent is the better way to go. For limited scope protection, the pros and cons are divided 50/50. For stronger protection, the patent should be sought.

Stability

Once a strategy is set, stick to it. Do not change it when circumstances are challenging or threatening. The implementation of the strategy's details will confer over time a precious sense of stability and certainty upon the employees, the shareholders, and the supply chain partners. The value of this stability cannot be overstated. It is the glue that will hold the vision together when times are tough. Inevitably, circumstances will arise that will challenge the validity of the strategy. These circumstances could come from within (frictions among the top line, high turnover, failed deals) or from without (a new entrant in the marketplace is creating immediate disruptions). It is essential that the leadership team distinguish between genuine challenges to the strategy and those stemming from a flawed or failed execution of the mission. In the case of the latter, the strategy must be kept; it is the people who are carrying it out who must be changed. There may be a disconnect between management's directives and people's interpretation of them. The communication needs fixing, not the strategy. On the other hand, external circumstances that put into question the correctness of the strategy must be carefully and methodically assessed by the leadership team. Questions may arise as to the underlying assumptions of the strategy, which may call for a review. If the strategy is deemed afflicted or conflicted, it must be adjusted accordingly to accord with the facts on the ground.

The bit about assumptions warrants a closer look. *All strategies rely on a set of assumptions that will either be proven right or wrong in the long run.* One must distinguish between an assumption and a prediction derived from it. For example, one must make the assumption that the innovative product will find traction in the marketplace (if not, the business is dead on arrival). That is a worthwhile and meaningful assumption. Selling 1,000 units in the first six months is not an assumption, it is a prediction that was derived from the accepted assumption. Therein lies the crux of the matter: when assessing a proposed strategy, one can either debate the assumptions or the predictions, but not both. The predictions always lead to revenue and profit projections in the future from which financial plans are constructed. Which is right then, the assumption or the prediction? The assumption, once accepted, is more inconsistent than the prediction, which suggests a large degree of variability.

> *Strategy discussions should proceed from the assumptions, not the predictions. Affirm the assumptions and let the prediction chips fall where they may.*

The Black Art of Forecasting

The use of the word *prediction* in the previous paragraph was a bit of a misnomer as it really came through as a forecast. A prediction is an outcome that has been *quantified* on the basis of calculations derived from an *assumption*. A *forecast* is a guess of an outcome dependent on one or more predictions. For example, an assumption suggests that a production process can yield one hundred parts per hour. The total unit production cost is a prediction that is calculated from the known logistical factors of the production environment, which could also include a statistical prediction that one out of 200 units will be rejected. These hundred units are then forecasted to sell as follows: 80% at full price and 15% at a reduced price. The assumption in this case guides the implementation strategy to put in place a production process that is capable of meeting the throughput rate. That rate is now assumed to be correct and serves as the basis of calculation for the predicted unit cost of the produced widgets. The revenues generated by the sale of those widgets are quantified by the *sales forecast*. We thus proceeded from certainty (assumption) to estimate (prediction) to guess (forecast).

Clearly, one can exert complete control over the assumptions and near-complete control over the predictions (variability, randomness, and unknown unknowns introduce the completion defect). The assumptions belong to the leadership team (top line). The *predictions* belong to the line managers who are

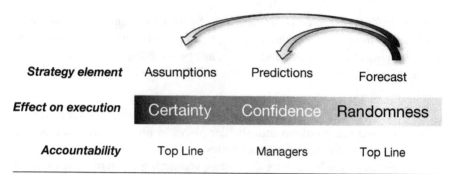

Strategy element	Assumptions	Predictions	Forecast
Effect on execution	Certainty	Confidence	Randomness
Accountability	Top Line	Managers	Top Line

Figure 10.1   The uncertainty principle applied to decision making: the growth in business uncertainty proceeds from top management to planning to execution; uncertainty is highest the closer to the ground of the market

reporting to each member of the top line. And the forecasts close the circle by belonging again to the leadership team, whose mandate is to put in place the management tools and processes required in order to deal with the inevitable randomness bred by the forecasts. This relationship is illustrated in Figure 10.1. The two top arrows indicate the feedback loops that must continuously occur to maintain congruence between the strategy and the facts on the ground (reality).

Firms get into trouble when they set arbitrary, wishful forecasts without tethering them to the strategy's assumptions or the operations' predictions or both. This disconnect is the customary progenitor of the hockey-stick delusion seen earlier in Figure 2.1. Given the import of the forecasts to the financial planning of the firm, the derivation of these forecasts deserves further discussion. The reliability of a forecast is rooted in the quantified knowledge (or lack thereof) of the market or markets that are being pursued by the firm. This is, of course, the realm of *marketing*, which is discussed later on in the chapter. One can never know with certainty what the market will bear or which proportion of that volume will accrue to the firm. Certainty comes with a signed purchase order (or any other variant of it), but remains a discrete forecast event that has little or no bearing on the market at large. Even when one has a thorough approximate understanding of the market, there will remain a guessing element to the formulation of a forecast. We are left with the issue of confidence in the forecasted numbers. How can one increase this confidence toward certainty?

Predictably, there is abundant literature on the matter; nevertheless, one recent text by Tetlock and Gardner deserves attention by the reader.[2] Entitled *Superforecasting: The Art and Science of Prediction*, the book offers battle-tested insights into the art of predicting the future. In particular, the techniques do not require high-powered computers but rely instead mainly upon compiling evidence from various sources, adopting a probabilistic thinking in group settings, keeping track of reality, and remaining open to being wrong and changing course accordingly. The method—in the grand scheme of things—involves ten steps:

1. Focus time and energy on forecasts that will yield the greater rewards
2. Dissect the problems into smaller pieces to uncover the assumptions, detect mistakes, and counter biases
3. Focus on the big picture first before wandering down into the weeds of a single case
4. Adjust your beliefs continually in small-step increments; big adjustments carry the risk of either over or underreacting to new facts
5. Look for the merits and tangible insights of contrary perspectives
6. Certainty is an illusion; get comfortable with the necessity of dealing with ranges of uncertainty and unknown unknowns
7. Be humble; do not bluster, but do not dillydally either: prudence of decision is best
8. Successes and failures are teaching moments; learn their lessons
9. When seeking the insights of others, be precise in your questioning; allow others to elicit your own insights for their benefits
10. Forecasting is akin to software development; start, test, and fail fast and, if necessary, tweak and repeat
11. The preceding rules are not all-powerful; question everything at all times

One little caveat must be firmly set at this time. The method is predicated on the availability of pertinent information and datum sets to formulate a prediction. The presence of data, facts, and figures instills the forecaster with an impression of unbiased attention. The forecaster may believe himself devoid of preconceived notions and personal bias in the act of reviewing the data. There follows a belief that the forecast (or decision) will be fact based. Beware the illusion of neutrality! In the years 2008 and 2009, neuroscience research[3] discovered a stunning brain process buried deep in a person's subconscious. Sophisticated MRI scans revealed that a decision first appears in the brain subconsciously before the decision becomes conscious to the person. In other words, people make decisions *before* realizing what choice they willfully made. A decision first appears in the frontopolar cortex of the brain and can *sit* there for seven seconds before the mind becomes aware of it. The same goes for the so-called *gut instinct* by the way. That is why a person's intuition appears to point to the right decision in the moment.

This subconscious operator leads directly to confirmation bias. It also silently steers a person toward the data that tends to corroborate the invisible decision. This action has immediate ramifications on people who are involved with making forecasts (or just facing a decision with several options). Unbeknown to them is an insidious impetus to migrate toward what *feels* right and find the information that strengthens the feeling. This brain mechanism is ancestral and therefore very arduous to overcome. The intensity of the stealth decision increases with the appearance of a threat around the decision to be made. Evolution is to blame—when our early ancestors faced a fight-or-flight situation, pondering the options was not an option. The brain moved to fight or flee in the blink of an eye. The carnivorous menace no longer lies in the shadows, but the reaction to the threat remains firmly anchored in the brain. That is why, when push comes to shove, even with the help of statistical data and quantitative facts, a person will be drawn to the factual information that converges toward the fully formed subconscious decision, especially if pain may result from a wrong choice. The feedback loop that is implied by Step 10 in the aforementioned list is the frontal countermeasure to neuter a brain's capricious proclivities!

The Labor-Forecast Tandem

The most difficult conflict that can arise from mismatched forecasts rests with head counts. A firm's staffing level carries a pronounced inertia against sudden needs for course changes. The level is proportional to the scale of the sales forecasts. However, while forecasts can turn, jump up, or dive down—seemingly at a whim—staffing levels are intrinsically harder to adjust in real time. Service companies are far more prone to personnel bottlenecks and shortages than their product counterparts. It is a juggling act that can derail the strongest of strategies if the head count fluctuations cannot be kept relatively in sync with the demands created by forecasts.

The labor-forecast tandem is exacerbated in small-scale companies. Should a firm staff up for maximum forecast contingencies or streamline their head count to sustain the minimum throughput demands of the operation? There are no formal rules on the matter, only suggestions. Generally speaking, it is always best to hire employees in numbers that support the minimum sustaining activities of the business. Small variations in demand can be accommodated through ad hoc overtime periods. When the overtime situation tends to move toward a permanent state, either the overall productivity has deteriorated or the workload consistently exceeds capacity. In that latter case, one should plan on expanding the head count. In the former case, better training, alternate processes, or reassignments might be in order.

When the forecast variations cannot be readily mitigated by the overtime policy, the better solution is a supplementary labor force tapped on a contract basis. Every company, no matter what its size, should in fact have a supplementary strategy of this kind, preferably developed when workloads do not require it. This can be the case of a mere handful of individual contractors invited to work on an assignment basis with the firm. For larger load cases, the supplemental resources are more efficiently provided by other firms retained on a contract basis as well. Keep in mind, too, that employing contractors in this way provides the firm with a unique recruitment opportunity without interviewing anybody!

Sustaining activities are best served by direct hires. Variability is best controlled through contractors.

It goes without saying that any labor variability strategy will come with a cost increase to the final product. Whether or not the cost increase is justifiable is a matter for the leadership team to assess. Myriad conditions render the analysis impossible to generalize. Some conditions (such as a contract) may not give the firm any option but to incur the extra costs. A key client may warrant the added expenses to nurture the long-term relationship. A growth strategy (the second path) will most likely drive the need, but a profitability path may argue against it. There is also the cold reality of the cash dictator depicted in Figure 8.2. As the reader can see, making a decision is as distinctive as the circumstances of the firm.

Profit Sharing or Profitable Shares

A happy workforce is a productive and resilient workhorse. Money is quite obviously a big player in the motivational arena. The leadership team may entertain the idea of implementing a profit sharing program or to establish an employee share ownership plan. Both are fraught with perils when expectations are not tightly corralled.

Profit sharing in particular has a dazzling way of instilling in employees a presumed sense of entitlement that was never meant to take hold in the first place. Employees differ from contractors in one very peculiar way: contractors understand intimately the relationship between their work and getting paid. Employees, especially established ones, not so much. So, if a profit sharing plan is put in place that will pay out every quarter or semiannually (or whatever other cycle), the employees are very likely to become accustomed to receiving their bonuses on the due date and grow to expect them *regardless of the financial circumstances of the firm at any point in time*. Worse, they may take offense at losing these bonuses in challenging times. And, never will they entertain a reduction in their base salaries when circumstances are dire (thinking that in good times they deserve rewards but not punishment in hard times that are outside of their control). If a profit sharing plan is to be put in place, the better policy is to avoid linking it to a predictable pay-out schedule. When times are good, dole out the money in safe numbers; in more difficult times, don't mention it at all. The same goes for salary increases; do not tie yourself to a fixed annual salary review, which will plant the seed of increase awards in the minds of people. Dole out salary increases on an individual basis when cash flow permits, staff performance warrants, and fairness to the rest of the employees suggests. Finally, be attentive and generous to your top performers; they are most responsible for the profitability of the firm.

One can avoid the expectation pitfalls of profit sharing by instead embracing an employee share ownership plan (ESOP). This approach requires much greater diligence by management than profit sharing. For starters, understand the critical difference (and associated motivations) between an employee and a shareholder: only the shareholder has skin in the game. This is absolutely paramount. Having skin in the game entails three built-in ramifications on the prospective holder:

- You will have a direct say in the direction of the company that affects the share price;
- You will get rewards in good times; and
- You will suffer financially in bad times.

The third caveat is the one most often overlooked. Highly paid CEOs with millions of share options on the line do not suffer the downside in a downturn: they lose none of their money, only the promise of future money. They therefore have no genuine skin in the game (and sometimes get rewarded with spectacular pay-out packages for having driven the company's stock price into the ground). A true shareholder is one who can be wiped out if the firm fails. The risk of losing one's money is a great motivator to do whatever it takes to avoid it—much more, in fact, than the promise of riches on the upside. Hence, if you decide to enact an ESOP, those employees who are invited to take part in it must—let me repeat—*must* put their own skin in the game. If the plan merely awards new shares to employees once in a while, these shares carry no risk of financial loss, only the loss of future possible earnings. Of course, the upside of a skin-in-the-game ESOP is a class of employees with an immediate vested interest in the success of the firm on a scale and magnitude beyond anything that mere hourly or salaried employees will espouse. ESOP employees will willingly shoulder greater sacrifices than non-ESOP personnel in hard times, but expect far more consultation and involvement in decision making with the leadership team.

MARKET STRATEGY

Three Pillars

Simply put, a market strategy aims to generate revenues from sales (in contrast, for example, to a financial strategy that seeks to generate earnings from complex financial instruments). This strategy is built upon three execution pillars: marketing, sales, and development. Marketing is the sum of the activities that generate sales leads. Everything that marketing does must be geared toward that singular goal (companies often go astray when they forget this simple rule). By extension, *sales* is the sum of the activities involved in converting these leads into revenues. Finally, development seeks to deconstruct a market into potential lead sources, to recognize trends, *and* to plan the evolution of the product offering to tap into these trends discussed in Chapter 7 under the heading *Product Evolution Strategy*. Obviously, the people involved in the three groups must work across their own boundaries to stay aligned on what the market is saying (leads generated), what it is doing (sales), and where it is going (development). For this reason, the three groups should always be hierarchically reporting to the revenue chief. The last two pillars have already been discussed at length in Chapters 7 and 9. Henceforth, this discussion will focus on the first pillar.

Success Factors in Marketing

In marketing, it is better to go narrow and deep rather than wide and shallow. This axiom harks back to the admonition in Chapter 5 to pick a specific market target early on and ignore the rest until cash flow warrants the expansion. A successful *sales* campaign rests on knowing precisely who the buyer is and why he will buy from you. This knowledge is derived in part from market research (one of the mandates of the development pillar) and in part from market reactions to the marketing campaign that put forth the value proposition (see *Diffusion Strategy* in Chapter 9). The *marketing* campaign must hone in on the target market and avoid drifting sideways into other potentially interesting markets. However, the characterization of the buyer will never become a certainty (unless you are, in effect, a monopoly or a monopsony). The buyer's profile is and will always remain an educated forecast. Never assume that you truly know the buyer or even the scope of the market. Always remain vigilant to new intelligence that surfaces, especially the bits that seem to contradict your original assumptions. Fight the tendency to be pleased with information that accords with your confirmation bias. Always question why facts on the ground seem to agree with you.

Viewed from within, marketing is the pursuit of truth as best can be approximated. It is not about the message or the sales pitch—this is the outward looking viewpoint. Sales success will accrue from knowing the truth of a marketplace and the truth of the facts on the ground. Don't be satisfied when your assumptions have apparently been confirmed by the market. Perhaps you just got lucky (which happens way more often than business personalities like to admit), in which case you have no idea if your assumptions are actually correct. Truth demands honesty and the courage to face reality as it is, not as it should be to fit your views.

Stay focused on a *reachable market*. It is futile to keep thinking about a market that is effectively out of your reach, whatever the reasons (for example, wanting to sell your newfangled drone jet engine to the U.S. Department of Defense). Do not let yourself be lured by the lucrative size of a distant market. If you are small, you are incapable of sustaining sales volumes that are common to multinationals. Find your niche first and strive to achieve an outsized success in it. Then, and only then, start planning an expansion.

A corollary of the reachable market is the *reachable sales goal*. It is imperative that a quantifiable goal be set for the sales targets (for example, 300 units sold in the next quarter). It is equally imperative that the goal be self-congruent—that is, the number is realistic relative to the forecasted share of the market available to the firm *and* is commensurate with the production capacity of the firm *and* is aligned with the costing reality of the order. The real-life example of Wells Fargo (mentioned in Chapter 8) serves as a cautionary tale to anyone thinking that goals can be picked out of the air, notwithstanding the reality surrounding it. If the goal is too low, the sales group will be unmotivated (low sales = low commissions). If it is too high, individual behaviors will somehow find a way to game the system even if the expedient is cheating. If sales numbers are achieved by lowballing competitors, the price will be paid in lost profits, which cannot be explained away with fast talking.

Do not confound customer relationship management (CRM) with marketing. The former is merely a software tool to manage the information stream that is generated by the three pillars. A potent CRM can never overcome a weak marketing strategy or a limp sales team. CRM is a tool, not a strategy; it is a process, not a solution.

Branding

Branding is a trendy topic that has taken on an academic life of its own over the past two decades. This is once again a topic that is amply written up in the business literature and is too broad to cover in-depth in the space available here. Suffice it to say that branding is important to firms that pursue the growth or exit paths. The value of a brand is the emotional connection to its customers, whose numbers, in turn, set an accounting value to the firm's financial status.

A brand is, quintessentially, a kept promise made to a buyer.

The promise is made by the firm under the guise of the value proposition. The manifestation of this promise lands in the hands of the buyer, who will in turn judge whether the goods live up to the promise (or hype). The brand is intimately associated with the buyer's understanding of what value means to him. When that value is realized, or better yet exceeded, the brand is confirmed while its emotional connection to the buyer is enhanced. The brand need not be defined by its colors, its flash, or its loud social presence. Industrial products very often benefit from branding that is stronger than the fickle tastes of retail products. Again, the essence of the brand lies in the manifestation of the promise, not the public persona that is often associated with it. A brand is not something that can be imposed from the outset by the firm despite the belief of many marketing professionals. Granted, the marketing campaign promotes and disseminates the message, which, in turn, engenders an expectation of value in the marketplace. But it is the marketplace that will, in time, cement the brand's promise or dilapidate it. A brand, in other words, is a long-term game, not a fast-buck tweeter storm.

The buyer, as ever, is front and center on this stage. The brand embodies the values of the innovator, but resonates only when it connects with the buyer's pain point. One will often hear that the customer is king, but this is incorrect. One should look upon the customer as a friend, a best friend in due time. You owe this friend honesty, even if this honesty requires you to let him down or tell him something he does not want to hear. Indeed, there are times when your buyer expects to do business with you at a particular moment in time when you are unable to deliver the value proposition unconditionally (for example, you are in the midst of a big order that has got your plant maxed out for the next two weeks). Whenever the need to say no presents itself, do so honestly and frankly with the buyer. Then, offer to find a possible solution outside of your walls, even if it means sending work to a competitor.

Never ever take on an order that you know will be impossible to fulfill without sacrificing elements of your value proposition or damaging the promise communicated by your brand.

The surest and fastest way to lose a customer—or at the very least damage the relationship permanently—is to refuse to say no to what should have never been a yes. If the delivery requires you to move heaven and earth and put the entire firm to work, the stresses resulting from the upheaval will linger long after payment has been received to the detriment of *all* of your other customers.

How does one reconcile this prohibition against a value-damaging sale and the primacy of the profit master? Recall that in the section *The True Master of Your Vision* in Chapter 8, revenue generation was given priority over preserving the integrity of the vision if a potential sale induced the conflict. In that case, it was presumed that the sale could be fulfilled by the firm without damaging itself, but had to swallow its pride if the sale did not align with the idealism of the vision. In our present case, we are pushing for the protection of the value proposition (which embodies the vision, incidentally) in the face of a threat from an order that could permanently damage the firm for the sake of an immediate revenue opportunity. The former case insisted on pragmatism to rule over idealism; in the latter case, we insist on the firm's integrity over temporary riches.

The Logo

The logo is the visual connection between the buyer and the brand. The opinions on what makes a good logo vary as much as the creators behind them. Some believe that the logo should *mean* something. Some firms will spend a fortune on the colors, the symbolism, the fonts, and the artistic value. Before the advent of smartphones, color selection was influenced by printing costs. Nowadays, it does not matter since people's dealings with logos come mainly from online interactions. It has been said that Bill Knight, the founder of Nike, was less than enthused by the logo proposed by its designer, Carolyn Davidson, a student at Portland State University. He reluctantly agreed to keep it and paid Davidson $35 for her services, thereby giving the world the famous Nike swoosh.[4] The logo became famous *after* the brand became so successful. Therein lies several valuable lessons for the reader:

- The logo follows the brand, not the reverse. It does not make any difference what the logo looks like if the brand is successful.
- Do not overthink the logo design or spend big money on it. Keep it simple, crisp, and pleasant to the eye. Remember that the logo will be seen most often on a screen.
- The logo cannot salvage a failing brand.
- Update at your peril. A bad revamp can hurt a firm overnight.
- Again, don't spend too much time and effort on this. There are more important things to worry about (like making a sale).

Pricing

The temptation of undercutting the competition is strong in the initial stages of an emerging business. After all, no value proposition exists independently of pricing. The pursuit of market share is especially prone to the chase for the bottom. One should resist this easy way out to the utmost. If the value proposition only boils down to being cheaper than the competition, the value that you are communicating to the buyer is that your business is purely transactional. This means that the instant a cheaper competitor shows up, you are out in the cold. Transactional relationships are not business relationships at all; they require neither personal contact, nor an exchange of intelligence, nor nurturing by either party. As long as the price is right, the deal is ripe. This is no basis to pursue long-term growth or, for that matter, commercial longevity. True longevity stands erect on the shores of genuine relationships that go beyond mere pricing. Higher profits *and* greater market stability are the natural outcomes of strong client relationships.

The right price is the value that the buyer is willing to pay for.

Never open up a conversation with a buyer by undercutting your price. You do not know what price he is willing to pay until you figure out what value means to him. When you firmly believe in the merits of your solution (in delivering the buyer-defined value), do not hesitate to stand up for your price and do not sell out just to seal a quick deal devoid of profitable logic. If a deal is not possible, do not waste your time or the buyer's time; decline the order (as discussed previously) and suggest a possible alternative.

The sale cycle is a related topic that goes hand in hand with the price. Any sale process that relies on a genuine relationship with the buyer will take time to close. It could be days, weeks, even months before a sale is final (commercial jetliners can take years). It is important to quantify what the sale cycle will be *for each prospective* client, which will in turn drive who will be given priority and who will be set aside. You cannot chase after all inklings of leads that come your way. You must prioritize them—first, on the basis of client importance (to your long-term bottom line) and second, in terms of likelihood of success. Outliers, tire kickers, unlikely enquirers, and foreigners are often looking to see what's out there without necessarily needing to buy anything right now. Do not waste time on dubious or incredulous would-be buyers simply because they contacted you. Things like a memorandum of understanding, letters of intent, and expressions of interest are a step above unlikely, but still wield little weight from the words they convey. Any form of commitment statement isn't worth the digital ink they are redacted on without cash up front to back up their claims of seriousness. Do not dismiss them—mind you—simply take them with a grain of salt until that salt has the taste of money. All the while, the rest of the firm is on pins and needles waiting to hear about the next order. The leadership team must work out a plan for keeping abreast financially while the sale cycle unfolds. There is little point in chasing after a twenty million dollar deal if you're going to go bankrupt while waiting to see it come true.

Teaching Is Selling

A highly effective way to expose new customers to what they could be missing by overlooking your product is to teach them what you know in order to let them figure out what they don't know. One way to do this is to publish white papers, technical papers, and other digital contents on the firm's website. You can take the process a step further and implement a newsletter (quarterly at the most) to communicate with clients. The web is replete with free or dirt-cheap apps to automate this process. According to the *MailChimp E-mail Marketing Company*, the best time to e-mail potential customers is between 2:00 p.m. and 5:00 p.m. on Tuesdays. Other juicy morsels of e-mail magic include:

- 33% of e-mail recipients open e-mails based on subject line alone, according to *Convince and Convert* marketing company.
- *ContactMonkey*, another marketing firm, observed that subject lines with more than three words experienced a drop in open rate by over 60%.
- Personalized e-mails that included the recipient's first name in the subject line had higher open rates as reported by *Retention Science*.
- For e-mails between businesses (so-called B2B transactions), a subject line that contains the words *alert* and *breaking* perform well, according to *Adestra*.
- *Adestra* also noted that B2B customers have become desensitized to the words *reports*, *forecasts*, and *intelligence*.

Remember to always insert the contact name of your marketing or sales group near the top of e-mails and other marketing and sale documents intended for public consumption.

The next step up is to organize lunch and learn sessions and short seminars. Some of them should be hosted on the firm's premises and be attended by invitation from the marketing group. Others should be held at a client's facility, typically as a breakfast or lunch event. Others, finally, should be done at conferences and trade shows. In all cases, the contents must be genuinely meaningful lessons. Topics should be as technical as the intended audience is and *never ever ever delivered as a sales pitch*. The value proposition is always about real knowledge transfer, not self-promotion. If you do the job correctly, chances are that someone will call you later to come clarify something or ask for help with a problem (leading to a sale).

The fourth and final level is the full-blown training seminar, ranging from half a day to a full week. Start offering them free of charge to potential clients. Keep the contents educationally rich, free of sales pitches, and of sufficient depth that your *graduates* will be able to put their newfound knowledge to work in their own environments. Eventually, the popularity of a seminar may attract more registrants than you can handle. At that point, you will be able to switch to a paid model.

When a seminar requires the participants to be away overnight, the organizers should plan to hold *fireside chats* at the end of the day where participants and firm representatives can mingle in a relaxed atmosphere. It is the perfect opportunity for soft selling to take place (whereby individual participants are engaged by salespeople to casually discuss their challenges and frustrations). These sessions cannot and must not become hard sale pitches—doing so will simply infuriate the crowd and destroy whatever goodwill was built during the day. The first day of a multi-day seminar should present the topics of discussion in terms of known and future pain points (to buyers). Speakers and trainers must be convincingly knowledgeable of the subject matter presented. Do not be afraid to highlight the individual accomplishments of the presenters. Introduce the firm briefly without fanfare or blatant self-aggrandizing declarations and always be ready to back up the claims you make. On subsequent days, introduce elements of fun each day that will occupy one segment of the course—things like golf, horseback riding, go-carting, archery, or any other unique activity that will broaden the individual experience. Another activity would be to invite unique individuals to speak about equally unique topics (without getting depressing, mind you). On the last day, in the last hour, someone from the leadership team (top line) should be present to close the proceedings. That will send a strong signal to the audience about the importance of this training to the firm. Obviously, the CEO is the best candidate; next would be either the technology champion or the operations chief. Avoid the head of sales—it will smell suspiciously like a sales pitch in disguise.

Success Stories

The last component of the market strategy is the success story. Many start-up gurus advocate that new firms strive to be the top, or at least the second- or third-best solution providers in their respective marketplaces. This is a laudable goal; however, when one competes against established companies with global footprints, such aspirations are simply untenable. You have no hope of being better than the recognized leader in your market segment, at least not initially. To be blunt, you just don't have the financial wherewithal to take on these behemoths head on—much like your Saturday afternoon baseball team could never beat the New York Yankees.

If you compete with a giant, you are outspent, out-staffed, out-resourced, and out of market presence. You cannot expect to thrive by excellence because the framework required to achieve excellence is out of your reach. That does not mean, however, that you have no chance of winning at your local level. You need to be realistic and focus on the strengths that can attract trust from your buyers. Building a long-lasting relationship is easier for a small firm than a commercial giant. Scale also plays in your favor; large companies rarely bother to chase small orders because they are not competitive at that scale. Ultimately, your value proposition will win on the back of the intangible benefits that it confers to the buyer (again, harder to do for the big boys).

You need not be the best in the world to succeed, but simply be the best in your own world.

NOTES

1. Hockey purists will no doubt have remarked on the missing goaltender in this lineup without whom championships cannot be won. In our analogy, the goaltender embodies the board of directors.
2. Tetlock, Philip E. and Dan Gardner. *Superforecasting: The Art and Science of Prediction.* Random House, 2016.
3. The extraordinary case of the subconscious making up its mind first was reported by Soon *et al.* in a paper entitled *Unconscious Determinants of Free Decisions in the Human Brain.* The initial research was corroborated by later findings by Joel L. Voss and Ken A. Paller (see *An Electrophysiological Signature of Unconscious Recognition Memory*).
4. Do not be outraged by the seeming stinginess of Knight in this matter. He would eventually grant Davidson shares in Nike worth $650,000. Note in passing that the catch line *Just Do It* came years after.

11

QUANTICO

"I have been struck by how important measurement is to improving the human condition. You can achieve amazing progress . . . toward that goal. . . . This may seem pretty basic, but it is amazing to me how often it is not done and how hard it is to get right."

—Bill Gates

PERFORMANCE IS METRICS

Assessments Rule; Measurements Govern

In this chapter, we return to the topic of money from the perspective of profits. One could say that the previous chapter also dealt with money, but from a revenue standpoint. Excellent exceptions like Amazon can afford to focus on a growth strategy to achieve market dominance at the expense of profits. For the vast majority comprising the rest of us, the pursuit of market share at the expense of sustainable profitability is a one-way ticket to bankruptcy. Indeed, it is utter folly to accept a billion dollar contract knowing that your margins at the end of the day will be near zero. Profitability underlined the motivation to turn down a brand-threatening order (see *Branding* in Chapter 10). It is safe to say that *anything done by a firm must be done to generate profits and not simply revenues.*

No profit, no business, no future.

It is the job of the leadership team to assess the health of the business from which decisions and choices can be made. The assessment governs the act of managing the business. The process is reminiscent of a patient diagnosed by a medical doctor. His vital signs will be taken—weight, pulse, blood pressure, temperature, lucidity (oxygen processes), and respiration. These signs will be measured quantitatively and assessed against established ranges. The same process applies to the business, whose corresponding vital signs are conveyed by the budget (allocations to operate), the profit and loss statement (pulse of the business), the balance sheet (the financial stability of the business), the gross margin (the value validated by buyers), the cash flow (the energy consumption of the business), and the backlog (the reserves ensuring the future). Each of these signs must be measured and quantified continuously in real time and assessed against the targets, baseline, and failure thresholds (set respectively by the vision, the mission, and the strategy from Chapter 8).

Clearly, the tabulation of these metrics is an accounting function, one whose extents are beyond the scope of this book. Our purpose is to emphasize the importance of these metrics to the leadership team and to make sure that the imperative is placed upon the team to take ownership of these metrics on a daily basis. The finance champion (see Chapter 10) is accountable for the tabulation of the metrics. The CEO is the probate authority for their release. The remaining top-line members (technology champion, revenue chief, and head of operations) are accountable for the assessment of the metrics and the decisions that flow from the assessments.

Necessary Evil

Marshall McLuhan, famous author of the maxim *the medium is the message,* offers another poignant piece of wit to our discussion:

> *"A point of view can be a dangerous luxury when substituted for insight and understanding."*

There is no glamour associated with financial reviews. The process can be a grind as it typically involves a plethora of minute details. Numbers can be confusing, intimidating, or riddled with complexity. The tale told by the numbers may be hard to understand. Above all, numbers (when honestly prepared) tell no lies: they are an instantaneous snapshot of the real state of a firm. The numbers may very well convey a message of dangerous conditions, a threatened immediate future, or impending doom. It is human nature to shun such potential bad news. But shying away from the reality that is presented by the numbers is no way to manage a business. To those who cling to the dictum, "If you are afraid of the answer, don't ask the question," the only retort needed is: "Volinescience[1] is dereliction of duty." Financial problems *never* go away by simply ignoring them. On the contrary, their ugliness[2] compounds every day until it becomes horrible and impossible to behold. The point to remember and to emphasize again and again, is this:

> *The review of the vital signs of the business shall not be delegated. It falls under the direct and recurring purview of the leadership team.*

It is indeed a necessary evil. Not only is it so, it also bears the hallmarks of a relentless, heartless taskmaster. The reviews are tactically essential to the growth of the firm with a frequency dictated by the state of flux of the business. In the early stages of a start-up, the profit/loss (P/L) statement, the cash flow, the gross margin, and the backlog should be reviewed at least every two weeks while the budget should be checked monthly. Later on, a monthly schedule should suffice except for the cash flow and the backlog, which should remain on a two-week period, and the budget moved to a quarterly recurrence. Later still, the period should be moved up to monthly for all except the budget (kept quarterly). The balance sheet is typically reviewed yearly, come tax time, but should be more frequent when new cash infusions are brought in from investors, banks, and government programs.

Nature of the Beasts

The use, and usefulness, of the various financial metrics are summarized here.

The *balance sheet* is a summary of a firm's assets, liabilities, and shareholder equity at a specific point in time. It is the primary indicator to outsiders of what is owned and owed by the firm. The balance sheet must balance at all times according to the formula: assets = liabilities + shareholder equity. A fictitious example appears in Table 11.1. The balance sheet is a dynamic document that will always change over time and require recurring reviews by the leadership team in order to stay on top of things.

The *P/L (income) statement* summarizes the revenues, expenses, and costs incurred by the firm during a *specified period of time*. The income statement is a qualitative portrait of the firm's ability to generate profits (or not). It says nothing about the efficiency of the sources of expenditures but informs the reader on the possible areas of improvements (whether to increase revenues or reduce costs). An example is shown in Table 11.2. This document is also dynamic and subject to recurring reviews by the leadership team—usually in parallel with the balance sheet review. Note that the statement is also used to determine the breakeven point of the operations; that is, the revenue generation level that is required to cover fixed costs (rent, leases, salaries, permits, and other expenses that do not depend directly on sales volumes).

The *budget* allocates the financial resources of the firm to its various operations. The original release of the budget is called the baseline, which can be set at the start of the fiscal year or mapped over from the actual budget figures from the last fiscal year. Once the budget is set, it will normally remain unchanged for the duration of the fiscal year, and it will be changed only when extraordinary circumstances have materially impacted its underlying assumptions. Note also that the estimates and allocations appearing in the budget can be made

Table 11.1   The balance sheet: this is a simplified example of a firm's balance sheet, which would be accurate on a specific date (included in its title). Note the equality between the assets and the sum of the liabilities and equity. The real thing will have several notes and annotations to explain specific details of the entries, where applicable.

Assets	
Current assets	
Cash	$319,000
Accounts receivable	$229,000
Inventory	$94,000
Work in progress (WIP)	$178,000
Other current assets	$38,000
Total current assets	$858,000
Total fixed assets	$123,000
Total other assets	$87,000
Total assets	**$1,068,000**
Liabilities	
Current liabilities	
Accounts payable	$44,000
Deposits on jobs	$90,000
Other current liabilities	$24,000
Total current liabilities	$158,000
Total long-term liabilities	$71,000
Total liabilities	**$229,000**
Equity	**$839,000**
Total liabilities and Equity	**$1,068,000**

according to various scenarios, each defined by a given set of assumptions. In the example shown in Table 11.3, two scenarios are illustrated: one based on optimistic sales and cost efficiencies; another on pessimistic assumptions. These scenarios help the leadership team determine the financial thresholds below which the firm could become threatened economically.

The *cash flow predictions* are compiled into a table. This document is the most dynamic one in terms of frequency of updates and reviews. This document sets out the spending patterns of the firm under controlled, scheduled conditions over a specific period of time (typically three months). The estimates are said to be rolling as each completed month becomes the starting point for the next one. If a firm generates revenues from several sources (as seen in the gross margin case which will be discussed next), the cash flow predictions should be made for each source. The overall totals must tie back to the budget document, which acts as the funding source. A single revenue cash prediction is shown in Table 11.4.

The *gross margin* report ties in intimately with the cash flow predictions. It informs the leadership team of the effectiveness of the deployment of the budget through the difference between the revenues generated and the cost of goods sold. The gross margin is not the same as the firm's profit margins, but it is the primary indicator of the ability of the firm to satisfy sales and generate positive cash flow. The profitability of the firm is measured with earnings before interest, taxes, depreciation, and amortization (EBITDA). EBITDA is calculated as the difference between revenues and the expenses other than ITDA. The value of the EBITDA metric is in enabling the comparison of financial performances of various firms by eliminating the effects of financing and accounting decisions. Table 11.5 shows an example of a firm with multiple revenue sources and their relative contribution to the whole. The numbers reveal immediately the importance of each revenue line to a company and the ones to be abandoned or sacrificed where performance is dragging the firm.

The *backlog report* is the final document in the financial reporting set. The backlog is a report on confirmed sales and their impact on the production capacity of the firm. The backlog is critical to the daily management of production activities (particularly labor). Lulls in certain periods may require dramatic adjustments to staffing levels or reassignments to other revenue lines. The variability displayed in the backlog also drives backup strategies for contractor activation, team mobilization, and personnel demobilization. In the example presented in Figure 11.1, the firm will face severe planning difficulties throughout the year, owing to the extreme changes in workloads from month to month.

Table 11.2 The P/L statement—also known as the income statement: this statement would, like the balance sheet, be issued for a specific date (included in the title).

Row		2017		2017	
		Year-to-date	% Revenues	Budget	Variation
	Income				
1	Equipment sales	$1,112,000	71.0%	$950,000	85.4%
2	Services	$435,000	27.8%	$345,000	79.3%
3	Travel (to jobs)	$18,965	1.2%	$21,000	110.7%
4	**Total income (rows 1 + 2 + 3)**	**$1,565,965**		**$1,316,000**	**84.0%**
	Cost of goods sold				
5	Material	$345,000	56.0%	$298,000	86.4%
6	Labor – equipment fabrication	$98,635	16.0%	$93,000	94.3%
7	Production overhead	$58,647	9.5%	$51,000	87.0%
8	Labor – services	$98,000	15.9%	$102,000	104.1%
9	Travel (to jobs)	$15,326	2.5%	$16,000	104.4%
10	**Total cost of goods sold (5 + 6 + 7 + 8 + 9)**	**$615,608**		**$560,000**	**91.0%**
11	**GROSS MARGIN (Rows 4 – 10)**	**$950,357**	**60.7%**	**$756,000**	**79.5%**
	Sales and marketing expenses				
12	Wages	$39,825	37.9%	$35,485	89.1%
13	Advertising and promotions	$65,287	62.1%	$63,220	96.8%
14	**Total sales and marketing expenses (12 + 13)**	**$105,112**		**$98,705**	**93.9%**

	R&D expenses				
15	Materials	$64,003	44.9%	$75,235	117.5%
16	Wages	$78,699	55.1%	$85,265	108.3%
17	**Total R&D expenses (15 + 16)**	**$142,702**		**$160,500**	**112.5%**
	Administration expenses				
18	Banking, insurance, and legal	$29,602	11.8%	$19,568	66.1%
19	Rent and offices	$34,521	13.8%	$32,512	94.2%
20	Wages and benefits	$186,877	74.5%	$179,650	96.1%
21	**Total administration expenses (18 + 19 + 20)**	**$251,000**		**$231,730**	**92.3%**
22	**TOTAL EXPENSES (14 + 17 + 21)**	**$498,814**	31.9%	**$490,935**	98.4%
23	**NET PROFIT (11 – 22)**	**$451,543**	28.8%	**$265,065**	58.7%

Table 11.3 The budget: this will normally be issued at the start of a fiscal year (FY). The baseline will remain constant through-out the year (here shown as the *previous FY*).

Row		Optimistic	Ratios	Pessimistic	Ratios	Previous FY	Ratios
	Income						
1	Equipment sales	$2,250,000		$1,800,000		$1,900,000	
2	Services	$700,000		$560,000		$550,000	
3	Travel (to jobs)	$65,000		$52,000		$50,000	
4	**Total income (rows 1 + 2 + 3)**	**$3,015,000**		**$2,412,000**		**$2,500,000**	
	Cost of goods sold						
5	Material	$650,000		$695,500		$530,000	
6	Labor – equipment fabrication	$200,000		$214,000		$175,000	
7	Production overhead	$75,000		$82,000		$65,000	
8	Labor – services	$220,000		$235,000		$215,000	
9	Travel (to jobs)	$30,000		$32,000		$35,000	
10	**Total cost of goods sold (5 + 6 + 7 + 8 + 9)**	**$1,175,000**		**$1,258,500**		**$1,020,000**	
11	**GROSS MARGIN (Rows 4 – 10)**	**$1,840,000**	61.03%	**$1,153,500**	47.82%	**$1,480,000**	59.20%
	Sales and marketing expenses						
12	Wages	$71,000		$74,000		$72,000	
13	Advertising and promotions	$75,000		$98,000		$74,000	
14	**Total sales and marketing expenses (12 + 13)**	**$146,000**	16.94%	**$172,000**	18.72%	**$146,000**	18.43%

			%		%		%
	R&D expenses						
15	Materials	$48,000		$51,000		$42,000	
16	Wages	$195,000		$205,000		$144,000	
17	**Total R&D expenses (15 + 16)**	**$243,000**	**28.19%**	**$256,000**	**27.86%**	**$186,000**	**23.48%**
	Administration expenses						
18	Banking, insurance, and legal	$47,000		$51,000		$47,000	
19	Rent and offices	$71,000		$75,000		$69,000	
20	Wages and benefits	$355,000		$365,000		$344,000	
21	**Total administration expenses (18 + 19 + 20)**	**$473,000**	**54.87%**	**$491,000**	**53.43%**	**$460,000**	**58.08%**
22	**TOTAL EXPENSES (14 + 17 + 21)**	**$862,000**	**28.59%**	**$919,000**	**38.10%**	**$792,000**	**31.68%**
23	**NET PROFIT (11 – 22)**	**$978,000**	**32.44%**	**$234,500**	**9.72%**	**$688,000**	**27.52%**

Table 11.4   The cash flow projections: this example is limited to a single revenue source and is issued for a rolling three-month period. The usefulness of the projections is granted by real-time updates to the data recorded on the sheet.

Row		June	July	August
1	Cash on hand at start of month	$263,000	$28,500	$157,800
	CASH INFLOWS			
2	Increase or decrease in customer deposits	$15,623	($12,000)	$3,458
3	Total cash receipts for the month	$145,869	$63,525	$185,698
4	Receivables to be collected during month (3 – 2)	$130,246	$75,525	$182,240
5	Total cash available (1 + 3)	$408,869	$51,525	$189,156
	CASH OUTFLOWS			
6	Advertising	$6,650	$1,053	$1,025
7	Administration labor	$6,200	$6,200	$6,200
8	Direct labor	$28,600	$28,600	$28,600
9	Insurance	$1,000	$1,000	$1,000
10	Interests and bank charges	$300	$300	$300
11	Materials, supplies, and consumables	$45,000	$40,000	$44,000
12	Meals and entertainment	$400	$400	$400
13	Office expenses	$500	$500	$500
14	Professional fees	$4,200	$2,000	$3,000
15	Rent and utilities	$18,000	$18,000	$18,000
16	Repairs and maintenance	$600	$600	$600
17	R&D labor	$11,000	$13,000	$15,000
18	Travel	$2,000	$2,000	$6,000
19	Income tax installments	$2,500	$2,500	$2,500
20	Other expenses	$500	$500	$500
21	Cash outflow from operations (sum 6-20)	$127,450	$116,653	$127,625
22	CASH ON HAND (5 – 21)	$281,419	($65,128)	$61,531

Table 11.5 The gross margin report: this report is constructed for a firm with six separate revenue streams. One could question the value to the business in continuing to offer equipment sales, given their minuscule contribution to the big picture. The cash projections for this particular business line may indicate that the firm is wasting resources that could be better employed on the other business lines.

Row	PRODUCT	TESTING	Operations Services	Operational support	Seminars	Equipment	Total
1	NET REVENUES	$2,678,500	$534,200	$958,000	$687,500	$214,000	$5,072,200
2	% total net revenue (1/total)	52.8%	10.5%	18.9%	13.6%	4.2%	1%
	Direct costs						
3	Labor	$532,000	$113,000	$154,000	$165,000	$14,000	$978,000
4	Logistics	$589,000	$36,800	$111,000	$135,000	$62,000	$933,800
5	Total direct costs (3 + 4)	$1,121,000	$149,800	$265,000	$300,000	$76,000	$1,911,800
6	GROSS MARGIN (1 – 5)	$1,557,500	$384,400	$693,000	$387,500	$138,000	$3,160,400
7	Contribution to total margin	49.3%	12.2%	21.9%	12.3%	4.4%	100.0%

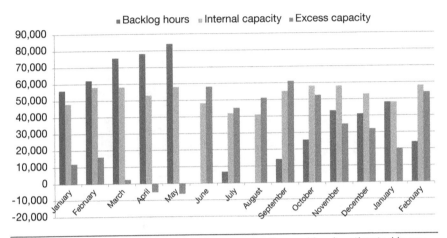

Figure 11.1 The backlog chart: in this example, the workload, estimated in production man-hours, is plotted over a 14-month period. The *excess* bars represent the sum of the internal resources and contractor capacity available

MANAGING BY THE METRICS

A Pirate's Life

The financial information set described above forms the primary toolset to analyze the health of the firm at any given moment in time. The toolset falls under the purview of leadership's time and nobody else. Its usage on a routine basis subscribes well to our recurring pirate analogy. The *balance sheet* quantifies the state of the ship, the crew, and the cargo before the ship sails—and after it has reached its destination. The *P/L statement* is a running tally of what has been consumed or acquired over time during the voyage. The *budget* is the ship's manifest, which describes in detail what has been loaded on board prior to departure. The cash flow predictions are the running tab on the amount being spent on fuel, food, and crew members. They can be summed up succinctly in these words: given what provisions remain unused today, can you still reach the destination tomorrow? The *gross margin report* delineates the fuel efficiency of the ship's engines and the productivity of the crew. The *backlog report* breaks down what tasks and activities remain to be completed by the crew before destination and the anticipated effort to be deployed at the destination to collect the treasure. The report also tells the captain whether or not the crew is sufficiently employed or stretched to the breaking point.

Continuing with our analogy, we can equate the firm's revenues with the treasure that has been accumulated along the way; the expenses reflect what has been consumed during the journey; and the profits are the share of the bounty that gets divided among the crew and the ship's backers at the end of the day.

Financial Literacy

The reader may have already deduced the importance of keeping the financial statements on board the ship. Unless the firm is a publicly traded company, its financial statements should never be allowed to seep into the public domain. They contain information that is utterly critical to the firm's business strategy. The fact that it informs readers on the profitability of the firm should suffice to convince the reader to keep the competition out of its affairs.

By opposition, it is a worthwhile endeavor to educate the firm's permanent employees on the basics of financial statements. They should be able to read and understand them on their own, which would lead them to the same conclusions that the leadership team has already reached. Obviously, the degree of details should be curtailed to avoid releasing critically strategic insights that must remain within the leadership team's grasp. Simplified versions of the financial statements will suffice to paint an adequately precise picture of the firm's economic reality. Even when the numbers are bad, the statements should be available to employees. This level of transparency will bring about additional expectations upon the leadership team, but the upside will be an informed workforce that will understand why certain actions must be taken to rectify nefarious circumstances.

If you must choose but one statement, pick the P/L statement. It is the piece that will tell the tale of the financial health of the firm. Employees will see whether the company is making money or losing it, and possibly deduce the reasons why (which may elude the leadership team, incidentally). One needs not be versed in the intricacies of complex financial management to get the profit message.

The next document on the pecking order is the gross margin report. This one is closest to the daily reality of employees, who live and breathe the factors driving its numbers. The gross margin is also enormously helpful to benchmark the firm against its competitors. Employees will readily see the ramifications of asking for widespread pay increases, for example. They will also see firsthand how their individual performances aggregate on the whole, relative to the competition. They may also discover that they are, in fact, in a better employment environment than that offered by competitors.

Setting the Targets

The imperative of measuring and tracking financial performance constantly should not be doubted by now. Running a business without conscientious attention to the numbers is like flying blind above a volcano that is itching to spew its mortal emanations. Nevertheless, measuring metrics is not, by itself, enough. One must also ascertain these metrics against clear, achievable, and quantifiable targets. A target is a number, not an opinion (*dominating the marketplace* is not a target—it is an intangible wish). Thou shall generate $250,000 in booked orders every month. Thou shall do so with a built-in 20% gross margin. Thou shall not exceed 26,000 man-hours of shop labor in any given month. These are the kind of targets that are needed. And the best place to define them and set them in stone is in the *budget's* baseline.

The budget is indeed the mechanic of choice for setting targets and assigning the right metrics to gauge their pursuit. The baseline captures the planned targets. The recurring reviews of the budget record the actuals achieved in a given time period and reveal the trend (positive or negative) over time for each string of actuals. These trends are what matters to the leadership team. If the actuals deviate materially from the plan (say, by one sigma in statistical analysis) and the deviation is sustained over time, the trend actually reflects the existence of something wrong or incorrect with the underlying strategic *assumptions* (pursuant to the context of Chapter 10). The first reaction from the team must be to look into the *assumptions* first before tweaking the planned targets arbitrarily. A change in the assumptions *must* be followed by a revision to the budget baseline and a recasting of the targets going forward.

In the event that the assumptions are deemed viable, the next area of investigation by the leadership team will be on the *predictions*. Is the labor utilization rate (intimated from the gross margin report) deficient or overprescribed? Is there a sudden surge in staff turnover? Is the supply chain delivering on time and on quantity? Is the production line suffering from intermittent shutdowns and unplanned maintenance? Are the production processes able to keep up with throughput? The answers to these questions will reveal potential solutions. For now, the budget baseline should not be adjusted until such time as it is shown that the existing production infrastructure is permanently constrained. In which case, a new baseline along with revised targets will be needed.

When the *predictions* are deemed to be adequate and not assessed as causes of the trend, the leadership team must keep the baseline intact and delve instead into the reliability of the *forecasts* (still pursuant to the definition from Chapter 10). It may well be that the forecasts were simply too optimistic. Or, the market research may be found wanting or the victim of honest misleading information. Whatever the reasons, these *forecasts* must either be revised appropriately without reissuing a new budget baseline or a new baseline may be called for.

Deciding What to Do About a Decision

Financial reviews guide the leadership team toward certain conclusions regarding the state of the business at a particular moment in time. When things are going according to plan, no corrective action is required—at least until the next review cycle. Sometimes, a change will be required, leading to the need to make a decision. Time will tell the merits of the decision. If things work out, you made the right choice. If they don't, acknowledgment of your fault will be required, and new corrective action will be necessary:

- The decision may result in an *honest failure*, whereby the facts on hand at the time of the decision were understood but some unknowns were unknown until too late
- The decision may result in a *false failure*, which means that something went wrong down the line but had no real impact on the initial problem
- The decision may produce a *blind failure*, in which case nobody understands why the failure happened in the first place
- The decision may end up in a *masked failure*, which is more concerning because nobody is yet aware that a failure has occurred despite evidence to the contrary (luck often plays a part in this one)

The response to a failure is invariant with the type. When the failure is observed, admit it and own it. Don't blame others—don't go around seeking guilty parties or outside culprits. You made the decision and it did not pan out. You were accountable and, consequently, you get to be nailed for it. Once you have owned it, you need to own it publicly—either within your firm to all employees or outside the firm to the clients and the media if need be. Be contrite about it. Next, take the time to analyze what led to the decision to being formulated the way it was and why it ended up in failure. The idea here is not a blame game; it is a root cause analysis. You need to really understand why the failure occurred. With that knowledge in hand, learn the lessons that must be learned. Make sure that you also understand those occasions when you got lucky in spite of yourself. Luck is a not a reliable partner. Afterward—and this is very important—get over it and move on. Nobody is perfect. Everyone makes mistakes. If you're lucky, the failure will turn out to have a silver lining.

The Success Crisis

The flip side of a failure is an unexpected success—sometimes unforeseen, sometimes on a huge scale, and sometimes without deserving it. A success will test the mettle of a firm in a similar way that a crisis will with one exception—it may result in an invisible crisis. Luck will always play a prominent role in this kind of outcome, even if you put your heart and soul into the venture. The crisis is one of delusion, one where the firm starts to believe that the success is its own doing. The danger, of course, is in setting oneself up for failure when the time comes to repeat the initial feat. If the firm was never set up to succeed *predictably at this level*, it will not be able to live up to its own billing. Complacency is often the residual, lingering mindset that survives beyond the celebration.

Big successes are like scary failures; they are fraught with risks that proliferate as soon as they are uncovered. If the organization's culture is fragile, those risks will propagate across its fabric like a fast-moving crack randomly attacking the weakest points. Risks come in all kinds of shapes, forms, and severity. Some are overwhelming, while others merely annoy. It is crucial to the economic health of the firm that the leadership team hones in on the biggest risks first and gets there quickly. Do not let a solvable risk fester and intensify. A risk is like a hand grenade with the pin pulled: if you wait too long to toss it, it will blow your hand and face to smithereens. When facing a plethora of risks, both small and large, do not waste time on the petty stuff in an attempt to create the illusion of proactive stewardship. Fix the biggest risks first and fast. Once they are corralled, move on to the next pressing risk.

To Stop or to Quit?

The dreaded tragedy of every business enthusiast is the day he realizes that the end is near. It may be a money-losing product line or the whole operation. No matter what you do, the financial story is the same: you can't keep throwing money at it. Other than running the thing into the ground, which is one option, the choice is between a hard stop, sell out, or quit altogether. What do you do? Well, the first thing is to not allow yourself to wallow in emaciating agony. Not everything works out in life or in business, and this is just life playing itself out. If your efforts have not turned things around, there is no point in stubbornly clinging to the blinding belief in the business. The financial statements will be trumpeting *softly* what is plainly obvious to a bystander: the time has come to pull the plug and move on to live another day.

- In the case of a failing product/service line, the hard stop is the most expedient option to implement by the leadership team. Terminate it now, but take care not to leave your existing clients in the lurch. The immediate priority is to stop hemorrhaging precious cash. The transition to a full stop must be carried out quickly and precisely to preserve cash. The hard stop implies a withdrawal of your solution from the marketplace. It also means that the competition is denied the opportunity to take it over.
- The other option to consider is selling the product line. You may simply be too under-capitalized to see it through commercial success. Or, you

may not have the marketing volume to impose it in the marketplace. *Selling can be a highly profitable exit strategy* (see Chapter 10) *when properly timed*. The key word is *timed*. Financial statistics will have already outlined a trend toward declining profitability. The sell decision is harder to make as a strategic change of direction because it requires the leadership team to anticipate the failure at some point in the future, but they agree to sell the product line now while it is still a worthy asset. You could, of course, wait until you don't have a choice anymore, but you will no longer have the negotiating leverage to maximize your asking price. The cautionary tale is the story of Yahoo! in this respect.

- The third option is to quit, which is different than the hard stop in that the leadership team actually ceases the commercial operation. This is a far more egregious outcome, given the likelihood that shareholders may be wiped out. Quitting is the only case of a bad strategic decision. The product line has effectively driven the firm to the edge of a financial abyss. It has no way to turn around and go in a new direction. At best, its assets will be liquidated to salvage some of the equity's remnants. At worst, it is a permanent closure following a bankruptcy.

The aforementioned analysis applies as well to the entire firm where the aim is to close shop rather than close a production line. In either case, the process will be neither easy nor painless. There will be additional costs incurred before reaching the end point, but usually these will be much lower than throwing money to try and heal the terminally ill patient. Egos will be bruised, dreams may be shattered, and visions may become disillusioned. These artifacts of the decision are still preferable to the more ignominious burial that bequeaths nothing to the survivor. The way that the firm and its employees survive the ordeal will be shaped by the honesty of the leadership team. The painful decision will be better appreciated by the troops if they were kept in the loop through the transparency of the financial statements. Pulling through this ordeal intact will, on the other side of the decision, strengthen the opinion of the staff in their leadership team—or permanently destroy it should the team seek to gain from the pain of others.

THE PRAETORIAN GUARD

Foul-Weather Friends

We segue with a commentary on three external sources of support that have the firm's well-being at heart. These entities are the kind of friends that bless a firm through their support and wisdom. They are very much like best friends:

steadfast in turmoil, loyal in adversity, and empathetic in victory. They are, in a historical sense, modern-day praetorian (body) guards of a roman emperor with the additional power of making their voices heard without fear of lethal retribution. The guard is led by the board of directors, manned by the accountant, and supported by the banker.

Board of Directors

It is lonely at the top. A leadership team is vested with enormous power and authority and acts accordingly. The danger with any power, however, is with the corrupting influence imbued in it. *Power corrupts and absolute power corrupts absolutely*—as the saying goes. But beyond the obvious, there is also the loneliness of the desert. A leadership team is a small island in the middle of a turbulent sea. One can only see so far and never beyond the horizon where storm fronts may linger. It does not take very long to walk the island and find all of its nooks and crannies. Likewise for the humans involved, the pool of insights, wisdom, intelligence, and creativity is entirely circumscribed by their collective minds. Try as they may, what lies beyond the horizon lies beyond their grasp. That's where the board of directors comes in. It is the bridge linking the island and the mainland beyond. It is the source of different insights, wisdom, intelligence, and creativity born of exposure to the bigger world. It is also the calm power that can stand up to the flights of fancy of the leadership team. This power is soft, hidden from onlookers, and matched in intellect with that of the team's five protagonists. The board of directors is the one venue where the firm's bosses can allow themselves to ask questions earnestly without inviting harch criticism or appearing weak. It is the one place where the bosses can ask for help truthfully and admit to their ignorance, yet remain unquestionably in charge (unless, of course, ego, stupidity, or *volinescience* gets the better of them).

The purpose of the board is to provide guidance to the leadership team and to hire or fire the CEO. The effectiveness of a board of directors to act as a sounding board is set by the choices of the individuals sitting on it. The worst possible setup is a board that is subservient to the CEO and made up of family members or friends and sycophants. That is not a board; that is a choir singing hymns of praise to the glory of their leader. The chairman of a board must be able to stifle the CEO if required; otherwise, it is better to skip the pretense altogether and let the CEO run the place like it's his playground. The other directors must be equally independent-minded and not be beholden to the graciousness of the CEO for their seats. Ideally, they will come from different backgrounds, have experiences from different industries, and be financially independent. The board should meet at least once a quarter. Its members should be available individually to the leadership team at any time in order to discuss issues of the moment.

The Accountant

Accounting is rarely at the top of a business person's priority list, except for the accountants themselves. The realm can appear difficult, futile, or even obscure to the untrained eye. It is utterly devoid of glamour, which is perhaps why it garners so few admirers from a firm's rank and file. Therefore, a little bluntness is in order: your accountant is a friend that you cannot afford not to have. The accountant is your Hermes, the messenger who can be trusted to deliver the news matter-of-factly, without tainting the message. The message, not the messenger, is the goal. Equally important is the neutrality of the messenger: his job is not to suck up to you but to paint your reality with fact-based pigments.

The accountant is your portrait painter.

This person may be your financial champion, someone who reports directly to this champion, or possibly an independent firm that has been retained to audit your books. Regardless of the accountant's station, the firm owes him the same treatment: transparency, naked honesty, and untainted data. The accountant operates on the principle of *garbage in, garbage out*. If you feed him anything other than truthful numbers, he can only give you garbled conclusions and timorous advice. Your accountant is your truth teller, which is quintessentially important to your interpretation and reaction to actual reality.

The Banker

The final piece of the trust triad is the banker, a name that can send shivers down the innovator's spine. The banker is your friend if only because he is in position to infuse the firm with fresh new cash. The downside is the mass of conditions, obligations, and interest payments that bind the firm to the bank. A bank loan may be preferable to undertaking a fresh round of private funding, which may be dilutive to the detriment of existing shareholders. Private financing obtained in extreme circumstances, when the firm is facing the prospect of stopping or quitting, may save the day for now; but keep in mind that the last investor is your savior, he may very well become the single majority owner since the pool of outstanding shares is effectively worth *nothing* at this point if this final tranche of financing is not awarded.

The bank may offer a firm the unique flexibility of running a line of credit, either unsecured or secured against assets (or receivables). Lines of credits are infinitely superior to credit cards in the management of large money transactions.

They can become lifesavers during short periods of difficulty (an industry downturn, for example) or simply to even out cash outlays when receivables are not coming in quickly enough to pay for expenses like salaries and rent. Their importance to the efficient management of the firm's cash flow is illustrated by the following example:

> *The innovator receives a purchase order for the design and fabrication of a piece of equipment. The project is expected to last two months. The work starts, and in the first month, the innovator accrues labor and material costs. He sends an invoice at the end of the month with payment due in 30 days. Unfortunately, the payment is made in 65 days (not an uncommon situation nowadays). Financially, the innovator's situation is this; by the time the payment is in the bank, the innovator will have accrued labor costs for 95 calendar days; during which time he will have had five pay periods. Material costs will also be accrued over that time, but payable on a deferred cycle in this case. Nevertheless, the investor will have had to pay all finishing costs and some of the material costs out of the firm's cash flow. If the cash flow demands over this 95-day period exceed cash on hand, money will need to come from somewhere—ideally from a line of credit.*

The ramifications should be clear to the reader: cash on hand must always be sufficient to cover fixed and variable costs (salaries, rent, phone, utilities, etc.) over a period of time that *is greater than the expected receivable payment cycle.* Practically, this means that cash on hand should be able to cover at least two and a half months of operation if the payment cycle is 30 days guaranteed. If not, add one month of cash reserves for every 15 additional days of payment cycle. This rule of thumb will give the innovator an idea of the reserve needed from a line of credit to cover operations safely. If cash flow demands cannot be balanced continually by available cash outlays (cash on hand plus credit limit), financial stresses will appear. At which time, unfortunately, the business will begin to operate under ill-advised constraints.

The key to a successful relationship with a banker is to secure financing when you do not immediately need it. Banks will not loan you money if you are facing a cash crunch or a bankruptcy. They will, however, be more than happy to extend you a loan when repayment is guaranteed. The line of credit should be the first instrument sought by the firm. Plan to apply for it when your cash flow is consistently positive and your revenue streams are stable. Consider a bank loan on a case-by-case basis. Loans are best deployed on one-time expenses like new equipment purchases, competitor buyouts, and market expansion campaigns. Once again, the firm will have to demonstrate a healthy financial position with predictable future earnings.

Dealing with a banker mimics the accountant relationship: honesty, transparency, and untainted data. The last thing that you want to do is to have a secret, ulterior motive that masks the genuine circumstances of your reality. Hell hath no belated fury as a banker scorned . . .

The Lure of Allure

We conclude this section, and indeed this chapter, with a counterpoint to the feel-good friendships previously mentioned. Sadly, we must acquiesce to the fact that a firm will have fewer friends than non-friends. Every competitor is out to get you—directly or indirectly. Regulatory bodies and licensing masters have no interest in your well-being. Even partners, contractors, and supply chain vendors may turn on you if their relationships with you have soured. Money mongers (angel investors, VC funds, banks, family) may have derived a very different picture of your credit worthiness than yours and stopped you from accessing critical funds. It is a harsh world out there as was mentioned way back in Chapter 1. The life of a pirate is never secure until he has achieved mastery of his seas. Getting money when the usual taps are closed will rapidly become stressful to the point of compulsive obsession. In those moments, the lure of alternative sources of funding may take hold of the desperate innovator's mind.

Needless to say, one should not venture to tread upon these roads carelessly. Unfortunately, in this day and age, the *status quo* in which we live is constantly being disrupted. Fintech, an acronym (for financial technology) that did not exist at the turn of the twentieth century, is here to stay and shake things up in the banking realm. Cryptocurrencies exploiting the towering power of block chains are *in vogue* and will continue to evolve until at least one form takes hold globally (just as Google, Facebook, and Amazon did in their respective spheres). Crowdsourcing and crowdfunding are giving people and organizations the opportunity to completely bypass traditional funding channels. Money is transacted through digital streams without regard to geography, national boundaries, or political powers. When looked upon from a distance, there emerges a picture of a mercantile framework that strives to thrive beyond the reach of regulators and regulations. We are witness to an extraordinary moment in history where internet money is becoming a cowboy frontier, where transactional power will accrue to the few, riches will flow to the many, and victims will flood the digital landscape. And while all of this is unfolding somewhat above the board, the much darker threat of the deep web appears to be experiencing a revolution on its own for which cyberattacks are the only visible manifestation. With everything moving to the Cloud, seemingly without giving any respect to those deep-web threats, the day is fast approaching when a firm's greatest threat to its continued existence will come from digital fraud and attacks.

Advice offered to the reader:

- Proceed with caution when intending to sail the internet seas.
- Assume as a starting position that a faceless digital counterpart that is interested in a relationship with your firm is, in fact, intent on wreaking havoc.
- Consider every unseen digital party as one who will harbor nefarious aims toward you until proven otherwise.
- Do not trust bytes, ever, when they introduce themselves to you.
- You will be hacked—someday, by someone, somewhere—plan accordingly.
- Internet money is intangible, frictionless, and leaks effortlessly in complete silence. Manage it accordingly.
- Some of this internet money is legitimate and worth pursuing. The trick is to confirm its legitimacy. Negotiate accordingly.
- The Cloud is like a cloud: without real boundaries and without real substance. Whatever data you put up there can and will be stolen. Decide what is worth this risk and what is not worth the risk. Archive accordingly.
- Artificial intelligence is coming. Do not fight it. Figure out instead what relationship you must nurture with it.
- Artificial intelligence is clueless. Nothing will ever beat person-to-person relationships for the continued prosperity of your firm. Meet accordingly.

CLOSING COMMENTS

The leadership team, especially the CEO, must be financially literate. Financial statements are not documents that can be delegated to subordinates for analysis. The onus is on the team to read them, analyze what story they tell, and mine them for deeper insights into the true health of the firm. They do not need to become financiers or certified accountants, but they must be able to read between the lines and derive a broader appreciation of the whole canvas, much like a reader involved with a literature classic. The six statements discussed in this chapter are the essential tools of financial management, but by no means are they the only ones. The nature of the business will dictate what they are (think production reports, inventory status, investment performance, receivables outstanding, travel expenses, etc.) and which may serve as information sources for the overall financial statements. Some may be generated by line managers and department heads and rolled up across the firm. The point to remember is this: financial performance requires constant vigilance over the ever-changing statistics that are generated in real time by the firm's activities. Performance must be reviewed at frequent intervals by the right people (defined as the ones who make decisions from the reviews) and gauged against the targets that were set by the leadership team. Financial management is *not* everyone's business, however. It belongs to the leadership framework of the firm, which in turn, requires a shared level of literacy by those who are called upon to make decisions from the numbers given to them.

NOTES

1. The word *volinescience* is a neologism coined by the author defined as *actively cultivated ignorance*. It is a contraction of the words volition (the act of willing, of choosing) and nescience (lack of knowledge).
2. Beauty, as the saying goes, is only skin deep. But ugliness goes right through the bone . . .

12

BEYOND RESILIENCE

"No plan survives contact with the enemy."
—Helmut van Moltke

NATURAL SELECTION

Rigidity Is Weakest

This chapter addresses a simple question that every business owner must face eventually: how to manage uncertainty and survive crises. As the previous citation[1] suggests, there is more to managing an unforeseen event than pulling out the old emergency response plan and hoping to fix everything with it. To paraphrase the language of mathematics about proofs, a response plan is a necessary condition, but not a sufficient one. The way an organization responds to a crisis must be bred into its cultural and functional DNA. No plan will ever be adequate simply because no one can possibly anticipate all possible contingencies and consequences. Business is a precarious world. There will be times when events will threaten a firm's status quo and its operating assumptions. Even the largest multinationals will have their day of reckoning with adversity. Some won't survive the encounters. Others will escape—bruised and battered, but still standing. Still, others will emerge stronger than before. What we want to know is how to mold an organization into one that can emerge stronger. In other words, we want to know how to turn adversity into advantage, conflict into supremacy. The answer is found in a word coined by Nassim Taleb[2]: *antifragility*.

The character of an antifragile organization borrows several insights from the theory of evolution. The building blocks of that character will be explored first using the evolutionary marvel that is DNA. The discussion will progress in small steps to elaborate a management framework within which extraordinary situations can be contained, managed, and mined for every nugget of survival insights possible. The first step of this discussion is to outline the lay of the land under crisis. We go back to this idea of a response plan, which encapsulates the theoretical features of a firm's action plan. Theory is no match for practice, however. What truly matters in a nonroutine situation is keeping one's attention on what's happening on the ground, instead of trapping oneself within the bounds of a theorized vision of how things should be. In a conflict, contestants will act according to their respective engagement strategies. There could be months or even years before a response plan needs to be activated. One is justified to ask how useful such plans can really be? Why even bother with any when you can rely instead on real-time reactions when things occur? President Eisenhower said it best when he spoke of the futility of plans but the necessity of planning. It is a question that has preoccupied war theoreticians throughout history, among them Caesar, Sun Tsu, Napoleon, Moltke, and Von Clausewitz[3] to name but a few. *One needs a strategy to anticipate the needs of the battle.* The strategy orchestrates the deployment of those resources in the right sequence at the right time. The plan, in turn, must above all else serve to inject flexibility into the proponent's response when things take an unfathomed turn. In any strategy, success lies in the flexibility element. The greatest of plans could plant the seeds of execution, then marshal the resources to join the battle. But these are not enough. It is possible to make no planning error yet lose the fight. A plan that is inflexible cannot hope to prevail over the random chaos of the reality.

> *The plan as well as the strategy need flexibility to adapt in real time to the changing circumstances on the field.*

This is crucially important to the would-be innovator. The lesson, forged across the millennia in the terrors of blood, fear, and destruction, fans far beyond the confines of guns and steel. It spans across all human endeavors. Sports, politics, business, religions, and free speech are subservient to its dictates. Rigidity is detrimental to survival. The military commander who insists on unconditional adherence to his plan can never prevail.[4] The coach of a football team who will not deviate from his game plan despite being behind by four touchdowns at the half will not have victory at the end. The CEO who insists on a rigid hierarchical structure to enforce a top-down, command-and-control management style will destroy shareholder value in the long run. Rigidity of thought coupled with inflexibility of decision making are the threads running through these examples. Rigidity is the Achilles' heel of any plan.

Elimination of the Weakest

For the innovation journey, the probability of success is inversely proportional to the rigidity of the firm's plans. Flexibility is paramount as is the importance of delegating decision making to those closest to the problems incurred. Flexibility is essential when confronted with circumstances that hamper, hold back, or even threaten the existence of the innovation journey—before and after technology readiness level 9. These circumstances are *inevitable*; there is no such thing as an emerging business that sails through its growth cycle smoothly, never to be challenged by externalities. Business owners may one day face the prospect of selling out to settle debts or the loathsome possibility of shutting down. The innovation game is doubly exposed to the certainty of randomness—first during the development phase, then during commercial ramp-up.

The world of business incarnates the theory of evolution, which predicts that the fittest will survive across time. The theory rests upon two foundational pillars: random genetic mutation and propagation of the mutation across generations. Dawkins[5] describes the two-step organic process in the following way. First, a genetic mutation appears at birth in an individual within a given population. The mutation affects the individual's competitive advantage (in the sense of gene propagation to later generations) in one of three ways: no effect, negative impact, or positive impact. A positive impact enhances the individual's survivability and probability of passing on its genes through reproduction (run faster, smell better, see farther, etc.). A negative impact handicaps the individual's gene propagation (heavier mass, bad eyesight, impotence, etc.). Over time, the positive impact mutations will spread throughout successive generations as long as they do not become impotent against a new change to the environment (the cheetah's speed is a handicap if the average daily temperature drops by 10°C). The appearance of a mutation and its propagation over time is the essence of natural selection. The gradual changes that have accrued over time from the successful mutations are the engines that power the evolution of a population over time.

Colloquially, natural selection is understood to mean survival of the fittest. Such an interpretation is problematic as it implies that over time a population will comprise only the best specimens. A quick glance at the internet will put an end to this spurious conclusion. The more appropriate interpretation is to regard natural selection as the *elimination of the weakest*. That which is not equipped to survive changes to its environment is bound to be eliminated from the gene pool. Consequently, the demands for survival are greatly relaxed to the less stringent requirement of being sufficiently fit to adapt to contemporaneous changes. The resulting population will contain a greater diversity of genetic contributors—which is readily observed everywhere we look. Diversity promotes adaptability, which is the forefather of flexibility, which in turn promotes survival. In complex populations, interbreeding reigns supreme (in opposition to inbreeding, which leads to genetic dead ends).

Free markets appear as instances of natural selection ecosystems. They encompass complex populations whose behavior and survival over time are governed by the theory of evolution. Innovations embody the population's response to changing conditions. They will come and go as mercantile genetic mutations that either propagate or get annihilated over time. These ecosystems are constantly changing from the interplay between innovations' struggles and the limits of the environment in which they grow. They will change their own limits from time to time (regulatory dictates, oil shocks, etc.), which forces their populations to either adapt (with new mutating innovations) or perish (remember typing pools?). Some individuals in their populations will not be able to adapt because their organizing principles are too rigid (taxis versus ride-sharing, for example). Others will muddle through the changes and survive to live another day. When pandemic changes occur, few will survive to make it through—the archetype example is the dinosaur extinction 65 million years ago (in market terms, think textiles in 19th-century Holland or coal mining in 20th-century Britain). Contemporaneous to us is the coming domination of electric vehicles at the expense of the venerable internal combustion engine. Dinosaurs did not possess the flexibility to survive the cataclysmic impact 65 million years ago, but tiny mammals did. And boy did they survive! We are a testament to their adaptive flexibility. The impact turned out to be a black swan event, famously explained by Taleb in his book bearing that name.[6] Closer to home, the 2011 Fukushima nuclear disaster is an imperfect example of a modern day black swan. Black swans are the great levelers, the ultimate arbiters of survival ability.

THE ADAPTIVE GENE

All Is Fragile, Until It Is Not

What does it take for a business to survive not only changes within their mercantile ecosystems but black swans as well? The answer is *antifragility*, which are the mechanics at the heart of the theory of evolution. Natural selection presents us with three possible outcomes to an external change: perish, survive, or thrive. These outcomes can be mapped onto a *survivability spectrum* as shown in Figure 12.1. The capacity to adapt is called the *capacity triad*, which includes fragile, resilient, and antifragile. The range of outcomes from a change is the *consequence triad*. Finally, the action taken to survive the change falls under the

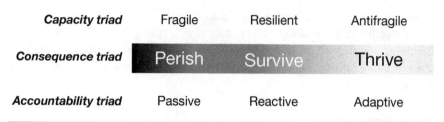

Figure 12.1 Survivability spectrum of natural selection: external changes propagated by the environment force the individuals living in it to react in order to survive

accountability triad. It spans an individual's innate ability to act, which ranges from passive (no ability) to reactive (able to withstand the change safely or injuriously) to adaptive (able to manage the impact of the change and shape its response positively).

The words *fragile, resilient,* and *antifragile* take on specific meanings. *Fragile* is defined as *a loss of functionality when stressed.* A champagne glass will shatter when dropped on the floor. It is inherently fragile. *Resilient* is defined as *a preserved functionality when stressed with cumulative degradation effects.* The same champagne flute, but made of plastic, will not shatter on impact. It could be dented, chipped, or deformed, but would remain functionally usable (if not quite presentable). Repeated drops would, however, cause more damage until one breaks the camel's back. That is the meaning of the caveat *cumulative degradation effects. Antifragile* is the literal antonym of fragile. It is defined as *enhanced functionality when stressed with cumulative enhancement effects.* In other words, the antifragile gets better, stronger, and more resilient with each new stress event. Virtually all biological systems operate on that basis (exercise stresses a body and increases its resilience, for example). In the mercantile space, the airline industry is an example of an *antifragile* system (Taleb first used this example to explain antifragility). Every time an incident or a crash occurs, an investigation is launched into the causes and the means of preventing it later. The airline industry keeps improving itself, a fact borne by its stupendous safety record (leagues beyond anything else in the road, rail, and sea transportation sectors). Note that antifragility does not imply that severe stress events will not occur. On the contrary, an antifragile system cannot thrive without stress events recurring randomly. The antifragile needs shocks to its system to remain healthy. A staid *status quo* weakens survivability.

It should be remarked that this fragility classification is not absolute. It is bounded by a body or system's ultimate stress limits. Anything will irreparably break given a sufficiently large stress. Put enough force on the plastic champagne glass and it will break into a thousand pieces. Put too much weight on when you bench press and you will tear your *pectoralis major* muscle. Crash a plane every day and watch the airline industry grind to a permanent halt. That is why fragility is the limiting natural state of everything. Calibrated treatments can move a system from fragile to resilient. Systemic engineering can take it to antifragile. But nothing can make it impervious absolutely. In the end, all is fragile.

State Transitions

The transition from fragile to resilient is a matter of material selection. What is made of matter is automatically limited by a physical limit—be it stress, heat, current, magnetism, or nonlinear dynamic instability to name but a few. When material bodies interact together as a system (the bits of an electric motor for instance) and systems into installations, these limits combine symbiotically to generate composite system-level limits of their own. In all these instances, what is of matter belongs to the realm of engineering. The injection of resilience into an object, a system, or an installation is therefore a question of engineering decisions over safe operational limits, design envelope, failure containment, and levels of redundancy.

The transition from resilience to antifragility starts with the engineered features although they are not enough. Antifragility requires several higher functions to create an autonomous feedback loop to react to a change, assess its impact, and devise the modifiers to the system to *increase* its resilience in the future. The reaction to the change will most certainly entail a (contained) failure of one or more components of the system. When the system is human-made, some of the higher functions must be invested with human decisions. The antifragile functions divide into three groups borrowed by the taxonomy of the nervous system: the sympathetic, parasympathetic, and somatic groups. Somatic functions mediate voluntary actions (i.e., activated by management decree). Fortunately for us, natural selection is our guide to discover what they are via the supreme antifragile system in the natural world—the venerable deoxyribonucleic acid (better known as DNA). Sympathetic functions are triggered to act in cases of emergencies while parasympathetic functions are the opposite: they come into play when the emergency is removed and the situation is relaxed.

THE ANTIFRAGILE PRINCIPLES

The Somatic Group

DNA is the ultimate survivor. It sits at the epicenter of our very conception of life. Its appearance on earth seems, by all measurable account, to have preceded everything. It has traversed the eons in exquisite style and patterned everything living under the sun or under the sea. As Dawkins puts it, DNA is the true meaning of life. We are but transmission vessels of its genetic code onto the next generation. Hence, DNA can teach us a thing or two about resilience and antifragility. DNA is first and foremost an information archive that is handed down to each successive generation with prodigious fidelity.[7] The information is written in a four-letter alphabet (A, C, G, T) standing in for the nucleobases adenine, cytosine, guanine, and thymine. These four letters can be combined into a possible total of 64 words, called codons. These codons form the totality of the dictionary available to the DNA molecule. Some codons are synonyms of others (lending the DNA the ability to self-correct and mutate without losing information). The codons can, in turn, be assembled into twenty different meanings, expressed as amino acids, plus one punctuation mark. The twenty amino acids can be strung together in long sequences numbering in the hundreds in the form of proteins. There is no known limit to the number of proteins that can be created. The proteins are sentences uniquely identifiable—the celebrated genes. These genes contain the instructions to construct living cells. In this way, we can say that while the chemicals of DNA are mortal, the information that they contain is eternal. As long as the reproduction cycle between generations is preserved, the information will flow forward in time. The copying of the information is guaranteed by additional molecular machinery that corrects errors during the duplication process.

We can infer eight lessons in longevity from this extraordinary antifragile molecule in terms of its physiological machinery. Taken together, these physiological features form the somatic group:

1. Prime triad
2. Clarity of purpose
3. History preservation
4. Message isotropy
5. Coterminous proximity
6. Incrementalism
7. Adaptability
8. Containment

Prime Triad

DNA is driven by three, and only three, primal directives: (1) keep a continuous record of its ancestors' information; (2) copy itself flawlessly when it replicates itself; and (3) perpetuate itself through reproduction by successive generations. This is the business of DNA. It does not anticipate the future. It does not willfully design new entries to its dictionary, nor does it change its grammar and syntax. It does not purposely tweak or adjust anything in response to changing conditions. It does not innovate anything proactively. And it does not operate a feedback loop to gauge the effects of a mutation upon its survivability. The analogy to the firm should be self-evident: the firm cannot seek to be everything to everyone, nor aspire to do everything for every opportunity. The antifragile firm must be thoroughly focused on the few things that it does best, and keep doing those things in the way that best insures its continuity over time. The antifragile firm is devoted to its vision unconditionally.

Clarity of Purpose

The dictionary is precise and compact. Four letters, sixty-four words, and twenty-one definitions suffice to create all life on earth in all its glorious diversity. This clarity of purpose and expression echoes this book's recurring calls for concise, prescriptive writing in everything that is published by a firm.

History Preservation

The information is never deleted. Each DNA molecule contains the protein codes of its ancestors. The majority remain dormant (*not expressed*, in the jargon) but maintain their ability to be activated at will. From an antifragile standpoint, this hoarding effect translates into the importance of keeping every learning event that ever occurred to a firm, be it positive or negative. The lessons of the past cannot be archived away; they must be kept current in the minds of everyone should one of those lessons prove suddenly pertinent to a situation.

Message Isotropy

The information is disseminated in its entirety without editing to every active cell in the body. For the firm, this speaks to the capital imperative of communicating the vision, the strategy, the mission, and the value proposition to each employee—regardless of their position in the pecking order. The communication mechanics are entirely subservient to the imperative for clarity of purpose and conciseness of expression—what we call isotropic messaging (that which has the same value in all directions).

Coterminous Proximity

The mechanics of duplication, error checking, and error correction are localized. There is no central, command-and-control type structure to oversee the DNA machinery. The analogue for the firm is obvious. Every operational function of the firm, either by an individual, a group of individuals, a department of groups, a division of departments, etc., must have the freedom to act and react to their immediate environments. Those closest to the action are the ones to act. And the outcome of every action must be preserved in the firm's information archive.

Incrementalism

The only mutations that survive the error-correcting mechanism are those whose impact is small. Dramatic mutations are not detrimental. The same, incidentally, is observed in nature. Dramatic changes in a newborn may leave the child unable to adjust against the constraints of the environment. The classic example is a genetic disorder at birth. In the context of the firm, this feature corresponds to the principle of continuous improvement.[8]

Adaptability

The specialization implied by the prime triad does not mean an absolute exclusionary principle for DNA. Its tolerance and indeed its reliance on incremental mutations are vital to its survival success. Over time, DNA preserves its vision (encapsulated by the three aforementioned prime directives) but embraces changes to the way it executes that vision on the strength of the mutations' impacts upon its continued survival. The corresponding character for the organization in this case was already explored in Chapter 10. That is, remain faithful to the vision but adjust the mission, strategy, and value proposition in real time in response to material changes in the marketplace.

Containment

The DNA molecule is fantastically good at containing errors and changes to within the smallest possible affected regions of its genome. Changes to a specific gene cannot cascade through the entire edifice. Integrity mechanics and codon redundancies are built-in. In the realm of the firm, containment is accomplished through a hierarchical structure that maximizes functional interactions in parallel while simultaneously minimizing them in series.[9] When an external change reaches the firm, whether it is expected or as a shock, its impact is immediately contained within the smallest possible affected *zone*, then countered by the functional elements closest to it.

Beyond DNA

The progression toward an autonomous, self-learning organization begins with the somatic functions. It is completed from the additional observations derived from DNA's complex machinery from which the sympathetic and parasympathetic functional groups are assembled. The primordial difference between the somatic group and the others is the DNA molecule's relationship with its environment, which is purely reactionary. Indeed, DNA is not equipped to respond dynamically to outside changes; it can only hope to survive the encounters. For that reason, somatic functions are inherently passive in character. On the other hand, antifragility requires proactive responses in a directed way. The proactive character is introduced in our context by the sympathetic and parasympathetic groups. Concretely, this response mechanic takes us beyond the structural limitations of DNA into the realm of intelligent evolution[10] for the organization. The sympathetic group assumes primacy when the organization is confronted by a sudden, threatening change. The change could be endogenous; say a bad production run or a spat of warranty claims—or exogenous; such as the arrival of a new competitor out of the blue or a thundering black swan like an earthquake disrupting the supply chain or poison discovered in bottles of pills for headache treatment. The parasympathetic group takes over from the sympathetic group when the crisis is settled and the time has come to learn from the experience and strengthen the organization. This is the point where antifragility is manifested through plans, actions, and transformations.

The Sympathetic Group

The purpose of the sympathetic group is to mount an effective organizational response *in real time* to extraordinary events along six response vectors:

- Immediate identification of the threat
- Immediate containment of the threat
- Rapid quantification of the extents and impacts of the threat
- Urgent countermeasures to nullify the threat
- Crisis management control with the outside world
- On-site after-action reviews (AAR)

These vectors will be familiar to readers who are cognizant of the art of crisis management, a topic that is highly recommended to all readers at this juncture.[11] Actually, the use of the word *crisis* is premature since the whole point of a coordinate sympathetic action is to prevent an event from worsening from emergency to crisis. Circumstances may not give the organization sufficient time to avoid the emergence of a crisis; nevertheless, the urgency of the action is always reinforced by the importance of containing the emergency. The priority, on the other hand, is to gain complete control over the situation. During an extraordinary event, one is not concerned about antifragility and adaptability; that aspect comes into full view under the guidance of the parasympathetic group. In the heat of the moment, all efforts must be focused on achieving mastery of the five action vectors that were previously listed. The mechanics involved are described in the next section (*The Response Framework*), which includes, incidentally, a learning component that is quantified during the event resolution and fed to the postmortem analysis that is being conducted by the parasympathetic activities.

Readers may not be as familiar with the AAR. It is a highly effective training mechanic that is triggered immediately after a course of action is completed within the coordinated response to an event. The point of the AAR is
to identify the pros and cons of the people and information associated with
the chosen action. It is *never* to assign blame. The AAR starts by convening
a meeting of all participants involved in the action. The meeting is bound by
four investigative paths:

- What was supposed to happen?
- What went wrong?
- What went right?
- Why things went the way they went, right and wrong.

The AAR mechanic will only work when blunt honesty is mandated while egos
are curtailed. In an AAR session, there are no titles, no bosses, no subordinates;
only participants. Respectful discourse is a requirement; the focus is on the
issues, not on personalities. Under these auspices, the AAR will always yield the
fastest route to the lessons that had to be learned without crippling the participants' self-worth. The AAR should be conducted as a matter of mandatory policy, not managerial whims. It is, effectively, a continuous improvement process
in the Toyota lean philosophy.

The Parasympathetic Group

Extracting the lessons and enhancements from an extraordinary event is the
reason that the parasympathetic group exists. During the resolution of an
event, the group's contribution is limited to keeping track of the data and information that is being generated as things unfold. The group is a spectator to the
drama that is being undertaken by the sympathetic group. Once the situation
is under control, it is activated while it progressively takes over the follow-up
mandate, which is to strengthen the antifragility of the organization. Unlike
the sympathetic group, this group is afforded the luxury to proceed at a self-
imposed pace. The functions of the group are divided into three stages: analysis, inference, and induction.

Analysis

This is the first set of functions that are executed by the group. Their common
purpose is to quantify retroactively the actions and reactions that are encountered during the event through the following tasks:

- *Event information*—gather all data, records, and decisions
- *Root cause analysis*—determine the true and possibly hidden reasons
  that enabled the event to manifest itself

- *Containment analysis*—assess the effectiveness of the organization in containing the spread of the event's consequences; determine what worked, what did not, and why; make a judgment whether failings were caused by human error, process/procedural deficiency, systemic obstacles, or organizational incapacity
- *Impact analysis*—put a price on the immediate effects of the event, on the response effort, and on the external damages to the firm
- *Channel analysis*—assess the organization's effectiveness in controlling the narrative, managing information flows, and maintaining clarity in communication across the parties involved
- *Framework analysis*—perform an independent review of the response framework's performance during the event
- *Previous metrics*—measure the effects of the previous round of antifragile countermeasures in dealing with this event (refer to the *performance metrics* in the induction stage, discussed later)

Inference

The second stage segues from the end of the first stage to extracting maximum knowledge from the circumstances surrounding the event. The findings of the analysis stage are used as inputs and transformed into deductions, insights, lessons, and inferences. The name of the game is *understanding*, as in why things went the way they went, and what can be changed to improve the organization's response to future events.

> *The target is not so much the details specific to the event but the underlying systemic features of the organization that characterized the response to it.*

These features will be discovered through the following inquiries:

- Why were known preventative measures (identified after prior events) not carried out (and the motivations why)?
- What were the plugs, bottlenecks, chokes, and ravines encountered during the event resolution and how could they have appeared undetected prior to the event?
- How did the previously implemented antifragile changes perform this time around? Did they produce the intended outcomes? Why?
- What lessons and knowledge can be extracted from the episode?

Induction

The third stage captures the essence of what has been learned and inferred from the episode, which culminates into a comprehensive program to enhance the antifragility of the organization. The program will include at least five components:

- *Antifragility requirements*—a compilation of the functional, technological, communication, information, and organizational requirements, derived from the inference stage, for enhancing the antifragility of the firm
- *Adaptation design*—to engineer the modifications, adoption, and abandonment of mechanics, mechanisms, and their underlying technologies, and to materialize the antifragility requirements
- *Performance metrics*—associated with the adaption design elements, established into a baseline of measurable performance criteria to assess the value of the implemented changes when the next extraordinary event occurs (refer to *previous metrics* in the analysis stage)
- *Evolution plan*—a governing document, approved by the firm's leadership, to manage and execute the implementation of the adaption design program, complete with scopes of work, budgets, and schedules; when the changes are extensive and company-wide, the plan should be developed in accordance with an *investment-centric project management execution philosophy*
- *Transformation*—the actual implementation of the scope of work specified in the evolution plan

THE RESPONSE TEAM

Managing by Message

The three antifragile groups define the orchestration of the organization's response to an extraordinary event. The number of activities is not insignificant and can easily monopolize the attention of the entire firm when the event reverberates outward in the public domain, at which point social media ramblings begin to take over control. The supreme directive for the firm will always be to do what it can to contain the ramifications of an event to within its walls. Managing a crisis is hard enough from within; doing so from without, under the relentless glare of prying eyes, worsens everything. Unfortunately, some events cannot be contained (as any airline dealing with a crash will attest). In that instance, the second directive in order of importance kicks in: control the message. This is, however, no call for duplicitous propaganda. Rather, it is a call to arms for the firm to mobilize its resources to stay on top of things. Staying on top means controlling the event and the consequences that sprout from it rather than being haplessly buffeted by the event. Only then can the firm hope to grasp what is truly going on and communicate its actions and decisions from a position of strength. That is the essence of message control. The pursuit of truth is primordial to the cause—not out of some righteous morality but because truth is the fastest route to resolution. If the event arose out of the firm's failure, admit it from the get-go without scapegoating or equivocation. Always remember the old political adage: the fall of a tainted politician is more often than not precipitated by the cover-up attempt than by the original misconduct.

> *When the sh*t hits the proverbial fan, stand erect and take it head on.*
> *The clean-up effort will be easier afterwards.*

The question that concerns us at this point is this: how does the firm manage the event? The answer is: with a standing *response framework*. The response framework is a functional structure that was mandated by the CEO. The framework's terms of reference include the orchestration of the activities undertaken by the firm to resolve an event; the containment of the event to within the firm's boundary (supreme directive); the control of the event's effects beyond the boundary (secondary directive); the articulation of the message within and without the boundary; and the enhancement of the firm post-event. The response framework lays dormant during normal business operations. It is activated following the occurrence of an extraordinary event and demobilized once the transformation (see *Induction*, the third stage presented earlier) is completed.

The Four Teams

The functions of the response framework are divvied up between four accountable teams: sentinel, prime, cadre, and master. The teams are arranged into a reporting hierarchy designed to manage risks within and outside the firm. The internal risks (visible only to the firm) fall under the joint purview of the *sentinel*, *prime*, and *cadre* teams. The same goes for the interactions and decisions occurring within the firm. The external risks (visible to outsiders) are assigned jointly to the cadre and master teams, along with the corresponding interactions and decisions with the outside world. The unbiased flow of information among the four teams is absolutely critical to the effectiveness of the response framework. The information must at all times be anchored to the truth, however ugly it may be. It must exclude the search for blame and assignment of guilt. Punishments of any kind have no place in an active response framework, especially when honest errors were committed. The exception is the instance when an individual behavior was found to be willfully egregious or contrary to the firm's policies and values.

The relationships between the four teams are illustrated in Figure 12.2. Each team is headed by a chief, who is assigned on a case-by-case basis for the sentinel and prime teams and permanently assigned for the cadre and master teams.

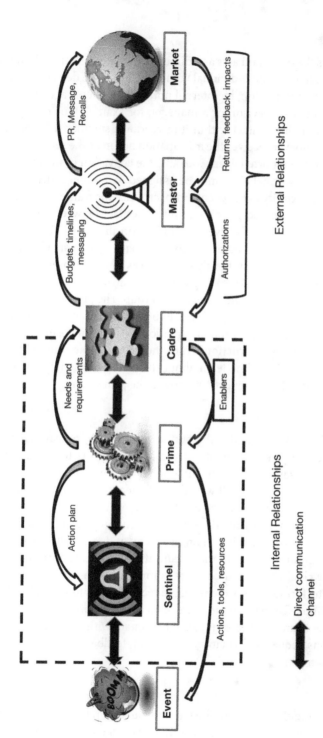

Figure 12.2 Response framework: the framework exists as an add-on hierarchical structure that is activated when an extraordinary event occurs. The actions of the sentinel and the core teams happen within the confines of the organization. The prime team coordinates the contributions of the various parts of the firm needed to execute the core team's action plan and sits on either side of the firm's boundary. The master team holds the purse strings and manages all relationships and impacts that are external to the firm.

Sentinel Team

The sentinel detects the event and acts as a direct conduit into the firm. Usually, the detection will be made by an individual within the firm. The detection could be triggered by direct observation, by internal notification (a colleague informing a lead, a foreman, a supervisor, or a manager, for example), or by a party outside the firm calling his contact within it (a vendor, a supplier, a journalist, an inspector, etc.). Whoever receives the information becomes the sentinel chief for the time being. If the reported event warrants the activation of the response framework, the role of sentinel chief may be assigned to another individual in accordance with its proximity to the event's impact. Once the framework is activated, the sentinel becomes the primary point of contact between the prime team and the people closest to the event unfolding on the floor. The sentinel team may be a one-person team led by the chief or made up of a small number of people assigned to the team on the fly on the basis of their closeness to the immediate effects of the event. These people may be drawn from any part of the organization, not just within the same functional group. The primary role of the sentinel chief is to act as a communication hub between the sentinel team and the prime team by providing real-time information to the prime team as to the status of the event, relaying instructions from the prime to the sentinel team, and passing feedback to the prime team about the effects of the implemented instructions. The sentinel team reports directly to the prime team.

Prime Team

The prime team is mobilized under the authority of the cadre team chief to whom it reports directly. The mandate of the prime team is to manage the event *within* the organization. The team will implement containment strategies; devise resolution options and consult with the cadre team to select the course of action to take; identify the resources needed to carry out the course of action; mobilize the approved resources and develop the execution plan; implement the plan; monitor the effects of the solution on the event; and formulate the proper message to be communicated within the organization as the response activities unfold. The prime chief remains in constant communication with the chief of the cadre team. The former passes the resource requirements to the cadre chief and provides continual feedback to the cadre team about the progress of the resolution. The prime team also keeps in constant contact with the sentinel team to issue instructions, request information, and obtain feedback on the effectiveness of its execution plan.

Cadre Team

The cadre team straddles the firm's inside and outside relationships. It acts as the central response center for the firm. It advises the master team on the requirements of the prime team; obtains the authorizations to proceed from the master chief; informs the latter on the effectiveness of the response both internally and externally; formulates the overall message to be conveyed externally by the master team; and gathers all data and information associated with the parasympathetic group. It falls to the cadre chief to determine whether the response framework should be activated or not in consultation with the master team. Once activated, the cadre team oversees *all activities implicated by the resolution of the event,* including the involvement of external parties (vendors, suppliers, regulators, etc.). After the event has been fully resolved, the cadre team initiates the activities involved with the *inference* and *induction* stages of the parasympathetic group. The onus for the execution of the parasympathetic stages falls to the cadre team. The cadre chief reports to the master chief.

Master Team

This team is an extension of the firm's leadership. It reports either to the CEO or the COO with a direct reporting line. The master team provides the authorizations to spend and mobilize the resources of the firm, which are managed by the cadre team. The master team owns the accountability for controlling the message to the outside world; enforcing the assistance of the pertinent supply chain partners; coordinating the firm's response with the applicable authorities; and orchestrating the public relations program. After the event, the master team continues its authorizing role over the cadre team for the execution of the three stages of the parasympathetic group.

The Activation Cycle

During normal operation, these four teams lie dormant. They are activated whenever an event warrants a response from the firm that is beyond the routine remedial processes. The activation is triggered when the firm becomes aware of an extraordinary event. The person who uncovers the event becomes the sentinel until the sentinel team is activated. This person advises both his/her direct supervisor and the cadre chief. The latter, in consultation with the supervisor, relevant manager, and all other parties invited to the discussion, determines if the response framework must be activated or not. If not, the problem solution is sent back to the supervisor for local remediation. Otherwise, the response framework must be activated. The mobilization unfolds in accordance with the flowchart in Figure 12.3.

The makeup of the sentinel and prime teams is decided by a function of the nature of the event, its initial impact upon the firm, and the anticipated character of the response. The two teams will remain dynamic as things unfold with various people possessing specific skill sets brought in and out as the circumstances dictate. The approval by the master chief in consultation with the cadre

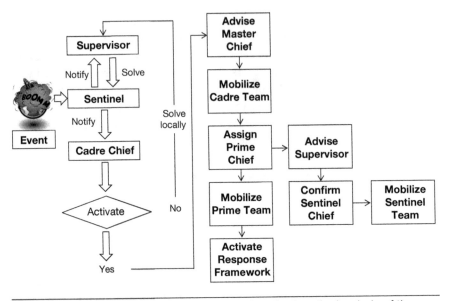

Figure 12.3 Decision flowchart for framework activation: the lynchpin of the entire process is incarnated by the cadre chief. Once a decision is made to activate the response framework, things happen in rapid sequence. The principle of direct accountability is embedded in the formation of each team (by the team chief, not by management edicts from high on down).

chief of the activation of the response framework triggers the cadre chief to mobilize the cadre team, and then nominates a prime chief. The latter nominates the initial prime team staff and mobilizes it. Concurrently, the chief confers with the supervisor of the initial sentinel to determine the logical choice for the sentinel chief. The sentinel chief in turn nominates the initial prime team staff and mobilizes it. The cadre team will normally be comprised of a permanently assigned staff and an ad hoc group of assigned personnel who are chosen in terms of the specifics of the event. The master team will be made up almost exclusively of permanent assignments (albeit amenable to additional temporary individuals as circumstances dictate). The permanent assignments of the cadre and master teams are intended to provide continuity over time, along with steady antifragile stewardship and conservation of corporate knowledge.

The four teams will be active during an event and occupied with activities of the sympathetic group. After the successful conclusion of an event response, the cadre team will immediately transfer its focus unto the parasympathetic group. During Stage 1 (analysis), the cadre team will usually enlist the assistance of the sentinel and prime teams to gather the information, compile the feedback, and complete the overall picture of the event's resolution. At the outset of Stage 2 (inference), the sentinel and prime teams are demobilized completely, although some may be invited to join the cadre team for the analytical work (ideally the sentinel and prime chiefs). The makeup of the cadre team will again change (and likely expand) as a function of the resources required to carry out the scope of work of the induction stage. Ideally, the prime chief will remain involved at this stage.

THE ANTIFRAGILE EXPANSE

The reader will by now have gained an appreciation for the extent of the ingredients that go into the survivability of an organization. A firm may well survive one crisis, another one, then perhaps a few more. However, the probability of coming out of each event unscathed is inversely proportional to the severity of each one. What's more, these odds *decrease* with every new crisis until one finally breaks the camel's back. The antifragile philosophy comes at a cost, obviously. Maintaining the elements described herein requires a permanent mindset, a budget, and a corporate discipline to follow through repeatedly and unconditionally. Lest the reader walks away overwhelmed by the foregoing, bear in mind that an antifragility program is at heart a potent continual improvement philosophy that aligns harmoniously with Deming's quality principles, Toyota's lean manufacturing principles, and the science of crisis management. It begins and ends with an unconditional commitment by the firm's leadership team with the CEO as cheerleader and enforcer. It will thrive organically through buy-in of all employees (those who don't, won't, and must be let go). The downside is a hit to the firm's overhead. And the upside? A permanent boost to the bottom line.

NOTES

1. See *Superforecasting: The Art and Science of Prediction* by Philip E. Tetlock and Dan Gardner, page 223. Tetlock relates the conversation that he had with General David Petraeus (Commander, 101st Airborne during the Second Iraq War) on his philosophy of leadership from which the mantra was quoted. Chapter 10 further explores the relationship between leadership and decision making in the face of certain uncertainty. The authors make a stalwart case about the sublime importance for leaders of organizations to formulate goals and objectives, but to leave the execution details to those closest to the theater of operations. History's greatest commanders from antiquity to now understood that the fog of war initiates randomness on the battlefield, which can never be solved *before swords are drawn*, through battle plans and theoretical musings.

2. Taleb's neologism was formulated to be the proper antonym of the word *fragility*, which is generally mistaken to be the antonym of *resilience*. See Taleb's *Antifragile: Things That Gain from Disorder*.

3. Caesar's insights come alive in his own words in *Commentaries on the Gallic War*. Sun Tsu's *Art of War* is the opus magnus of military strategy. Napoleon's genius as a military commander and master of logistics is expounded in James N. Wasson's *Innovator or Imitator: Napoleon's Operational Concepts and the Legacies of Bourcet and Guibert*. And the classic *On War* by Carl Von Clausewitz is a must read for a modernization of remaining concepts.

4. This is not technically true. The battle of Stalingrad offers us a counter-example where Soviet troops prevailed over the Nazis' onslaught, but at a horrific cost in human lives. Napoleon, a century or so earlier, failed in his own Alexandrian aspirations for similar reasons. One may indeed gain the upper hand when human lives count for nothing except as expendable commodities to be thrown into the throes of battle. This is the advantage of heartless dictators who view their personal glory as the only end that counts. Juxtapose this into the business arena where layoff-happy corporations dump people to protect their stock price. Sound familiar?

5. The inner details of the mechanics of natural selection are superbly illustrated by Richard Dawkins' many classic tomes on the subject, among them: *The Selfish Gene*, *The Ancestor's Tale*, and *The Blind Watchmaker*.

6. See *The Black Swan* and *Fooled by Randomness* by the same author. Taleb described the black swan with a non-zero probability of occurrence that cannot be metricized and which has a huge, immediate impact when it happens.

7. Richard Dawkins, *The Ancestor's Tale—A Pilgrimage to the Dawn of Life*, p. 18.

8. Continuous improvement as a management principle was first posited by Edward Deming during his work in post-war Japan in the 1950s and 1960s with *Out of the Crisis* cementing it in print. Toyota took Deming's concepts further, down the path of lean manufacturing, through the authoritative text *The Toyota Way* by Peter Senge.

9. Mathematically, we would speak of the *reliability* of a system or systems, which can be defined as the degree to which said system can be relied upon to perform in accordance with expectations/specifications and expressed quantitatively as the probability of nonfailure (between 0 and 1, 1 being the certainty of nonfailure). For a system with components connected in series, the failure of any component will cause the failure of the whole. For a system with components connected in series, its overall reliability is given by the product of individual component reliabilities.

When they are connected in parallel, the overall reliability is expressed by the product of the component unreliabilities (given by 1—probability of nonfailure). The parallel arrangement will always be more reliable than the series configuration.

10. A suitable alternative would be *intelligent design*, which would be literally and operationally correct. However, that expression suffers from its association with hostile religious connotations that render it unusable in a rational context.

11. The business literature covers this topic widely. An excellent primer on the topic is *Crisis Management—The Art of Success and Failure: 30 Case Studies in Business & Politics*, by Yunus Saleh, published in 2016.

12. See Keays' *Investment-Centric Project Management*, Chapter 17 and Geoff Colvin's *Humans Are Underrated: What High Achievers Know That Machines Never Will*. The technique was pioneered by the U.S. Navy in the 1960s. It is one of the key ingredients of the success of the U.S. Navy's acclaimed Fighter Weapon School, made famous by the 1986 movie *Top Gun*.

13

CURTAIN CALL

There is no such thing as a glass half-empty. There are only gradations of fullness. Because half of zero is still zero. Ergo, carpe diem to your heart's content!

THE EYE OF THE BEHOLDER

A Tangled Web Woven with the Thread of Time

The ease with which our lives interact with the myriad innovations that populate our existence is the stunning conclusion of an evolutionary process that, until a mere century and a half ago, was mired in a permanent state of stagnation. Peer through the pages of history back to the 1860s: the world then was as distant from ours as it was to the dawn of civilization. Over the past ten millennia, the march of humanity across time and space barely dented the realm of technology, whereas our age witnesses the advent of some new gadget or some newfangled idea every day of every week. But what we don't even take for granted anymore—because it is so ubiquitous to our daily experience—was for the longest time a source of considerable unrest among populations. Innovations were, in the grand scheme of things, rare and few. Most would spring up in throes of ignorance's twilight, amidst fear and fright, each time threatening the tenuous state of survival that was at least known to the people. Each one seemed to signify grave upheavals to those eking out a substance from a harsh ecosystem. A simple thing like fire forever changed human nutrition and led to the growth of the human brain as we know it today. The wheel helped humans defeat gravity. Agriculture led to cities, civilizations, and specialization, but also to earth-born diseases and plagues. Cities led to armies, religions, money, and technological arms races. Wars required resources and logistics, which led to the invention of governments. Governments led to laws, power bases, political thinking, corruption, and messaging. Messaging led to widespread reading, writing, propaganda, human rights, and the printing press. Presses created books that led to the downfall of the middle ages, the rise of secular thinking, renaissance, projective geometry, accounting, and mercantile pursuits. And on and on and on.

A Number Heretic

The ways by which these innovations came about, for they were all innovations in the truest sense, is profoundly enlightening. Take the humble number zero. It is startling to realize that what we call zero did not exist as a proper number in the ancient world. Neither the Egyptians, the Greeks, the Romans, nor the Persians had zero in their numbering systems. The ancient Babylonians did make use of a placeholder that functioned as zero in giving the scale of a number, but it was not used in their calculations. Would you believe that our calendar is also built on a time sequence that did not start at year zero, but year one? It would take the Indians, sometime in the sixth century CE, to devise a positional number system that began at zero as a genuine number on par with 1 and 2 and the rest. Most people are familiar with the system, which goes under the wrongly named Arabic numbers (0 to 9). The misappropriation was caused by the rapid adoption and diffusion of the system by the Arabs as Islam rose in ascendancy in the eighth, ninth, and tenth centuries. It would be several more centuries before the system made its way to Europe via the genius of Fibonacci (of the golden ratio series fame) who taught his contemporaries the rudiments of algebra that he learned from his travels to the near Orient.

How could such an eminently essential concept take so long to be discovered and as long to find market acceptance? Religious edicts, theological dogma, and fear of change are to blame. We discern from this epic battle between *status quo* and progress, the classic character of a marketplace whose *buyers* refuse to see the value on offer (as discussed in Chapter 2). Here was an infinitely better mousetrap than everything else in use at the time; yet, it had the hardest time making its case on its own merits. There is a delicious irony in the fact that the early adopters were the merchants and bankers who immediately grasped the superiority of the system and adopted wholesale against the dictates of the religious authorities, self-appointed keepers, and arbiters of acceptable knowledge. To hell with dogma, we're in it for the money!

Gutenberg Is Pressing

An illustration of the incremental character of the innovation process comes down to us from the printing press. Back in the day, in 1439, the business of printing facsimiles, posters, and books was in full swing. Granted, the production runs were minuscule, but many of the elemental processes involved in mechanizing the placement of ink unto paper were in use. Adjustable molds, image blocks, movable types, oil-based ink, and the screw-type press could be found in many reputable shops. Gutenberg's flash of genius was to combine all of these elements into a single, integrated product called the printing press. The whole system exceeded the sum of its parts. For the first time in history, a single page could be printed in any number of copies *in an economical fashion*. This was a truly disrupting technology—one that birthed an entirely new industry: book publishing. The second flash of genius displayed by Gutenberg was his pick for the first target market (see Chapter 5): the bible. This was an inspired choice. With this one selection, Gutenberg reached the maximum possible market anywhere, across any topic, by any audience. Even today, the Christian bible remains the most published book in the history of the world. That is what we call knowing how to pick a winner!

Lead Balloon

The elusive flying car stands in diametrical contrast to the printing press. Here is an instance of a need, or at the very least a strong wish, that has existed in the marketplace for decades. Ideas and prototypes have come and gone during that time, never able to solve the technological conundrum of a transportation device that can perform two independent tasks. What would-be innovators have failed to understand all along is a very simple fact of life: a flying car can never be a car; its aerodynamic accessories are incompatible with a vehicle that can drive 120 mph down a highway. A flying car, in other words, is really just an airplane with a different configuration. The day that someone figures out a way to negate gravity (rather than fight it with wings) will be the dawn of a new day for flying cars. Until then, it will never become a commercially viable reality. Nobody wants to parallel park an airplane!

A Humble Forecast

If any doubts linger by now about the characterization of the innovation game as a battle to the death, they should be squelched by the epic war that is being waged right now about the electric car. The marketplace for this confrontation was global from the get-go. There are no clear winners yet except in the realization by everyone that electric vehicles will conquer all roads in our lifetime. Technologically, there is no contest: the electric powertrain offers a hundred-fold reduction in the part count over the gasoline approach. Hybrids *add* to the gasoline part count and can therefore not hope to be anything but a transient configuration in the evolutionary trajectory. Energetically, mechanically, operationally, and reliably speaking, the electric approach will win as a matter of certainty. The energy supply, however, is another story. The battery solution is unlikely to steal the crown from gasoline and will also be but a transitory milestone to the evolution. When we look at typical market metrics (see *The Landscape Basis* in Chapter 4), the energy density of conventional hydrocarbons is at least one order of magnitude higher than for lithium-ion batteries. Compressed hydrogen is even higher. Refueling times are also utterly out of meaningful comparisons: minutes for gasoline and hydrogen versus hours or days for car batteries. Logistically, no electrical grid anywhere on the planet is capable of coping with the current densities that would be required to electrify a country's entire vehicle park. Unless a technological breakthrough can simultaneously increase the energy density of batteries by 100 and reduce the charging current density by at least 100, there is simply no path forward for batteries to conquer that arena. The most likely permanent solution will be a combination of a hydrogen supply and high efficiency fuel cells.

NATURAL SELECTION

Evolution Has No End Point

Humans are the product of evolution and natural selection. The same can be said of human *advances*, be they political, philosophical, artistic, or technological. Starting with a given population (a gene pool, a set of ideas, a widely distributed technology, etc.), a mutation appears in its DNA (randomly in nature, by volition in advances). This mutation can be innocuous to its holder, it can negatively impact the holder's ability to survive in its environment or it can give it an advantage that will enhance its reproduction (or wider diffusion within the population). A rabbit born with the white fur gene for winter conditions in Canada has increased its survival probability. The same gene acting in the summer has the opposite effect by making the rabbit stand out in a predator's eye. In this simplistic context, evolution spurs the mutations while natural selection determines its propagation into the future. The dual process governs all that surrounds us. Really. Take any example of innovation, any whatsoever, whether it succeeded (the smartphone) or not (the original personal assistant PALM). Look at it from the sequence of mutations (changes, features, capabilities) that occurred to it and you will see that natural selection (incarnated by the marketplace) led some of these mutations to die and others to thrive. Dramatic mutations can occur but rarely survive. Natural selection, it would seem, favors incrementalism over quantum jumps in matters of progress. This book, in effect, was an investigation into the means and ways that are available to the innovator to reduce the randomness of the mutations and increase their chances of survival (i.e., propagation) into the marketplace.

Richard Dawkins often points out one feature of evolution that is overlooked by people: evolution has no end point.[3] Humans, for example, are not the final chapter in humanoid evolution. Evolution did not unfold in some directed way to produce us. We came about through natural selection.[4] Neither evolution nor natural selection is subject to some invisible directing force pushing toward some presumptive end goal. Sometimes, evolution even goes into reverse! There are fish species for example that have, over the eons, gained then lost then regained eyesight. The whale's closest relative is the hippopotamus, which seems to imply that a land mammal devolved back to a seaborne existence. Once again, the same conclusion applies to the *advances* of mankind. Over time (we're talking decades here, not the next software update cycle), technology progresses unpredictably on the back of innovations that survive (or not) the natural selection pressures of the marketplace. That is why the future is impossible to predict. Not convinced yet? Consider this: nobody in the 1980s fathomed the internet. I learned computer programming on punch cards. Today, we have software that designs other software.

Great Expectations

The fact that evolution, technological or otherwise, has no end point represents an extraordinary future for innovators and business owners alike; the innovation game is never over and never stops. It gives hints as to where things might be headed, but it sets nothing in stone. Since nothing is irremediable, everything is possible, including a reversal of progress (witness the resurgence of the vinyl record)! This is fantastic news. It means that there will always be an opportunity for someone to gain by taking on and defeating the *status quo*. This is perhaps the deepest insight into the innovation paradigm. Our existence appears to be geared *toward* progress through innovation. Even better, this progress carries a higher level of probability when it occurs incrementally (just like evolution in nature). Seminal innovations that divide history into before and after their appearance are rare (again, exactly like natural selection to quantum mutations in nature)[5] which is phenomenal news to would-be innovators—success is more likely in small progress than costly and expensive moonshots. In other words, you do not have to aim at changing the world to succeed, only at changing *your* world.

The never-ending cycle of renewal and destructive creation promises the world but comes at a price: the prohibition against stagnation. The most dangerous moment in the life of a business comes after a long period of commercial success (cue the Nokia's cell phone saga here). Getting accustomed to success breeds complacency and entitlement sentiments across the hierarchy from top to bottom. Complacency leads to bureaucracy and rigid management structures. The very thing that made the original success possible—the innovative spirit—is the first victim to be sacrificed upon the altar of quarterly results. Complacency signals the beginning of the end, ignominious or otherwise, unless someone summons up the courage to rebel against the *status quo*. Progress never stops, never ends, and never hesitates. It will move forward of its own accord, impervious to the objections of its antagonists. It will stumble, hit dead ends, and get off track; but it will always find its way back toward long-lasting mutations. The innovation game, in other words, never ends; which marks a fitting end to this book, summed up by the immortal words of Winston Churchill:[6]

> *"Even though large tracts of Europe and many old and famous States have fallen or may fall into the grip of the Gestapo and all the odious apparatus of Nazi rule, we shall not flag or fail. We shall go on to the end. We shall fight in France, we shall fight on the seas and oceans, we shall fight with growing confidence and growing strength in the air, we shall defend our island, whatever the cost may be. We shall fight on the beaches, we shall fight on the landing grounds, we shall fight in the fields and in the streets, we shall fight in the hills; we shall never surrender, and if, which I do not for a moment believe, this island or a large part of it were subjugated and starving, then our Empire beyond the seas, armed and guarded by the British Fleet, would carry on the struggle, until, in God's good time, the New World, with all its power and might, steps forth to the rescue and the liberation of the old."*

NOTES

1. The word *volinescience* is a neologism coined by the author, defined as *actively cultivated ignorance*. It is a contraction of the words volition (the act of willing, of choosing) and nescience (lack of knowledge).
2. Beauty, as the saying goes, is only skin deep. But ugliness goes right through the bone . . .
3. See for example *The Blind Watchmaker*, *The Selfish Gene* and *The Ancestor's Tale* by Richard Dawkins.
4. The anthropological evidence indicates that fifty thousand years ago humans coexisted with Neanderthals and *Homo Florensis*. And, the Neanderthals had bigger brains than humans, which have not changed in size since then.

5. Even the internet, incidentally, was in the end an evolution of an earlier variant called Arpanet.

6. This is part of a speech spoken by Winston Churchill to Britain's House of Commons on June 4, 1940. On that occasion, Churchill had to acknowledge a recent military disaster and warn the nation of the potential for an invasion by Nazi Germany. Things looked dour, almost hopeless. His speech roused the nation. "He mobilized the English language and sent it into battle," as U.S. President John F. Kennedy would later say.

BIBLIOGRAPHY

Arthur, W. Brian. *The Nature of Technology: What It Is and How It Evolves*. Simon and Schuster, New York, 2009.

Bessant, John and Joe Tidd. *Innovation and Entrepreneurship*. John Wiley & Sons, 2007.

Cameron, Gordon. *Trizics*. Gordon Cameron, 2010.

Collins, Jim. *Good to Great: Why Some Companies Make the Leap . . . and Others Don't*. Harper Collins, 2001.

Collins, Jim and Jerry I. Porras. *Built to Last: Successful Habits of Visionary Companies*. Harper Collins, 2005.

Colvin, Geoff. *Humans Are Underrated: What High Achievers Know That Brilliant Machines Never Will*. Penguin Publishing Group, New York, 2015.

Dawkins, Richard. *The Blind Watchmaker: Why the Evidence of Evolution Reveals a Universe Without Design*. WW Norton & Company, 1986.

Dawkins, Richard. *The Selfish Gene*. Oxford University Press, 2016.

Dawkins, Richard and Yan Wong. *The Ancestor's Tale: A Pilgrimage to the Dawn of Life*. Hachette, UK, 2010.

Deming, W. Edwards. *Out of the Crisis*. MIT Press, Boston, MA, 2000.

Drucker, Peter. *Innovation and Entrepreneurship*. Routledge, 2014.

Fox Cabane, Olivia and Judah Pollack. *The Net and the Butterfly: The Art and Practice of Breakthrough Thinking*. Portfolio/Penguin, New York, 2017.

Hipple, Jack. *The Ideal Result: What It Is and How to Achieve It*. Springer Science & Business Media, New York, 2012.

Holiday, Ryan. *Growth Hacker Marketing: A Primer on the Future of PR, Marketing, and Advertising*. Portfolio/Penguin, New York, 2014.

Holland, Frederick (translator). *Caesar's Commentaries on the Gallic war*. Translation Publishing Company Inc., New York, 1918.

Karlsson, Charlie. *Innovation Adoption and the Product Life Cycle*. University of Umea. Sweden, 1988.

Keays, Steven. *Investment-Centric Project Management.* J. Ross Publishing, Plantation, FL, 2017.

Keeley Larry, Ryan Pikkel, Brian Quinn, and Helen Walters. *Ten Types of Innovation: The Discipline of Building Breakthroughs.* John Wiley & Sons, 2013.

Kelley, Tom. *The Art of Innovation: Lessons in Creativity from IDEO, America's Leading Design Firm.* Crown Business, 2007.

Kelley, Tom and Jonathan Littman. *The Ten Faces of Innovation: IDEO's Strategies for Defeating the Devil's Advocate and Driving Creativity Throughout Your Organization.* Crown Business, 2006.

Kim, W. Chan and Renée Mauborgne. *Blue Ocean Strategy, Expanded Edition: How to Create Uncontested Market Space and Make the Competition Irrelevant.* Harvard Business Review Press, 2014.

Konstam, Angus. *Pirates: The Complete History from 1300 BC to the Present Day.* Rowman & Littlefield, 2011.

Liker, Jeffrey K. *The Toyota Way: 14 Management Principles from the World's Greatest Manufacturer.* McGraw-Hill Education, 2004.

Mankins, John C. *Technology Readiness Levels—A White Paper.* Advanced Concepts Office, Office of Space Access and Technology, NASA, April 6, 1995.

Martin, Robert C. *Clean Code: A Handbook of Agile Software Craftsmanship.* Pearson Education, 2009.

Mil-Std-973. http://everyspec.com/MIL-STD/MIL-STD-0900-1099/MIL_STD_973_1146/.

Moore, Geoffrey A. *Crossing the Chasm: Marketing and Selling Technology Project.* HarperCollins e-Books, 2014.

Nakamoto, Satoshi. *Bitcoin: A Peer-to-Peer Electronic Cash System.* http://bitcoin.org/bitcoin.pdf.

Osterwalder, Alexander, et al. *Value Proposition Design: How to Create Products and Services Customers Want.* John Wiley & Sons, 2014.

Payne, Mark. *How to Kill a Unicorn: How the World's Hottest Innovation Factory Builds Bold Ideas That Make It to Market.* Crown Publishing Group, New York, 2014.

Piketty, Thomas. *Capital in the Twenty-First Century.* Harvard University Press. Cambridge, MA, 2013.

Ries, Eric. *The Lean Startup: How Today's Entrepreneurs Use Continuous Innovation to Create Radically Successful Businesses.* Crown Publishing Group, 2011.

Rogers, Everett M. *Diffusion of Innovations.* Simon and Schuster, 2010.

Salamatov, Yuri and V. Souchkov. *TRIZ: The Right Solution at the Right Time: A Guide to Innovative Problem Solving.* Hattem: Insytec, 1999.

Saleh, Yunus D. *Crisis Management—The Art of Success and Failure: 30 Case Studies in Business and Politics.* Hillcrest Publishing Group, 2016.

Sawyer, Ralph D. (translator). *The Art of War*. Westview Press, Boulder, CO. 1994.

Schwaber, Ken. *Agile Project Management with Scrum*. Microsoft Press, 2004.

Senge, Peter M. *The Fifth Discipline Fieldbook: Strategies and Tools for Building a Learning Organization*. Crown Business, 2014.

Silverstein, David, Philip Samuel, and Neil DeCarlo. *The Innovator's Toolkit: 50+ Techniques for Predictable and Sustainable Organic Growth*. John Wiley & Sons, 2013.

Soon, C. S., M. Brass, H. J. Heinze, & J. D. Haynes. *Unconscious determinants of free decisions in the human brain*. Nature Neuroscience 11 (5), 543–5, 2008.

Stone, Brad. *The Upstarts—How Uber, Airbnb, and the Killer Companies of the New Silicon Valley Are Changing the World*. Brown and Company Publishers, 2017.

Taleb, Nassim Nicholas. *Antifragile: Things That Gain from Disorder*. Random House, New York, 2014.

Technology Readiness Assessment (TRA)—Guidance. Prepared by the Assistant Secretary of Defense for Research and Engineering (ASD(R&E)), revision posted May 13, 2011.

Tetlock, Philip E. and Dan Gardner. *Superforecasting: The Art and Science of Prediction*. Random House, 2016.

Thiel, Peter and Blake Masters. *Zero to One: Notes on Startups, or How to Build the Future*. Random House, 2014.

The TRL Scale as a Research & Innovation Policy Tool, EARTO Recommendations, April 30, 2014.

Von Clausewitz, Carl and James John Graham. *On War*. Vol. 1. London, N. Trübner & Company, 1873.

Voss, J. L. and K. A. Paller. *An electrophysiological signature of unconscious recognition memory*. Nature Neuroscience, 12, 349–355, 2009.

Wasson, Lt.-Col James N. *Innovator or Imitator: Napoleon's Operational Concepts and the Legacies of Bourcet and Guibert*. Pickle Partners Publishing, 2014.

INDEX

Note: Page numbers followed by "*f*" indicate figures; and those followed by "*t*" indicate tables.